THE
SPIRIT *in the* CAGE

Peter Churchill

THE ELMFIELD PRESS

PETER CHURCHILL

THE SPIRIT IN THE CAGE

Originally published in Great Britain
by Hodder and Stoughton Limited, 1954

This edition 1974
ISBN 0 7057 0033 X

A Morley Book published by
The Elmfield Press, Elmfield Road,
Morley, Yorkshire, LS27 0NN,
in association with Shire Publications Ltd.

Printed in England
by Stephen Austin and Sons Ltd., Hertford

THE SPIRIT IN THE CAGE

TO

ODETTE

WITH LOVE

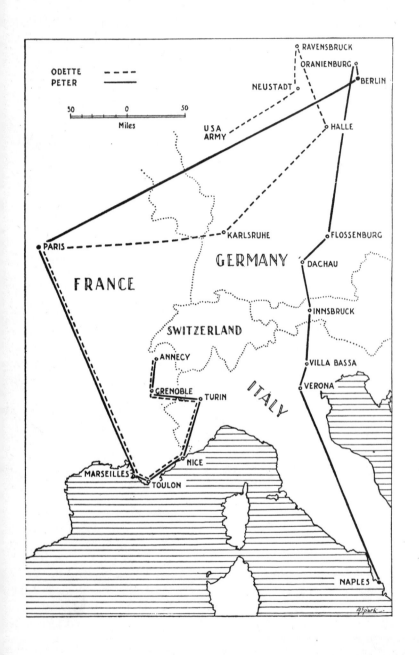

PART ONE

CHAPTER

I

THE door slammed behind me and the grating screech of a rusty bolt put a full stop to my activities as a saboteur.

My spirits sank to zero. Doubly so, for somewhere nearby lay Odette—captured with me—and I despaired at the thought that my beloved and sparkling courier should also have had her wings of freedom clipped. Perhaps we would never meet again, perhaps never know each other's fate.

It was midnight of April 16th, 1943. My 225 days behind the lines—made up of four clandestine visits to France by submarine and parachute—were over, unless I could escape. Out in the yard I had taken good note of the beam that stretched from the cell block to the boundary wall beyond which lay the main road linking Annecy with Geneva. It stood some seven feet from the ground and a simple gymnastic movement would get me astride it. This meant fixing the guard, so I had better start studying the hours at which they changed. Fortunately they had left me my watch, an oversight which I felt the Germans would never have made, had I first fallen into their hands.

My present gaolers were Italians, for Annecy was inside the Italian occupied zone of France.

When my eyes grew accustomed to the dark I took stock of my first stinking hovel; stinking because I found there was no toilet and previous tenants had attended to their needs—as perforce I must do—on the floor. A wooden board some six feet long and two and a half feet wide represented my bed. There were no blankets. So this was it. All the honour in which one was held by one's friends, all the love of one's family were now of no avail to stop the implacable march of doom that awaited the saboteur, captured out of uniform, in occupied territory. Beyond the merciful reach of the Geneva Conventions this was the beginning of the end. My gloomy thoughts were in no way dispelled by lying down on the hard boards. Sleep was out of the question. I simply lay there wallowing in my first cloud of despair and that cloud had no silver lining. At times I thought I should choke with panic and claustrophobia. I simply had to get out, yet I must remain calm and study the beam carefully by daylight.

At 2 a.m. the guard was changed and the new one passed his entire spell of duty either jangling a bunch of keys or opening and slamming back the bolt of his rifle.

The Annecy barracks which had formerly been the home of the 27th battalion of the Chasseurs Alpins was now, ironically, occupied by their Italian opposite numbers—the Alpini.

My mind kept running over the fateful details of our arrest, the ignominy of being trapped whilst I was asleep, Odette's coming into my room and asserting that we had been betrayed, her uncontrollable outburst against Louis le Belge, the upsetting of all my affairs onto the floor, the search for compromising papers, guns, lethal tablets, etc. I thanked my lucky stars that my obsession for tidiness had been responsible for the disposal that very afternoon of half a dozen new radio crystals, half a million francs of French currency, two Belgian automatics, a Sten gun, 200 blank Identity Cards and dozens of French ration books.

The only thing that Henri—the German counter-espionage Agent—had found was my diary and this would not prove very helpful to him or the Gestapo, for I was not in the habit of keeping a log of the kind of events that we had lived. I tried to think what, if anything, I had put down in that diary. God Almighty! There were three telephone numbers of people I had worked with three months before in Cannes; numbers that were far too long to memorize for they went in series of six in that part of France. I had put down only three names with their corresponding numbers and since there were so few the Gestapo was sure to ask me the significance of the names Antoine, Suzanne and Catherine. It would be some time before these interrogations could take place, as we still had to be transferred into German hands, but it was on the cards that Italian Security Officers might have a shot at extracting this information, *inter alia*, before we were handed over. As for my wallet, containing the last five compromising messages that my radio operator, Arnaud, had passed me on the previous day, as well as some 70,000 francs, I never saw it leave the inside pocket of the jacket I was now wearing; yet that pocket was empty. The thoughts of the contents of those decoded messages gave me the shivers. I was thankful that I had refused Arnaud's pressing request and quelled my own private wish that he might stay at the hotel and prolong the first happy evening of our reunion after my parachute drop in the mountains.

Into my mind's eye there returned constantly the picture of Odette placing my Canadian fur-collared coat over the coat I was already wearing before they had put the handcuffs on my wrists. I saw her moving about amongst my scattered clothes deftly picking up an article here, another there, and stuffing them all into a small canvas bag; all the things a prisoner would require. She went about it as though she had rehearsed the scene all her life.

I let my mind run over the short drive from St. Jorioz with one guard in the front to protect the driver from any funny business and the other seated between us in the back. When the barrier had dropped behind us at the entrance of the barracks another nail had been driven into the coffin of our captivity. I wondered how many nails there would be and if they would always be accompanied by the same pang of foreboding before the coffin was brought to its final resting-place.

When Odette and I had got out we had stood close together and as she squeezed my hand I could feel some of her strength pouring into me. Nearby I overheard Henri saying to the OVRA (Italian Secret Police) Officer, "Take good care of these two, we can't afford to lose them."

What would happen to Odette if I ever managed to escape? They would only double the pressure upon her and add to her restrictions. Where did my duty lie? If I got away, could I get the

Maquis of the Plateau des Glières to ambush whatever convoy took her to the next stopping place of her Calvary? If only I could think clearly and stop my heart panicking at this new fear and feeling of powerlessness. This was something I had never before experienced even when waiting to drop from the blacked-out fuselage of a bomber onto a mountain ridge at some 200 miles per hour.

Here then, at last, was the fear that I feared most of all; a fear such as my imagination had never foreseen except in nightmares. But this was a living nightmare and something told me it would last forever. The vision of this kind of eternity sent me off into another panic. I simply had to get out.

With such thoughts as these the first night dragged endlessly by before the faint light of dawn began to filter through the cracks in my door.

Coffee was brought to me at 8 a.m. and towards noon I was allowed out into the yard to eat my lunch. This I did in the company of an Alpini soldier who had spent the night in the neighbouring cell. My lunch companion was a cheerful individual and we conversed together in French. He gave me to understand that he spent half his life in the "pound" as he was always up to some mischief.

Throughout lunch a vulture circled above the yard and, to add to this evil omen, came the guard's unreassuring remark, in Italian:—"Funny thing. . . . That's the first time I've seen a bird like that in France. . . . Wonder what it hopes to pick up down here." I was painfully reminded of Ernest Hemingway's description of the smell of death in *For Whom the Bell Tolls*.

Although I spoke Italian I decided to pretend not to, in the hope that the guards might give some indication as to our next destination during their conversations, for many of them gathered in the yard during this short interval. I also had plenty of time to study the height and thickness of the beam. As to its solidity, no better proof could have been given than when it stood the gymnastic display of one of the men.

After lunch, which consisted of a copious helping of well-prepared rice with bits of meat in it, plus a large roll of white bread, I was transferred to a larger cell with an adjoining toilet. Three large biscuits (portions of mattress) were laid on some straw and a small window high up in the back wall gave some light to this comparatively luxurious cell.

Throughout that afternoon and the following night I thought of what I had to do. If only the panic would leave me and I could remain calm and firm of purpose. I had never known such jitters. What was the matter with me? Why did confinement make me chicken-hearted? I was an expert at close combat and in the peak of condition. With the side of my hand I could put the average man to sleep, yet all night I had to talk myself into it. This action was to be vital; my life probably depended on it.

At 6 a.m. came the change of guard I had been waiting for and yet it took me a whole hour before I could sufficiently control my jangling nerves and start the thing.

Poking the stub of a half-smoked cigarette through a hole that had been previously bored in the door I asked for a light. The guard got up and came towards me. Seeing the tiny stub, he changed his mind and instead of lighting it he slipped back the bolt on the door and came inside. I took his measure carefully and decided that an upper cut would have to take the place of a clip across the temple, since his helmet protected the upper half of his head.

At this moment he pulled up his jacket, drew out a chrome-plated cigarette case, opened it and held it out to me with a beaming smile. All the fire of my intention was suddenly damped by this friendly gesture and instead of giving him a knock-out blow, I merely pushed him roughly into the back of my cell. However, I had not counted on his thick rubber-soled boots and he never skidded as I expected, so that I could run to the door and lock him in.

I soon found that I was dealing with a young man of considerable strength and determination and his resistance to my intentions fired me once more. A battle royal ensued. In a twinkling he had his rifle off his shoulder and was going at me for all he was worth with his short round bayonet. I closed with him before he could use it effectively and, holding the bayonet off with one hand, I gave him a smashing blow in the face. Whilst he staggered about I pulled the rifle out of his grasp and broke the bayonet on the ground. Then, picking up the rifle by the muzzle I broke it in half and threw the débris into the corner of the yard.

Whether it was the sight of the rapid destruction of this soldier's "best friend" or the realisation that I had not even bothered to break it over his head, but was coming for him as though to give him the same treatment, young Angelo wisely began to bellow, "Help! Help!"

His cries of "*Assistenza!*" were soon cut short by a blow to his solar plexus followed by another to the chin which put an end to a scrap that seemed to have lasted for five minutes but which, in all probability, had only been a round of less than two.

With no time to take off my three-quarter length Canadian coat I rushed towards my beam, only to hear the clatter of boots and shouting of angry voices coming towards me. Angelo's yells had spoiled the show.

The first rescuer was well ahead of the pack, and as he rushed me in a headlong bayonet charge, I side-stepped and came back with a hard blow to the face. The man crashed to the gravel and his rifle skidded into the wall.

Two steps and my hands were over the beam. And now, with sheer terror gripping at my throat, I put the last ounce of my ebbing strength into the frantic up-thrust of the legs so as to swing them over the top and bring them back into line with my inturned fingers. Just as I was straightening up at the top I felt a hand grab my coat and knew it was all over. I was brought crashing to the ground and automatically scrambled to my feet in a daze only to find myself pinned to the wall by nine bayonets. A little way off I saw the Sergeant of the Guard pulling at the pin of a hand grenade. Something told him at the last moment that this bomb was hardly the right implement in the crowded circumstances and he tucked it back into his belt.

Brushing aside two or three soldiers who were hemming me in, he eased his frustration with a straight right that brought me to my knees. I was then kicked and dragged into my cell where I remained on the floor in a state of semi-consciousness.

For half an hour the uproar continued in the yard as more and more soldiers came to see what had happened and the wounded were being helped away. Animal instinct told me that I should not hear the end of this fracas for a considerable time. Nor was I wrong.

Presently the door was flung open and twenty faces peered in at me, headed by a young Duty Officer. Instead of being clubbed to death as I expected, a sudden surprising hush came over the excited assembly and, thanks to the light, I saw what I could only suppose must have stilled the hubbub. My hands were covered with blood from bayonet cuts and I strongly suspected that the same applied to my face where I had gingerly touched a closed eye.

I heard the Officer say, "Double the guard. . . . Put a padlock on the door as well as using the bolt. . . . No food for two days. Keep his glasses and shoot at the slightest provocation. No medical attention and no one is allowed in."

The door then closed and the noise simmered down. I began to lick my wounds and assess the damage. Four bayonet cuts, a black eye and parts of the face rather tender. I had lost my glasses and wrist-watch in the fray.

An hour passed before the trouble began. It was announced by a third Italian voice joining those of the two guards.

"Let me have a look at this bastard," it began.

"No one's allowed in," came the answer.

"Don't be a B.F.," said the voice.

"Sorry, chum. Orders."

"To Hell with orders!" spoke the rising voice. "Have *you* seen Angelo?"

"No."

"Well, *I* have. He's in hospital with his face bandaged up. You open that bloody door before I break it in!"

A rattling of keys announced the worst. I looked towards the door to see a large, swarthy, open-shirted soldier standing in the gap, the black hair on his chest rising half way up his neck.

Snatching one of the guard's rifles he bent down the folding bayonet and came in with a muzzle grip.

"By Christ, I'll kill you, you bastard English spy!" he yelled before proceeding to carry out his threat.

I warded off the blows as best I could but I took a terrible beating. When I recovered consciousness the man had gone and my head was splitting with pain. It was only later that I discovered that the joints of two fingers had been crushed, one of which had swollen up most painfully owing to a Provençal ring Odette had given me in Arles. Pains in my back which lasted for three weeks probably indicated two fractured ribs.

Lying on the floor I wondered what Odette was thinking about all this, for the tale would certainly have reached her through some well-meaning but ill-advised Italian. She was sure to imagine I was at death's door. If only the man had polished me off, I thought, selfishly. I knew then that I was never made for the tombs of the living dead, that I should never be resigned to the endless monastic solitude that stretched itself out before me like an eternity.

Anyone with the most meagre knowledge of the military situation was bound to realise that except for some miracle the war would drag on for at least another two years and in all that time the odds could only point to my being condemned to death and executed.

Everyone who has to face the possibility of a violent end has his own preference in the matter. My own choice would have been like nectar compared to the daily poison of impotent waiting in squalor and degradation which was to be my lot. I had already chosen, as I was to choose in my mind, a thousand times over, to end—if I must—with a Sten gun in my hands and surrounded by a handful of trusty companions. My plan to do so had already been accepted in London and if I had failed in my design by a matter of a few hours and now railed at my fate, perhaps my dismay was understandable, even if wrong; but curse my fate I certainly did—and bitterly so.

I heard the key rattling in the lock again. In a bleary daze I watched the OVRA man come in with a folder of papers. He sat down on the straw beside me and opened up the dossier. I raised my head three inches onto an elbow and looked at him through the slit of one eye. I must have presented a pretty grizzly picture and, like a wounded animal, I was just in the right mood for an interrogation.

"*Now* do you feel like answering some questions?" he began weakly, without any preamble.

"Go to Hell!" I said.

He closed the dossier and got up.

"I'll be back later."

"You're wasting your time," I said. "Forget the paper work. The Germans will only do it all over again."

"What makes you so sure we'll hand you over to the Germans?" he enquired, without much conviction.

"It's pretty obvious, isn't it? They command and you obey."

"We work on an equal footing."

"And do your troops occupy Berlin as theirs occupy the whole of Italy?"

"It is a reciprocal arrangement."

"Go tell that to Mussolini," I growled.

The wretched man who had merely had the i's of his previous shameful convictions dotted, shuffled dejectedly out of the cell.

If only, I thought, I could be in this mood when I had to face the real thing, all would be well. The trouble was that I was so dependent on moods. It would be difficult to whip up a rage at any given moment and keep it up for hours at a time. It wasn't in my nature. What a prospect lay ahead for every waking hour; thousands of endless hours in all probability. God, what one must go through for an ideal! However, the longer it could be put off the greater the chances that our friends outside could cover their tracks and carry on their subversive activities from a new base.

I was certain that Jean Cottet, the Proprietor of the Hotel de la Poste at St. Jorioz, must have got word through to Arnaud not to come to the rendezvous we had fixed for the day after our capture. Arnaud would tell London what had happened on his

B

radio and they would instruct him what to do. By now our names would already be sponged off the French Section's blackboard where they had stood for so long and gained for our group such a high place in the statistics of parachutings for the concerted railway plan and the recent delivery—not three weeks past—of 168 containers to the Maquis of the Plateau des Glières. If some of these efforts were to bear fruit, our work would not have been in vain. As far as I could see, this was about the only consoling thought that remained to help me face the unknown span of empty days until the dreaded end would put a merciful stop to the torturings in my mind.

I imagined the blow our capture would cause at Headquarters and the temporary gloom cast over my friends Colonel Buckmaster, Major Jacques de Guélis, Jerry Morel, Vera Atkins and perhaps a few others. A gloom to which they would never become wholly accustomed through further arrests despite the comparatively heavy losses of the Section. But the work must go on. Fresh plans must be made and new men take the place of the departed. Only a strengthening of their resolve, a confidence in the ultimate outcome and a strong heart were of any use if the briefing of new men were to carry any conviction.

The hopeless hours dragged by and day turned into night. The guards kept themselves awake—as well as me—by talking and endlessly rattling their keys. I thought I should go mad and give myself away by yelling in Italian my one thought that had turned into an obsession: "For God's sake, let me sleep! You only have two hours on and four off. I'm here for life. Let me at least reduce my sentence with a few hours of blessed sleep."

Although I was sure Odette must be facing all this with a certain equanimity, the thought of her anguished expression, which I had occasionally glimpsed in our shared moments of danger, or the faraway look which had spelt a moment of painful yearning for her three little daughters in England, was so grievous that I could not prevent the tears from pouring down my face.

My despair was presently interrupted by the advent of several drunken soldiers who began by addressing the two guards in much the same manner as my previous bravo. It was nearly 2 a.m. and I had wrongly supposed that the heavy punishment I had already received might serve to avoid any repetition.

Having whipped themselves up with alcohol these men were clearly determined to finish off a job that had been previously mishandled. They would not listen to the guards' half-hearted complaint that they would get into serious trouble if their prisoner was done in during their tour of duty.

Inexorably the key searched out and opened the padlock, the bolt was drawn and the door flung open. My good eye was blinded by the lights from four torches. I shaded it and sat up, alert to all that this could mean.

A strong smell of scent came to my nostrils, so far accustomed only to the acrid smell of ammonia.

"You prince of bastards!" opened up their spokesman in a deadly voice. "He offers you a cigarette and you slug him while his hands are opening the case. We'll fix you properly for this."

I was trapped. With the four shafts of light on me I could not see their faces. They would either shoot me or beat my brains out. I had to say something and say it fast. The business of not speaking Italian had suddenly lost all importance, even if it meant more trouble later on. Streams of perfectly comprehensible Italian poured out of me.

"I didn't hit him when his hands were opening the case. It's true I had intended to, but it was precisely because of his friendly gesture that I merely tried to push him into the corner of the cell. He had plenty of time and fair warning of what was going to happen. You ask him. He'll tell you that that's the truth."

"We've just returned from leave and that's what we were told."

"You ask him tomorrow," I repeated.

"D'you realise what would have happened to him if you'd got away?" asked another of the four disembodied voices. "He'd have been shot."

"I can hardly believe that," I replied. "In England they don't shoot guards if a prisoner escapes."

"In our regiment they do, and you would have been responsible."

"Gentlemen," I pleaded, "if you were in my position, wouldn't you try to escape?"

This remark seemed to ring a sympathetic bell in the scented bosoms of my four invisible persecutors and from then onwards what had started as a vendetta turned into a ghostly scene of alcoholic commiseration.

As they left the cell each man threw me a cigarette.

I lay back and drew deeply on the perfumed East African tobacco. I wondered what the next day held in store. The thought also crossed my mind that an Italian saboteur—if such a thing existed—might have fared less well than myself if similar events had occurred in a British cell.

Towards three o'clock I managed to fall asleep and when I awoke it was to discover that my outburst in perfectly good Italian had classed me as a first rate double-crosser. I became an unpopular object of scorn, a twister who could not be trusted. This unsavoury yet justifiable reputation was to follow me from place to place for quite a while. I thought it a reasonable price for a performance that had probably saved my life for the time being.

In the afternoon another prisoner was bundled into my cell. I soon rumbled this smooth man as a stooge, despite his glib story of having been caught crossing the Swiss frontier on some black-market errand. His copious private rations which he offered to share and I gladly accepted, his concern over my plight, offers to help—once outside—and his well-acted show of impatience to be called for questioning clearly indicated that he had been introduced by my OVRA friend for the purpose of getting something out of me. I easily avoided this trap.

After three pleasant hours of this game and the smoking of several Balto cigarettes he was yanked off and I never saw him again.

Time crept by and I remained in a state of unshaven filth until the tenth day when I was shaved and permitted to spruce up. Perhaps something was going to happen. Indeed it was.

Towards evening a truck was backed up to the door of the yard and I was taken out of my cell and led to it by the entire guard. Despite my previous unpopularity, such was the rapid and total change of heart from mortal rage to a state of warm friendliness in these Italians that most of them came and shook my hand and wished me luck. The first to come was the young guard I had knocked out at the door of my cell.

Standing before me with a smile from ear to ear he put out his hand. Smiling back out of a rather bloated face I shook it warmly. No word was exchanged between us.

A very agreeable Sergeant who had returned my glasses after I had spent two days without them and who had also accelerated my return to normal feeding hours, informed me that Odette would be travelling with me.

I climbed in and there she sat. It was almost too good to be true.

The lorry filled up with a dozen Carabinieri armed with Schmeissers. Two of the men—my particular enemies—took up positions by the back-drop with their guns across their knees. We set off and a second lorry load of troops fell in behind us in case the Maquis should try to ambush us.

CHAPTER

II

WHY the Italians allowed us to sit together and talk all the way to Grenoble I could not understand, but the two hours' drive beside Odette made of this—as of the few other meetings we were lucky enough to have—an oasis of happiness such as I had never known and her moral courage and fearlessness were like a fountain of strength upon which I was to draw on many a future occasion of black despair.

She filled my pockets with cigarettes that she had accepted

from the guards, merely lit and then stubbed out as soon as the guard had gone, in order to keep them for me. She also put some eggs into my hold-all.

Seeing my face and hands a little worse for wear she implored me not to get myself killed in any further scraps. As I had suspected, she had been given fairly precise details of most of what had transpired. She told me of her conviction that we had been betrayed by Roger Bardet who was behind Louis le Belge. I replied that it seemed of little importance who had betrayed us and that I was certain to be executed on any one or all of a dozen counts.

Odette said: "I know that you will survive all this. Promise me to face it with patience. I shall be thinking of you and praying for you all the time, but particularly at 6 o'clock each evening."

I knew then that she did not consider her own chances of survival to be as good as mine. What gave her this notion I could not imagine, nor could I elicit any good reason for her views. Maybe she was working on premonition or maybe she was hatching some intricate plot. Whatever it was I felt sure that, as far as it was in her power, she would do everything she could for my sake.

The drive ended all too soon and once more came the sadness of separation. Odette was taken to a room in the Grenoble barracks which she shared with two or three other women and I was led off to a cell very similar to the one I had so recently vacated in Annecy.

My evil reputation had followed me with a vengeance. Before my door was barred the Guard Commander chained my ankles together and took away my glasses. But what did I care? I lay still on the straw and digested every unselfish word, every affectionate look and gesture of my indomitable Lise.

I always thought of Odette by her war-name—Lise. It now seemed right that she should have two names, for here was a girl quite different from the one I had known in the Resistance. There she had proved to be a carefree courier who, whilst capable of taking important decisions and able to march with the best, never really took the thing seriously; whereas the Odette I had just left was a person facing a situation that required moral fibre and in this lonely contest she had clearly revealed herself as a winner. Here, at last, was a reality that she understood, something that she could put her teeth into and it seemed odd to me that it should require such a predicament as this to bring out her finest qualities. It was still more curious for me to think that not until now had I fully realised the extent of my admiration and love for her. Surely, I thought, few people could ever have known such a boundless measure of love as that which had been transmitted to me under the scowling gaze of the Military Police by a woman weighed down by the knowledge that she might never again set eyes on her own children. My longing to live and to find her again seemed all the more dreadful in our gloomy circumstances.

In the morning my ankles were freed of their chains and I was taken outside to wash at a tap. So fierce was my reputation that a Sergeant stood in attendance the whole time, pointing a revolver at me.

On the way back to my cell I heard Odette hailing me and, looking up, saw her through the wired window of her room. I walked up to the window but was shoved away by the guard. We waved gaily to one another. Back in my cell I found that by standing on tip-toe I could see Odette through my tiny window. She caught sight of me and from time to time we waved at each other throughout the day when there were no guards about. In this way the days that we were to spend in Grenoble passed in a state of being so near and yet so far. Still, it was infinitely better than not being able to see each other at all.

On the second day my door was opened and I was surprised to see the entrance crowded with officers and men. They came up to me in a rather menacing way and the first man bawled:

"What's your name?"

"Chambrun," I replied.

"We know all about that, but what's your real name?"

"That is my real name," I said, somewhat nonplussed.

"No, it isn't. Your name's Churchill and you're related to Winston Churchill."

"What makes you say that?" I asked, a trifle crestfallen at the thought that my fully-tested and seemingly foolproof French 'cover' should suddenly have vanished into thin air, now leaving me to face the charge not only of being a British officer but one bearing the name of the best-hated man of the Axis Powers.

"Never mind how we know, we just do. You sign your real name here and insert your rank and number as well."

Now the fat was in the fire. When the Italians had ceased gazing at me in wonder and gone off with their piece of paper I reflected how my fighter pilot brother and I had discussed the pros and cons of being captured with such a name. My brother claimed that the hatred for this name was such that whenever he went on fighter sweeps he never wore his identity disc and was prepared to give another name. As I generally agreed with his judgment in most matters I still harboured the conviction that this fresh evidence would bring about my end more quickly than anything else.

I was not aware at the time that Roger Bardet knew my real name and that when betraying me as Chief of the south-east zone of France he had divulged it and tried to increase the importance of his betrayal by falsely stating that I was a nephew of the Prime Minister. But this was not responsible for the Italians' knowledge. It was due to an entirely different cause of which I was likewise ignorant and was only to discover some time later.

The boring business of being cooped up in a darkish outhouse dragged on interminably for, of course, no one ever took the trouble anywhere or at any time to let prisoners know where or when they were to be moved until the very last moment. Odette's birthday on April 28th came and went like the travesty that all anniversaries are when you do not know if you will ever live to see another in freedom. It is not impossible to have a small gift delivered, but to see someone on such a day behind a wire cage and to say "Happy Birthday" requires a certain art if you are not to have the reverse effect.

On the morning of our tenth day at Grenoble I was again handcuffed and taken off to another lorry. Odette was already seated inside but the guards would not let us speak to each other, so we had to content ourselves with smiles until we were deposited at the station.

When the train came in we were placed in separate compartments and accompanied by about seven guards apiece. Thus escorted, the journey to goodness knew where began. As the train climbed up to Modano I knew we were going to Turin. I kept up intermittent conversation with my guards whilst the tightly drawn chain gnawed at my wrists.

At Modano the word soon got round who the prisoners were and one or two Carabinieri took the trouble to come into my compartment and spit in my face. My own guards looked sheepish at this cheap performance and they made up for it by allowing me to share their bottles of Chianti on the run down to Turin. We reached the station in good spirits. Here Odette and I were left together in a waiting-room whilst the guards telephoned for transport. Now that we were far away from officer supervision they gave way to their natural good nature and left us alone for a wonderful fifteen minutes.

"It was I who told them your real name," said Odette.

"Why did you do that, for goodness sake?" I asked.

"Because the Germans are the most frightful snobs. I told the Duty Officer at Grenoble that you were closely related to the Old Man and that's a piece of information he'll never be able to keep to himself."

"Well, bang goes my cover story," was my first reaction.

"Never mind about that. They'll be so pleased with Henri for capturing you that they'll probably give him the Ritterkreuz and keep you as a hostage."

"So that was the idea," I said. "Maybe you're right. We'll soon know. But I always thought it rather a dangerous name to travel under these days."

"Wrong psychology altogether. You'll see," said Odette confidently. "I told them something else, too," she went on, looking at me sideways.

"What?" I enquired, now quite prepared for anything.

"I said I was your wife, and that we'd been married since 1941."

"Well," I laughed, "that certainly shows your confidence in this plan. I begin to like the idea, Lise. Yes, I like it very much. Sink or swim we shall be together."

At this point a Turin Carabinieri joined the two guards who were with us in the waiting-room. After whispering together and looking in our direction the Turin man came across and, shaking an admonishing finger at us, said:

"*Niente politica*, eh!"

" As though reunited lovers would waste their precious moments in conspiracy and treason," I said. "Why, all we're doing is whispering sweet nothings to each other."

He seemed satisfied and, having fulfilled his duty, returned to his companions.

"Naturally," went on Lise, as soon as he had gone, "I need hardly add that this stunt is merely a war-time measure."

"If I ever get the chance I shall ask you if you'd care to make it a lifetime measure."

Our transport had arrived and we were driven off to our respective jails. Odette, I discovered afterwards, spent the night in a place where they ran in the women of the streets whilst I was locked up in a Police Station.

Before going to sleep I worked out the answer to every possible question that might trip us up in this fresh by-play that Odette had foisted on me as a *fait accompli*. I simply had to speak to her somehow and the sooner the better, for if our answers did not coincide we should soon be tripped up by separate interrogations.

In the morning our Grenoble Carabinieri came to fetch me, but the Police had lost the key of my grilled door. The noise and recriminations of this comic half-hour filled me with adolescent joy.

With the eternal chain around my wrists and a coat through my arms to hide it, Odette and I were taken by tram to the station. The citizens of Turin averted their eyes from a scene they had grown to know only too well.

The guards told us that we were now heading for Nice. Once again we travelled in neighbouring compartments.

The entire journey passed in a friendly and even jovial atmosphere. After my guards had changed places with Odette's and were later chased out on the grounds of priority, I joined in with this nonsense by saying:

"You're doing all right, aren't you, rushing in and out to have a look at my wife? How about letting me lean out of the window and talk to her through hers?"

"Fair enough," was the general comment which gave us our golden opportunity.

After the first few moments of normal happy chatter, I said to Odette:

"Keep up exactly the same tone and smile when you repeat what I'm now going to tell you. It's this . . . first of all we shall be confronted with captured friends who know perfectly well that we were never married. The answer to this is that we kept it a secret in view of the fact that most of our colleagues had left their womenfolk at home, so we didn't wish to make a display of our happy state. Have you got that?"

"Yes," answered Lise with a gay smile and a wave of her handkerchief.

"We were married on the 24th of December, '41, in a Registrar's Office at 60 Baker Street. There probably isn't one there, but it doesn't matter a hoot and it's easy to remember."

"A lovely idea, Peter. Who were the witnesses? Let's have my aunt, Mrs. Geary of Kensington, as one of them."

"Fine, and the other can be my dark slim 26-year-old brother, Oliver, whom you can say you only met twice in uniform. The rank doesn't matter. He went off to the wars after that."

I gave Odette the names and addresses of the principal members of my family and she gave me hers so that we could both practise this fresh knowledge and later speak intelligently on the whole subject. In this manner we tied up all the loose ends we could think of, questioned each other back and forth, making necessary amendments here and there to suit the new circumstances and, trusting to luck that enquiries would not be pressed too far we both took an oath to stick to this marriage lie to the bitter end.

With this vital and well-rehearsed agreement behind us it only remained for us to hope that we could make our inquisitors swallow it.

At Nice we were driven up to a villa high up in the hills where Odette was taken to an upstairs room and I was kept in the cellar which had been cleverly converted into several cells easily supervisable by one guard. Here the electric light was kept on day and night, for no daylight could penetrate the place.

In this well-appointed cellar the beds and food were excellent and the place was spotlessly clean. My first impression of these improvements was that if one must be locked up, here, under the Italians, was a spot I might choose for a lengthy stay. But it was not long before I radically altered this view. The OVRA men had an unpleasant habit of walking round the eight lattice-doored cells and picking out a victim for questioning with the same relish as the previous owner might have selected a choice wine from the same cellar. The hapless individual was then led away by a special guard and only returned many hours later. I never knew when my turn might come.

On the ninth afternoon a new prisoner was brought down the stairs. I recognised him immediately as my old friend Louis of Antibes. Before he could distinguish all the faces intently watching him he was put inside the next cell to mine. I hoped we might have the chance of a few moments' talk if we were lucky enough to be taken to the washing-room together.

During the ninth night nobody who was in the cellar could sleep and I had the painful opportunity of seeing the OVRA methods applied to two of my fellow prisoners. For reasons that I never knew—but in all probability because they would not answer questions—these men were made to walk round their cells all night without stopping. One of these was an old man who naturally began to flag towards 1 a.m., and tried to rest against the wall. He was shouted away several times before finally sitting down, exhausted. The guard then threw buckets of water all over his cell floor. To have to watch this was one of the first degrading things of my prison experience. The wound to my self-esteem for not having shouted out my disgust at this vile treatment of an old man, and because I had been cowed into silence through fear of reprisals made me quite disgusted with myself. But there it was. The first downhill step had been taken because I was not in the mood. A new set of values was being taught me and, for the first time, I knew that a real man was the man who kept himself constantly in the mood and who overcame the fear of reprisals either because it was in him or because he made it his business to do so. There were a few such men and women. They were the shining examples of the superiority of the human spirit over the weakness of the flesh. Those who survived have won the greatest battle of all—the victory over themselves. Those who died never tarnished their souls.

The second prisoner who had to walk through the night was Louis of Antibes. At 6 a.m.—after 11 hours of this performance— he suddenly sat down.

"None of that!" shouted the guard, "or you'll get the water treatment."

"Let's have it," said Louis in a firm and quiet voice. "A cold bath is just what I want, you big bully."

I rejoiced that my bald stocky friend Dr. Lévi, whose Jewish forebears had lived in and loved France over the past 300 years, this respected citizen of Antibes, good husband, loving father and ardent patriot, should, in his hour of trial, be undefeated.

By now I could no longer restrain myself.

"Bravo!" I called out and would have liked to add Louis' name but knew this would raise suspicions that we had worked together.

A general murmur of protest from all the cells saved me from the reprisals I was by now in the right mood to face.

At 9 a.m. on my tenth morning in the cellar I was taken out of my cell, but it was for the next leg of our journey; a journey that I could feel in my bones must eventually lead to Germany.

Odette and I were now driven by lorry to Toulon. This time I was not handcuffed. Out of the back of the lorry on this sunny morning in early May we were to see many of the places we had known so well. One after another the roads we had cycled over a hundred times swept under us as though in reverse through the long nightmare of this bitter drive.

As we sped along the Rue d'Antibes, which runs through the centre of Cannes, Odette's hand sought mine and in silence, without daring to look at each other, our dilated eyes and tortured minds recaptured a hundred scenes that had been shared during the months we had worked together in this hub of the south-east zone. Here, six months ago, we had first met and here had been cemented the everlasting friendship between Arnaud, Lise and myself. A dozen staunch Frenchmen and Frenchwomen were interwoven in this tapestry, just as we made up part of the picture in which they were centred. Here on this very road we had watched the Italian troops passing through the town to occupy the southern zone of France. I had laughed then at the discomfiture of an Italian officer who, walking backwards whilst exhorting his troops to march at attention, had fallen into a low trailer. I was not laughing now and all these thoughts were but a jumble of misery swirling round in our cup of woe. Along the whole length of the Rue d'Antibes the wheel of fortune ran over us with a crushing weight, leaving a mark in our lives when we had suddenly grown older.

At la Bocca the lorry veered off along the interior road. We were swirled from side to side as the driver screamed the tyres round every corner. It was all we could do to hold on.

Eventually we reached Fréjus where the road to Brignoles straightens out and the ride became easier. We stopped before turning left for Toulon and I was allowed out to relieve myself. Two guards stood on the road ten yards away, their light machine-guns slung over their shoulders.

At this moment, squatting behind a bush and looking at the guards over the top, I knew that had I been alone I should have made a dash for freedom. Five yards behind me was the cover of some thick bushes. It was a risk well worth taking. But I was not alone and it was at this point that I decided that I would face whatever was coming and share, for better or for worse, the same destiny as the woman I loved. I had had plenty of time in which to reflect on the feelings I should have in freedom whilst imagining Odette in continued captivity and had realised that the mental torment would be too great to bear.

Yet as I returned to the lorry, my nostrils full of the warm scent of Provence—a mixture of thyme, laurel, pine, mimosa and eucalyptus—my feet dragged with the agony in my soul and I looked straight at my companion for I was too immature to make so big a sacrifice without being tempted to look over my shoulder.

At Toulon we were handed over to two S.S. Sergeants who escorted us by car to Marseille. Neither of these men spoke anything but German, so we were reduced to the language of signs. During the ride they understood that Odette was suffering from a racking headache and stopped in a village to get some aspirin tablets and a glass of water.

Throughout the twelve hours' train journey to Paris they allowed us to sit together and talk. They carried out their duties punctiliously and with humanity.

We were joined by two other prisoners at Lyon. Chained to their guards these new arrivals filled our compartment and brought home the fact that, by degrees, we were to become two tiny elements in the vast throng of German captives.

Next morning, as dawn crept over the landscape it was an unhappy group of unshaven humanity that awoke from its fitful and uneasy sleep. Odette felt it like the rest of us. She squeezed my hand and smiled bravely, saying:

"*Bonjour, mon Pierre.*" From her handbag she then produced a tiny crucifix which she gave me.

Presently the train was slowing down to enter the Gare de Lyon. Once more I was handcuffed; the sweetness of Odette's proximity was almost over.

Henri met us at the station and having acknowledged the safe receipt of his pet captives he sent the S.S. men ahead and led us along the platform. Having welcomed Odette with a certain courtesy he turned to me and said:

"Although your capture took me several months I confess I'm rather surprised to see you now."

"Why?" I asked.

"I should have thought you would have managed to give the Italians the slip, somehow."

I said nothing.

We were handed over to two Gestapo guards whom we were to see quite frequently as time went by and driven through Paris to the big prison of Fresnes. Passing in front of Notre Dame and crossing the Seine was an added pang. The sunny streets were full of people going about their business whilst we were to be put away.

The twelve painful kilometres to Fresnes were all too soon over before we were passing along the private road leading to the prison gates. Outside these gates stood two Sisters of Mercy. I wondered how much mercy we should find inside.

Odette and I were signed in and then led to a set of tiny wooden cubicles from which we were extracted in due course to be searched and to have certain possessions confiscated.

On hearing Odette's brisk steps outside my cubicle I felt a stab at the knowledge that this was the end of our many hours together. I called out automatically.

"*Bon courage, Odette chérie!*" but she had to remain silent in the presence of her tight-lipped woman guard.

Whilst I waited for my turn to come I had plenty of time to study some of the thousands of remarks pencilled on the walls. One of these impressed itself on my mind above all the others. It had been written in English and read: "Oh, my beloved France, what has happened to you?"

CHAPTER

III

AFTER the search, during which I was deprived of all my cigarettes and lighter but managed to persuade them to let me keep the ring and crucifix Odette had given me, I was led through the ghostly underground passages of the prison towards the second division. I saw armed guards standing at all strategic points. Many doors had to be opened and then locked behind us before we reached the ground floor of this mighty jail.

Above me I counted four cat-walks, thus making five floors in all. I did not yet know that there were two more identical blocks housing in all some 3,000 prisoners.

I was led up to the second floor and taken into cell No. 220. Once more my belongings were carefully searched and then the door slammed behind me.

I looked at my new pen. It was a well-lighted and reasonable-sized lavatory with an iron bedstead against one wall, a wooden wall-table and stool opposite and large double windows of frosted glass with a plain glass over-window which could be opened or closed by a control lever. One of the square panes of frosted glass was partially broken and through it I saw the exercise cages below and the grey mass of the first division opposite and perhaps 70 yards away.

My door had the usual ticket office slot carved into it at chest height but this, I found, was never opened. The German regulations insisted that any communication or passing of articles between guard and prisoner should be done through the open door. This increased security measures and allowed the guard a full view of the cell's interior.

Above the slot was a spy-hole. Remnants of chipped glass in the circular groove told me that my predecessor had been busy. With my finger I tried moving the small circular plate which I

C

presumed had an external control for the guards' use. It moved aside with ease. Through the gap I got a good view of the two floors above and below me. As for the cell doors opposite I could see at least a dozen of them. Above each I noted various cryptic signs which, I imagined, told the guards what restrictions were being enforced, or what privileges were allowed to the man within.

Presently, above the low hum of prison sounds to which my ears were only too soon to become attuned, I heard the clear untroubled voice of a man somewhere below me declaiming a news bulletin, just like a radio announcer. I could hardly believe my ears. Here, in the middle of nowhere, the war report, with a definitely allied bias, was penetrating my cell as though it were the most natural thing in the world.

From the equable tone of his voice I imagined the purveyor of these bright and encouraging advances on all fronts must be somewhere in the cloisters below and that the Germans allowed this sort of thing. I walked over to the window but could see no-one.

At the end of the news the voice said: "That is the end of this morning's bulletin. Pass it round, chums." Then, after a short pause, he continued, "Here are some personal messages: Paul sends his greetings to Jacques and says he had rather a rough time with the Gestapo, but there's no need to change anything in their previously agreed defence. . . . Robert asks his friend Loulou if he got a parcel this week," etc. . . . etc. . . .

The repetition of the news around the walls of the second division rang out and echoed back from the opposite wall. I turned round and had a look at my bed. There were three blankets and one undersheet. A hard, stale straw mattress and an apparently cast-iron pillow were my bargains in this direction. Opposite, below a disused gas-bracket, was a typed notice under the heading: RULES OF THE HOUSE. I glanced through the paragraphs, the general gist of which was that there was to be no singing, shouting, tapping on the walls or any communication whatsoever with people in other cells. I listened to the rumpus outside and thought to myself: "Oh, my beloved France, I have not yet lost my faith in you."

In the midst of this babble of voices, one voice stood out above the rest and kept repeating:

"Hey, you, the new man! You with the broken pane of glass on the second floor, come to the window!"

After a few repetitions it dawned on me that this might refer to me and I went up to my broken pane and shouted:

"Hallo, there, do you mean me?"

"Yes, of course," said the voice, "What's your name?"

"Pierre," I replied after some hesitation.

"Well, you'll be known as Louis. Those who stay in your cell are always called Louis so that the guards can't guess to whom we're speaking. Where were you captured?"

"Annecy," I replied.

"Oh, we've got a couple of your group here already. Riquet and Marsac. I'll put you in touch with them presently. Where do you come from?"

"My home town, d'you mean?" I asked.

"Yes."

"Well, oddly enough I come from London."

"What, are you English?" enquired a voice of open amazement.

"Yes," I said, feeling a little dubious myself after masquerading for so long as a Frenchman.

"Well, you mustn't mind if we put you to the test. I'm sure you'll understand that we have to protect ourselves against possible stooges."

"Go ahead. I understand perfectly."

"Hang on a moment then," said the voice and in a little while I heard it again somewhere in the corner of my cell. Looking round I saw that it was coming from a rectangular hole set high up on the wall. The voice was calling out, *"Emile, allo Emile !"* several times before another replied, *"Allo Michel, c'est toi?"*

"Oui. Voilà de quoi il s'agit. . . . Le nouveau—à mi-chemin entre nous—se dit Anglais. Parle-lui un peu en Anglais pour t'assurer que ce n'est pas un mouton."

The sound of a plank being replaced told me that one of the speakers had covered up his hole in the shaft.

Now Emile's voice came to me quite clearly and in good English with a slight French accent I heard him say:

"Hallo, down there, get your stool and stick it up against the wall at the foot of your bed. Have a look around first through your spy-hole to see if any Fritzes are prowling about. If all's clear climb up onto the back-rest of the stool. In this way your mouth should be on a level with the central heating exit."

I went through the motions and soon found myself in the required position to prove my nationality.

"Hallo, Emile," I began, to show him that I had got there.

"Hallo, friend," replied the pleasant voice of my upstairs neighbour. "I hear you're English. When were you last in London?"

"About a month ago I should say."

"From the way you said that I should say you were English all right."

"You bet your boots I'm English."

"I'll be back to you later on when it's safer for you to talk. The soup trolleys are getting on the move, so I'll just tip off Michel that you're O.K. . . . So long."

I climbed down from my perch and overheard Emile now telephoning down five floors to the redoubtable Michel.

"This chap's all right. English as boiled cabbage."

"Well, I'm certainly relieved to hear that. His French is good enough to evoke a dish of snails and garlic."

I laughed out loud. There was nothing wrong with the morale inside this inverted catacomb; in fact, the living-dead seemed very much alive. I wondered how Odette was faring.

Having hung up my two coats on the pegs and laid out my few belongings on the shelf above and pinned my crucifix into the chalky wall, I began to munch a piece of what looked like an 8-ounce hunk of bread which I had been given on the ground floor. When my cell door opened for the first time and a second half-loaf was planked on the door-shelf I felt that with such rations as these there could be no complaint as far as the food was concerned.

A quarter of an hour later I watched the soup trolley passing the opposite cells on my floor through the spy-hole. Seeing which of the three aluminium containers was produced by my neighbours. I stood by the door with the correct article at the ready.

With one deft movement, resulting no doubt from much practice, the guard rammed home his key into my lock, turned it and the door was open. Standing aside he gazed in at the new occupant of No. 220, but I was more interested in the closer view of the two men on the trolley. They were both prisoners and whilst one of them pushed, the other sat behind a giant soup cauldron containing maybe 50 quarts. A swift dip and my billy-can filled with about one litre of the precise ration of thick and thin that the disher-up intended me to have. He took a swift glance at me and winked with the eye hidden from the guard by his nose. My door closed and the trolley moved on to the next cell. The whole thing had lasted perhaps ten seconds.

I took my soup over to the table and ate it with my tin spoon. It was reasonably hot, rather thin and not very interesting. However, the quantity seemed sufficient. I drank the last drops out of my upturned can and then washed the can under the tap placed over the w.c. I noticed that the flat end of my spoon had been sharpened down against something until it had quite an edge. I could use this for cutting my bread. Further inspection of my cell showed the main purpose for which it had served my predecessor. Through the broken pane of glass I saw the mark where he had been sawing the end bar. Looking over to the left I saw the two walls of the prison, the outer one some 30 feet high. I was almost immediately above them, being only two cells away from the end of the block. Two guards passed at this moment between the walls. They were accompanied by an Alsatian dog. Some optimist—my predecessor—I thought; and yet I supposed it could be done.

My thoughts were interrupted by the opening of my door and there, framed in the entrance, stood the suave Henri.

"I'm afraid I've got some bad news for you, Pierre," he opened.

"What?" I asked.

"Arnaud's been captured."

"I don't believe it," I said.

"Why did you say you only brought back 70,000 francs from London?"

"Because that's what I did bring back."

"Well, Arnaud was caught with a suitcase, which he claims was yours, and there was a million francs in it."

"What nonsense!" I said, in a tired voice. "You've simply invented the whole story. You can't possibly find a million francs where no such sum has ever existed," I continued, with the confidence of the person who knows that the sum hidden was half a million.

Henri offered me a cigarette to change the subject, lit it and went over and sat on the bed.

"What would you say to the idea of being exchanged for Rudolf Hess?" he queried.

I roared with laughter, then said:

"A wonderful idea, Henri."

"It seems reasonable to suppose that Winston Churchill would be glad to give up a person of so little real importance to get his nephew back."

"I somehow feel that because of the enormous distance of the relationship between us the Old Man might view this proposition as a badly balanced exchange of values," I said.

"Don't forget," said Henri, slowly and with meaning, "that the closer your relationship with Winston Churchill, the further your distance from the firing squad."

"Suits me all right," I replied, "so long as the Gestapo will swallow it."

"I'm sorry to see you in this plight, Pierre," said Henri, in all apparent sincerity. "Now that I've captured you I should like to do everything possible for your comfort. I was a prisoner in similar circumstances during the '14-'18 war and the British treated me very decently. You'll be interrogated fairly soon, but in the meantime what can I do for you?"

"Arrange for me to meet Odette as often as you can," I said.

"That will be a little difficult but I shall manage it somehow, and you shall see her next time I come. I'll be back very soon."

Henri threw a packet of ten High Life cigarettes onto my bed and went out.

I had hardly the time to digest this rapid and extraordinary conversation before Michel was calling me through the window. I walked to my broken pane and called back.

"Who was your visitor?" asked Michel.

"How did you know I had one?" I asked.

"I could hear your voices through the central heating vent."

"Oh yes, of course," I replied. "That was the man who caught us."

"What d'you mean, us?"

"My wife and me," I explained.

"Is she here, too?"

"Yes."

"Would you like me to try and get a message through to her in the third division?"

"Please. Just say Pierre sends his love to Odette."

"I'll do that. . . . What did your chap want?"

"He wanted to exchange me for Rudolf Hess."

"That's a laugh . . . unless you're some big shot. . . . Are you?"

"That's just the joke. I'm not, only my name—for the sake of the record—is the same as that of the Big Chief who makes all the decisions back home."

"Gosh! What a name to carry!"

"I'm beginning to think it is."

"Well, good luck to the exchange, Louis."

"Thanks, Michel."

"Louis," came back Michel, after a short silence, "Has the Old Man launched any more of his pile-driving speeches lately? We hang onto every word he says."

"I was only home for a short time in April and the last one I heard was over here on the radio somewhere around March 22nd. Did you hear that one?"

"Heavens, yes. A long time ago. You see, new chaps are coming in almost every day. That's how we keep abreast of the news."

"I see. Well, all I know is that the R.A.F. raids are being stepped up over Berlin and Germany in general and that there'll be a landing in France as soon as we're ready. The whole of the United States and Britain are geared up for this big event, but personally I can't see it coming off until the spring of next year, at the earliest."

"That's just about the way we figure it, too. Well, patience, Louis. Roll on the mighty ship of victory!"

Later on in the afternoon I was put in touch with Riquet and was just able to hear his voice some twenty cells away along the wall.

"Hallo, Louis," came the faint sound of his well-known voice. "How are you?"

"Fine, thanks, Riquet," I shouted. "How are you?"

"Tip top. I've been interrogated and they didn't connect me with you. Don't worry. Everything will be all right."

"Good for you, Riquet. I won't know you when questioned."

"Marsac sends his best wishes," he went on.

"I don't want any messages of any kind from him," I said. "He gave Henri a letter with my name and St. Jorioz address. It's probably thanks to him that we were put in the bag."

A heavy silence followed this categoric remark and no more voices shouted through the bars of this particular section of the grim walls of Fresnes for the rest of the day.

I walked up and down my cell like a trapped animal, but like a very average trapped human being I began to lay all my misery, fear and anguish at Marsac's* door. When Marsac was caught on March 24th, or thereabouts, and put straight into Fresnes, Henri had entered his cell and told him the tale that, as an Abwehr officer, he could not abide the Gestapo and that all he hoped to find was a Frenchman belonging to a Resistance group to which was attached a British officer sufficiently influential to get the War Office to send a four-engined bomber to pick him up and bring him back to London, where he would gladly expose the best way of bringing the

* See Appendix.

war to a rapid end. Yes, if such a man could be found and even if that man were imprisoned in Fresnes, he—Henri—would know how to get him out and take him back to England in the same aircraft.

I imagined Marsac's reaction to this line of talk, this tale so incredible that it might almost be true. I proceeded to imagine his reply as being:

"Why, Henri, I'm the very man you're looking for. I happen to be the chief of one of the most powerful sabotage groups in France and our British liaison officer is none other than Captain Peter Churchill, the nephew of the Prime Minister."

No doubt, I thought, Henri had hoped for something of this nature and his reply to it was probably along these lines:

"Well, before I can get you out I must get the aircraft and before that can be done I must get into touch with Peter Churchill."

The rest had no doubt followed like clockwork and I had seen it in the shape of Marsac's letter to Lise explaining that if he had given Henri our address at St. Jorioz it was because Henri was a German one could trust implicitly. The letter proceeded to outline the Abwehr's hatred for the Gestapo and closed with the hope that the bomber operation could be arranged in order that Marsac's liberation from Fresnes could be swiftly followed by the end of the war.

This was the impossible mess which Lise had had to face single-handed during my short absence in England. She had handled it rapidly and well, reporting the situation succinctly to London. Had I not been so stale I, who was at Head Office at the time, should have advocated a clean break from the whole Annecy set-up and a fresh start elsewhere. But I *had* been stale and my return by parachute to the danger spot was a fatal error. I had lulled myself into believing that a change of address before finally joining the Maquis of Glières would solve the problem. The very fact of contacting a single person of our contaminated group was a madness against which my long experience should have warned me as clearly as a rolling ball across his path warns the alert motorist that a child will soon dash after it.

Of course Marsac had been foolish. Of course he had fallen for Henri's tempting bait. Of course he had given away our hide-out. But was it a betrayal in the strict sense of the word? Such as Odette laid at Roger Bardet's door. Who was I to judge, anyway? The thing to have done was to expect this kind of folly, to provide against it by the simple expedient of anticipating and avoiding it. There were no Queensberry Rules in this dangerous game. But I had not done either of these obvious things and here I was and here I must remain until I had paid the awful price of my blunder.

My hatred for Marsac was the instinctive reaction of finding a scapegoat to carry the blame that I was hiding from my own conscience. As I walked up and down my cell I railed against him and my thoughts tore round and round inside my stricken mind like motor-cyclists round the "wall of death". I saw the war ending with a British Tommy opening up my cell. I imagined every word of our moving conversation and then I saw myself entering Marsac's cell and, scornfully rejecting his outstretched hand, I heard myself saying:

"You Judas Iscariot! You belong to the only class of individual whom even Christ could not forgive."

I heard myself saying all this because I was talking to myself aloud. So that was it. I was round the bend already. 'In Heaven's name,' I said, 'you'd better pull yourself together. You're not alone in a solitary tomb; there are thousands like you all around and most of them are probably worse off than you. Some of them must be old men and others sick in health, whereas you are young, and strong.' But alas, that was just the trouble. Still young, I must be deprived of all the sweetness of life and wait endlessly, cooped up in solitude, for a lonely death. Waves of despair enveloped me.

By now the sun, which had had its rays diffused by the frosted glass of my window, was going down and I watched its mark rising on the wall above the door. It must be getting late. The actual hour was no longer of any importance to me. I did not even know what day it was. I had no train to catch, no rendezvous with any of my men. Never again should I look at a watch and know that perhaps in a quarter of an hour Odette would be chattering gaily at my side. 'But wait, oh fool! She was due at six and you weren't there to meet her.'

My vision of Odette sitting on her bed in a similar cell and thinking of me whilst I had missed the one sacred hour of the day worth living for was too much for my distracted mind and I gave way to a flood of tears.

*   *   *

I was awakened on the following morning by the rumble of the trolleys bringing round the acorn-juice which represented the morning coffee. It had a queer yet not altogether unpleasant taste. I drank it while it was still hot and then did about half an hour's physical exercises, interspersed with greetings through the window.

My door was opened and a French prisoner accompanied by a guard explained that I must be ready every day at this hour with a little pile of sweepings off my floor and that my cell brush served for that purpose. This, too, he explained was the moment to mention any fault in the water system and ask for medical attention, if necessary. After he had gone I was left alone for the rest of the day.

I had nothing to read, as this was a privilege I had not yet earned, and I was never allowed pencil and paper. As I had eaten all my food there was nothing to do but fill in the time as best I could until the bread came round.

With my cake of national soap that resembled a piece of slimy pumice-stone, I washed myself in cold water from head to foot, drying myself on the cleaner of the two towels in my cell. I was pretty sure I was only entitled to one of these but thought it wiser to hang on to the second as it might serve some useful purpose. I washed some of my underwear and hung it up against the window.

As I walked up and down the cell wondering how I should fare at my first interrogation I began to feel really hungry.

By now I had recovered from most of the damage incurred

in the Annecy battle and although I had a five days' growth of beard it was good to feel clean elsewhere. My crêpe-soled shoes were a perfect fit despite the absence of laces which had been confiscated and my walking about could not annoy the man below. As I never wore either belt or braces, the absence of these articles, which so complicated other prisoners' existences, did not arise in my case. I felt light, springy and well, far too well for anything evil to befall me.

Whilst I still had half a stick of the shaving soap Odette had packed for me I decided to use it only for washing my hair. It would probably have to last a very long time. In the absence of a toothbrush I rubbed my teeth with a damp corner of the towel and then worked on them from time to time throughout the day with a piece of wood that I found.

When my hunk of bread came I began to suspect that the eight-ounce half-loaf was, after all, the day's full ration and that the two halves I had received on the previous day had been but a lucky mistake. I placed the bread on my shelf and every time I came back towards the door on my short prowl I tried to avert my eyes from it. But it was no use. I picked it up in the end, smelt the black crust, baked almost to a cinder, inspected the way one piece had been half cut and a small piece of margarine inserted in the cleft and I examined the ridiculous little piece of meat, the size and weight of a double biscuit with sugar icing between. Never had I smelt such wonderful bread. I cut off the first slice and tasted it. No roast chicken in the world was ever better: no oysters, caviare or quenelles inspired such a gastronomic thrill. I must leave the larger portion for the long evening, so I began to walk up and down some more. I drank some water to make the bread swell out like a sponge inside me and give me a better impression of having eaten something, but it was of no avail. Back went my eyes to the remaining piece. I might as well eat it all at one fell swoop and be certain, at least once a day, that I had had enough to eat.

By the time the soup came round I was thoroughly ashamed of myself and knew that I should have to pay for my gluttony. I wisely limited myself to drinking the liquid and keeping the vegetables for the evening. This action saved me from the pangs of hunger which were to grip me henceforth—however cunningly I divided up my food—and which forced me to think and dream about food almost to the entire exclusion of everything else.

During the afternoon my neighbours spoke to me again. I was eternally grateful at all times for any interruptions of my solitude and I wondered what I should do when these spirited men were whisked off to Germany, particularly if those who replaced them were not of their calibre.

A call to the central heating exit brought me up onto the back of my stool.

"Would you like to help us keep 'cave' at this end?" asked Michel.

"Certainly," I replied. "What do I do?"

"If you rummage about inside your straw mattress you'll find a length of string at one end of which is a running noose and at the other a piece of steel wire. The steel wire is just the right length to go over the vertical shaft of this hole. You can feel its size and distance from you by stretching out your arm."

I did so and felt the rectangular space.

"I get it," I called down.

"Right. You simply unwind the string so that the loop at the end goes down the shaft. It's long enough to reach me down here. When I see it I shall attach a small gadget like a lorgnette with a tiny mirror fitted into some twisted wire. By opening your spyhole and sticking this through the gap you'll be able to see all the way along your cat-walk to the very end of the block."

"How long does this 'cave' business last?" I enquired.

"Only during the news and exchange of messages."

"What do I do if I see a Fritz coming?"

"You whistle '*J'attendrai*', and when he's passed you give a rendering of '*Tout va très bien, Madame la Marquise!*'"

"Fine. I know them both," I said. "And what do I do with the mirror if things get really hot and the chap comes in here?"

"Drop it down the can. They never look down there."

I opened the seam of my mattress and there, sure enough, was the very article about which Michel had spoken. Climbing back up the wall I lowered it down the shaft and fished up the minute mirror. I then rolled up the string around the rod and placed the rod over the hole. In no time I had the hang of the mirror and its fantastic range.

By using the shaft I was now able to get Michel to light me one of the cigarettes Henri had left me. I smoked it from the back of my stool, blowing the smoke into the shaft whilst keeping an eye on the spy-hole and listening intently for the sound of approaching footsteps. All went well and, thanks to the soothing intoxication of the tobacco, I managed to sleep for a while.

When I woke up it was still mid-afternoon. I was fully rested but the pangs of hunger were gnawing at me once more. I took a drink of water and did some walking. I measured the cell by placing one foot in front of the other. It was exactly fourteen feet long by eight feet wide.

On enquiring if we were ever allowed to exercise in the cloisters below I learned that this sometimes happened once a week, sometimes once a month, all depending on the mood of the guards.

I now began to think of the cigarettes, the drink, the food and all the other joys of life that I had always taken for granted. Now everything was a luxury including food. With the meagre rations I supposed that one could just about keep body and soul together. I had read Victor Hugo's *Count of Monte Cristo*, and so already had a fair notion of what dungeon existence was like but, try as I might, I could not remember a single passage that had dealt with the gnawing pangs of chronic hunger. Perhaps man's power of evil had increased since the days of the Chateau d'If. Perhaps this was a calculated torture, a Teutonic sublety designed to soften up the prisoner before his interrogations. If so it was having the wrong effect on me, for the hungrier I got the less inclined I felt to co-operate with my tormentors. Had they, on the other hand, fed me with reasonable rations I might have been led to believe that the Gestapo were not as black as they were painted.

That evening when I thought it must be six o'clock I projected my mind into Odette's cell and spent a happy hour in imaginary conversation with her. This moment of concentration was like a prayer made easy by her comparative proximity and my clear vision of her face. Without shame I accepted the waves of strength and sound counsel I seemed to receive from my frail partner. We had not had much opportunity to talk during the feverish activity of our Resistance days, but although I knew Odette to be a non-practising Catholic I had always felt in her a spiritual strength which her role in the "underground" had never required her to exert. But now that her hour had struck, her power was a very real thing, and on this, as on each successive spiritual meeting, I knew her strength was enough for two, and to spare.

True to his word, Henri was back within a few days and I was fetched down to meet him in a private cell on the first floor of the third division. I noticed that we were in the women's half and saw a huge wooden partition separating it on the ground floor from the men's.

Henri began with the same assertions about Arnaud's capture and the money that had been found. I replied as before. Whilst we smoked together in an atmosphere of comparative amity he warned me again that my interrogation was imminent and said that the Gestapo were putting their best man onto me. He also informed me that Berlin had put through the exchange proposal. Having had time to read the Italians' reports he challenged me on the question of our marriage. I told him that we had kept it a secret, but that if he wanted corroboration he had only to ask London. I ended our somewhat pointless but not unpleasant conversation by asking if I could see Odette.

Henri opened the door and sent for her. He did not shout out an order but spoke his request quietly.

Presently the door opened and there stood Odette, immaculate from head to foot. She had on her one and only dark grey suit, silk stockings and rather square-toed shoes. Above a spotless blouse, poised on her slim neck, was the head I knew so well with her thick light brown hair in a rolling quiff above her rounded forehead and falling down at the sides to rest on her shoulders.

On seeing me rise from the table beside Henri a shy, happy smile spread over her small features and brought light to her eyes that had come in dull with uncertainty as to what awaited her behind the door. Unconcerned at Henri's presence we embraced each other warmly whilst he stood by and then walked over to the window.

Seeing a bruise on Odette's wrist I asked her what had caused it. She told me that a wardress had come into her cell one night and started beating her with a brush, as she suspected her of talking through the window. She somewhat calmed my rage by explaining that although she was a frequent window-talker, her innocence on this occasion had so provoked her indignation that she had reported the incident to the Captain of the prison and that this very decent white-haired German had issued a stern admonishment to the culprit.

Although Henri's presence prevented us from saying all the things we should have liked to say, the quarter of an hour we spent together was another of those precious milestones I was to live over and over for many a day to come—despite the almost unbearable pain of parting.

Back in my cell I now began to work up my courage to face my first Gestapo interrogation. As I paced up and down I tried to think of all the men or legendary figures I knew of who had had to face a similar trial. If only I could concentrate better and keep my mind from flitting off down the sloping avenue of self-pity or along such dead-end lines as that this could not have happened to me. If only I had paid more attention at school. If only I could remember the story of St. Paul. Yes . . . if only . . . but there it was. Like the average Public School product of my day, my mind had wandered in the classroom and chafed impatiently until I could get onto the football field. Following up this athletic craze until at twenty-one I had exceeded my ambitions by becoming Captain of the Cambridge University Ice-hockey team and an International, it was easy to see that my mental equipment—left so far behind as to be practically non-existent—was not of much use to me in my present plight.

I seemed to remember vaguely that St. Paul had once been a Roman Centurion, that he had had a hand in persecuting the Christians and that suddenly, on a solitary journey, he had received the call. I could understand how, from then on, his life had undergone a complete change and how, thanks to the immense power of his religious fervour, he had passed through the fire with equanimity.

But I had no religion. Sunday School and services had meant less than nothing to me. The repeated prayers of a Chaplain of my youth had seemed mere empty mouthings, nor had they prevented *him* from being relieved of his duties for behaviour that, if reprehensible in a layman, was beyond the pale in a member of the "cloth". I had not noticed any difference in the behaviour of boys after they had been confirmed. In short, I was at a loss as to what it was all about. But then no St. Paul had, as yet, crossed my path.

My mind sought something nearer to hand, something I could hold onto for strength. It fell with gratitude upon the memory of my fighter-pilot brother. Walter's was the firm character I had always tried to emulate; his was the death I might have chosen. With the increasing conviction that I should shortly be joining him in the hereafter, I now pictured him in Valhalla, where the Norse Gods kept an ever-expanding Hall for the World's heroes. I saw him, as I was always to see him, pointing at an empty chair beside him and trying to say something to me: but I never heard what he said and only guessed what I hardly dared believe. Turning away from this swiftly vanishing image and joining my hands in my first serious prayer, I said out loud: "Oh God, let me behave with dignity that I may deserve such honour."

As I said these words I was aware that, for the first time, I had invoked God's help. Up till then I had thought I was self-sufficient. It had been all right for those who could not stand on their own two feet to bolster themselves up with prayers to the Almighty, but such weakness was not for me. And now that I had joined the ranks of frail humanity I realised the conceit of having set myself up as a judge of my fellow creatures. In my gratitude for this first lesson in tolerance—one that I might never have received but for the fact of captivity—I gave thanks to the Lord.

Though the thought of God as a person was quite beyond me, I could better understand and admire the life of Jesus Christ. His voluntary sacrifice, his human temptations, his cry—"Take away this cup from me"—all these things suddenly took on real meaning for the first time. Here was the consolation of all consolations. Here was a man who had passed through it all and faced it well. Surely this was the outstanding hero of all times; a hero one could worship with admiration, a Deity who would listen to one's prayers with understanding, for had he not passed that way himself—and voluntarily?

The words that came to me that night were simple, brief and to the point, nor did I have to search for them. I said: "God give me strength, courage, patience and good judgment." As I heard myself utter the last two words, I smiled and added, "We'll forget about the good judgment since, in my case, I feel that a whole lifetime will not be long enough to develop such a quality."

I then recited the Lord's Prayer. I was in no hurry and took each phrase slowly, trying to weigh up its meaning. "Our Father which art in Heaven. . . ." Here was a poser. Was he a bearded judge in flowing robes, sitting on a throne? Was he the final arbiter to whom the Saints turned when they themselves were in doubt? Was he a person who had the time and capacity to listen to the individual and collective prayers of some 2,000 million souls? I remembered reading a book by Denis P. Hadley, entitled *Towards the Stars*, in which the author, on one occasion, put the following question through a writing-medium to a contact in the spirit world: "Have you ever seen God?" The answer came back pat through the swift writing of the medium, "I have been in the second sphere for close on 2,000 years and shall not begin to understand the meaning of God for at least another 2,000." This was quite enough for me and I passed onto "Hallowed be thy Name." No difficulty about this. "Thy Kingdom come"; how I agreed! "Thy will be done on earth, as it is in Heaven." Quite all right, and the more who strove for this the better. "Give us this day our daily bread." I stopped and said that again. The words almost choked me. Never had this simple request borne such meaning. I vowed that if ever I survived I should never tolerate waste again.

"Forgive us our trespasses," I went on, wondering if it always required a major catastrophe before one began to ponder the sense of words one had so often repeated meaninglessly. It was not surprising, I concluded, that the Zen Buddhists packed off their novices into the Himalayas to spend several years on a snow-capped mountain peak simply to contemplate the sound that would be made by the clapping of one hand, before they were considered fit to come down and be initiated in the fundamentals of this sect. " . . . as we forgive them that trespass against us." That clearly meant that if I did not forgive Marsac there would be no salvation for me. This thought would require some heavy consideration and I decided to keep it for a particularly rainy day.

"Lead us not into temptation." What were the temptations here? I could not really see any unless it were the temptation to abandon oneself to despair. Well, I had covered that contingency in my previous short prayer. " . . . but deliver us from evil." Ah yes, there was another winner.

" For thine is the Kingdom, the Power and the Glory, for ever and ever. Amen."

CHAPTER

IV

I was very fortunate in one thing. Every night I slept solidly and although the guards had an annoying habit of switching on the light at odd moments and peering at me with a fishy eye through the spy-hole, I managed, nevertheless, to put in many hours of sleep. Almost every morning I would wake up to the sound of the trolleys, and the pleasant dream I was conscious of having dreamed would vanish as my eyes caught sight of the grey walls and my mind came back to the awful reality.

After I had passed some six days in Fresnes the inmates of the second floor were privileged to the singular treat of being allowed to shave. It was astonishing what one could do with a worn out brush boasting about eighteen bristles, non-lathering shaving cream, a blunt blade and cold water. The uplift of this operation was remarkable.

It was the day after this great event that I heard the hated and dreaded sound, "Tribunal!" shouted at me after the key had rammed my lock shortly before the coffee was due. A particularly horrible-looking Kraut, whom I had never seen before, seemed to be enjoying the startled look that must have spread over my face as I was woken out of a deep sleep by his foul greeting. He shouted it again, stressing the last syllable in the German accent that murders the French language.

I washed and dressed quickly and stood by, listening for the heavy footsteps that would bring someone to fetch me. I was wide awake, hungry, alert and terrified. Over and over I murmured, "Give me strength and courage."

It was too early to shout at my unknown friends through the window, and I did not want to start their day with bad news. Fortunately the wait was not long before I was led downstairs to the ground floor where all those in the same boat were being drawn up in two lines facing each other. As I joined these ranks I instantly spotted Eugène, an old acquaintance; he was one of the two radio-operators I had landed in Antibes Bay from Alastair Mars' submarine, the *Unbroken*, over a year ago. When the guard's eyes were elsewhere I gave him a sly wink to indicate—as though it were necessary—that we did not know each other. Presently I felt a dull thud in my heart. Odette had joined our grim party. Here, however, there was no need to wink and we smiled openly at each other for mutual encouragement and to hide the fear each of us had that the other might be tortured.

On our way through the subterranean passages of the prison we managed to get close to one another so that we could whisper *"bon courage, mon chéri."* At the gates we were separated and put into two different "Black Marias"—each prisoner being locked into a tiny cubicle with a forward-sloping tin seat. Presently my van moved off on its twelve kilometres journey, bearing its load of isolated anguish. We were deposited at the elegant gates of 84, Avenue Foch on a May morning of brilliant sunshine.

It was incongruous to think that this lovely building in this equally elegant and majestic Avenue should now house the most brutal elements of Nazi Germany.

We were ushered individually into the rooms where our fate would be decided. I was taken up to the fourth floor and shown into a small room that had probably served as a maid's bedroom in happier days.

A tall man of maybe forty, in a dark lounge suit, looked up at me out of a grey intelligent face. His high forehead and protruding ears gave him an intellectual aspect, but his cold eyes gave me the shivers. He waved me to the vacant chair before his desk and started in without any sort of preliminaries.

Name; date of birth, nationality, father's full name and profession, names of brothers and sisters; their doings. Schools attended, University degrees. What had I done since then? All these questions on my life's history were put to me in flawless French after my interrogator had enquired whether I preferred the interrogation to be held in English. All the answers were taken down in quintuplicate on a typewriter operated at lightning speed by my enemy. When he reached the foot of the page, he pulled out the sheaf of papers, laid them out in five different piles and with deft fingers reinserted the four carbons between the five fresh sheets.

Having swept the decks of my early life and reached the war period, he stopped and leaned back in his chair. Pulling open a drawer, he drew forth a wad of some ten typed pages of single-spaced information on my sabotage activities. He fanned out the pages like a pack of cards and it seemed hopeless to try and double what was obviously a grand-slam in no-trumps.

"You see, Mr. Churchill, or Monsieur Chauvet, or Monsieur Chambrun, alias Raoul or what-have-you," he said slowly. "We

know absolutely everything about you. . . . Three visits to France
—one by submarine and two by parachute." (I was glad that my
fourth visit by submarine was unknown to my betrayer; this gave
me hope that there might be other discrepancies.) "You organised
fishing-boat landings of men and material in the south of France,
aircraft landings for the exchange of personnel, parachute drops
all over the place for the railway sabotage plan and you were
responsible for the arming of the Maquis of the Plateau des Glières
by twenty-five British bombers."

"Who gave you all that exaggerated information?" I asked.

"I don't think you quite understand our respective roles today," he said, suavely. "It is I who ask the questions and you
who do the answering. Is it true that you were the Chief of the
south-east zone?"

I had fortunately remembered our training in how to answer
Gestapo interrogators. Two courses were open to us, we had been
told: one, to answer rapidly, which required a very alert mind,
and the other to speak slowly and pretend to be the village idiot.
The main point I had to remember in the second course—my
obvious and natural choice—was that at all costs I must not show
any more enthusiasm or indignation when denying a false charge
than a true one. In this way it would be difficult for my interrogator
to assess where the truth lay. Before the day was out I should know
the results of such a method.

In a monotonous voice, therefore, I told my first half-truth.

"There was no such thing as the Chief of a Zone. Each officer
was in charge of the district to which he was sent. The south-east
zone is full of such districts."

"Tell me the names of the British officers in charge of your
neighbouring districts."

"I never knew them. We worked in watertight compartments."

"Ever seen any of the men who travelled in the Black Maria
with you today?"

"No."

"We shall see. Some of them know *you* all right. You'll have
a chance of meeting them later, in my presence."

There was a short pause, then, tossing a small collection of photographs across the table, he asked, "Ever seen any of these men before?"

I spread them out and ran through them once, slowly. I had met four of these men before, one of whom was the radio-operator who had travelled with me that morning.

"Never." I shook my head.

"So you don't know any of these men, you never knew any of your neighbours and you weren't the Chief of the south-east zone," he said, sarcastically.

"No," I replied in a dull voice.

He clicked his teeth and typed a short paragraph.

"This affair of the Maquis of Glières, are you going to deny that you arranged for their being armed by those twenty-five bombers?"

"Yes. It was a de Gaulle operation," I said, in what seemed a hopeless attempt to minimise the heavy load of charges standing against me.

The interrogator jumped up and stormed round the room shouting, "What do you take me for?—a complete ninnyhammer?"

"Not in the least," I answered, slowly and with what I profoundly prayed might look like innate stupidity. "But the man who gave you all this information seems so pleased at laying it on with a trowel that he has placed every single incident he has ever heard of since the beginning of hostilities at my door."

My interrogator shut off the steam of his wrath abruptly, to say, "You realise what to expect from your stupid attitude in denying what is already known against you?"

"I am your prisoner," I said, "but I cannot accept the responsibility of all the things my enthusiastic betrayer has pinned on me."

"Then what do you accept?" he said.

"That I came over here to sabotage the German war effort, that I did my duty as a British officer, that I lived with forged papers in civilian clothes, was prepared to blow up anything and everything I was told to blow up, but that in fact I have never sabotaged anything, never carried arms and never killed a single German."

By this slow-witted statement which was enough to show my opponent that I knew myself liable to the extreme penalty I hoped to avoid some of the painful ordeal of being asked the names and addresses of my companions. How long I could keep the man jumping unmethodically from one subject to the next was impossible to tell. Yet so sure was he of the veracity of the typed words before him that he picked out another winner which could only have been known to Frager, Marsac and Roger Bardet.

"Are you going to deny that on March 2nd of this year you wrote a letter to one of Carte's Chiefs who had stolen arms, intended for your group, threatening him with the sternest reprisals of the War Office unless these arms were handed back?"

"I've never heard of such a letter," I replied, praying that the original was not in his possession.

"Well, you wrote that letter," he said.

"I shall believe it when I see it," I said, hoping that if this letter was lost, some doubt might begin to enter my interrogator's mind as to the reliability of my betrayer's report. Maybe he was already beginning to think that I was not quite such a big fish as he thought to have caught in his net.

Changing the subject again, he blurted out, confidently, "What's the idea of trying to make out that you and Lise are married? Everyone knows that she joined you for the first time on November 2nd 1942 as your courier."

"We are married," I said quietly.

"When were you married?" he asked, thinking to floor me with this simple query.

"On December 24th 1941," I said at the same dismal studied pace.

My lifeless replies seemed to be having the desired effect and this subject, like the others, was not pursued. A good deal more of this kind of thing filled up the rest of the morning, along the same dreary lines. At the end of it my interrogator got up slowly. "I'm wasting my time with you," he said. "I'll see you another day when you've had a little more time to reflect on what you're letting yourself in for by this stupid attitude of non-co-operation. You needn't expect any privileges so long as you remain in your present frame of mind."

I breathed an inward sigh of relief. I simply could not understand why the man had not tried out any one of a dozen tortures that were practised here daily. Perhaps the name of Churchill was responsible for this. Perhaps the senior Gestapo Official had issued the directive that I was not to be touched. Who could tell?

My sharp-witted opponent looked at me with a mixture of hatred and disdain. I could not make out if he thought Allied help to the French Resistance must be pretty paltry if they sent out dullards like me or whether he thought I was stalling.

I had no particular satisfaction from this slothful performance. Its mediocrity might have been pierced by torture; no one can tell his own or other people's reactions to torture until this horror has become a reality.

I wondered if I should catch sight of Odette on the way back. No such luck. The few seconds that it took between the entrance of the building and the Black Maria were just sufficient for the shaking prisoner to catch a nostalgic glimpse of elegant French mothers pushing perambulators along the sun-drenched Avenue Foch. The carefree indifference of the passers-by strolling below the chestnut trees was not for him; in his dark tin box he must return to his tomb with his black thoughts, his hopes and his despair.

I wondered if Odette had already returned in another van or if she was being kept so that my interrogator could attend to her during the afternoon. The latter seemed the more reasonable supposition.

Back in my cell I ran over every question, every answer. I must memorise it all. Whatever my own views on the efficacy of this line of stone-walling might be, I must say the same things next time so as to be consistent.

I could only suppose that any point in questioning me must be for corroboration of my acts and in order to extract names and

addresses of those with whom I had worked. So far, from that
standpoint I had incriminated no one. The interval before my
next visit might be vital to the continuation of our survivors'
work. My stalling had diverted all questions as to our contacts
anywhere in France. Only a few names had cropped up, amongst
which came inevitably that of Arnaud, whom I admitted as my
radio-operator and whom the interrogator—in collusion with
Henri—said was captured. (He was already across the Pyrenees
on his way home.) When asked where he worked I had said that
he never intimated where he transmitted and had received another
glowering look of disbelief. When faced with the fact, known to
too many people, that Paul Frager, the French Chief of our group,
had returned to England with me in a Lysander on March 23rd,
I had realised the madness of trying to deny it, but when asked
where and when he would return, I had invented the reasonable
tale that owing to the danger in which our group found itself at
the time of my capture London had decided to keep him in England
until the situation became clearer.

The name of Carte—the ex-Chief of the group, who had been
supplanted by Frager and Marsac—cropped up, but had tailed
off on my assertion that he had gone to the U.S.A. Finally, I made
no bones about my association with Marsac, but when confronted
with the name of Roger (Lt.-Col. Francis Cammaerts) who had
got out of the same Lysander that had taken me home, in order
to carry on in my absence, I was able—quite truthfully—to dis-
claim any knowledge of his whereabouts.

There had been no mention whatsoever of any of the dozens
of people with whom I had been in contact either in Cannes,
Antibes, Arles, Aix-en-Provence, Marseille, Toulouse, Lyon,
Clermont-Ferrand, Tournus, Annecy, Faverges, Perpignan,
Paris or Estrées-St. Denis. If the village-idiot act had been to
some extent instrumental in side-tracking my able interrogator,
it could not possibly have been responsible for this gigantic list
of oversights. There must be a catch somewhere. Perhaps I should
be enlightened before long or perhaps I should remain forever in
the dark.

The anchored hours ground by. With a pin I managed to scratch a calendar on the wall beside the door and crossed off the days I had spent in Fresnes. The empty days lying ahead until the end of the year would take a hundred years to pass at this rate. I ran over the interrogation until I had it well-nigh off by heart. I became hungrier and hungrier until my principal thoughts centred around food; and the more I thought of food the hungrier I became. I began to plan my condemned man's supper in terms of kilos of nourishment rather than in a series of delicacies. It started with a tureen containing a gallon of thick vegetable soup followed by two 7 lb. roast chickens with a kilo of roast potatoes and brussel-sprouts. The table was stacked with long French loaves which I would spread from a pound of butter. Two simple bottles of Châteauneuf-du-Pape were to help wash down this feast and, after a large cup of sweet black coffee, I chose a gold-fish bowl of old Marc de Bourgogne as the final balm against the ugliness of the morrow.

Nothing could relieve the strain of this black day and my misgivings, fears and uncertainty as to the outcome of Odette's interrogation kept up their throbbing tempo all through the night.

CHAPTER

V

NEXT morning the habitual noises of prison life and the calls from my friends through the window helped to ease the pangs I had felt on the previous day. Through the broken pane in my window I watched the white fluff from the ash trees (from which the name of Fresnes originated) blow like snow across the intervening space between the two divisions. How could anything be seriously wrong on such a glorious day? How could there be torture and sudden shattering death against the wall?

Presently the regular crump of the guard's key announced

something out of the usual. I dared not use my mirror, as the opening of cell doors was coming closer. Now I heard the yell of "Promenade" and clattering feet began to pass along the cat-walk on the far side of the prison-well. I glued my eye to a slit in the door and studied my passing floor-mates. As they poured down the open staircase at the end of the building a babble of conversation ensued, interspersed with vain shouts of "Silence" from the guards. Soon I joined this lively crocodile. In front of me, in riding breeches, walked my fifty-year-old neighbour of No. 221. He turned and gave me a friendly wink. Although in the very next cell to mine, we had not yet been in touch with one another, for his window was blocked and, so far, we had not discovered any means of communication.

"*Comment t'appelles-tu?*" he asked, when we reached the stairs, using the intimate "thou" that unites all prisoners of whatever rank or class. We exchanged names without moving our lips and then entered neighbouring open-air cages. Locked, like wild animals, inside these barred squares, a new world opened itself to our enchanted gaze. A tingle of liveliness invaded one's soul at the sight of the scudding clouds above. A quick glance showed that the door to this open-lidded box also had a spy-hole and a second trap awaited the unwary in the shape of guards patrolling a raised cat-walk to prevent talk either between the cloisters or between those being exercised and their friends above on the fourth and fifth floors who were entitled to open their windows.

From somewhere nearby I heard a voice singing an English song and changing the words to ask if anyone understood. I burst forth into "I can't give you anything but love, Baby", which lends itself to this sort of thing, and with a guard in full view leaning over the rail and listening to my rendering and my unseen friend's completion of the lines—not certain whether he ought to stop this nonsense or not—I had exchanged names with a bomber pilot and been able to tell him that after three months in this hole he would be sent to an R.A.F. camp where his troubles and starvation would be over.

All this took place during the short ten minutes to which we were entitled. Others had to be exercised here, too, and the guards were in a hurry to get it all over.

On our return to our cells I recognised my young friend, Marcel Fox, an escaped French prisoner of war at the time of the fall of France. He had been a gay companion in Lyon, sixteen months before. Then, as on every subsequent occasion on which we were to meet, Marcel's morale was always exemplary.

I just had time to hear my immediate neighbour, Marzelle, ask me to talk to him that night by tapping on the wall. He said, "It's very easy; just knock once for 'A,' twice for 'B' and twenty-six times for 'Z'. We did it for months in the Toulouse jail."

The short ten minutes in the fresh air was a joy that remained with me for the rest of that day. I spoke with my neighbours through the central heating gap and through the window, I kept "cave" with my little piece of mirror, whistled the right tunes as they fell due, crossed another day off my calendar, thought of this and that and Odette in particular, and knew that at the end of the day I could look forward to a new game with my neighbour.

In this manner, with practically nothing to eat, nothing to smoke, nothing to read and deprived of everything to which one is normally accustomed, I managed to pass one single day in a state of comparative equanimity.

When darkness fell I got into my hard bed and, with Odette's ring, I set to on the tapping business. I soon discovered that this was a hopeless means of communication since the French language contains far too many letters requiring twenty-six taps. After half an hour we gave it up and I drifted off on my endless imaginary motor ride to the most beautiful spot I knew in the world—the south of France. All the way Odette and I laughed and chatted gaily together and the dreadful war was over.

Next day I managed to shout to Marzelle through the window and teach him the morse code. By the simple device of tapping once for a dot and twice for a dash I gave him the alphabet. Marzelle was no dullard and that night we had a slow but intelligible conversation, for he had got the hang of it in one day. As time crept by he got faster and faster until, in the end, his effortless tapping reached my own speed. For two hours every night we conversed with each other and thousands of words penetrated our communal wall beside which we lay comfortably in bed. Although the light snapped on from time to time we were never caught, as the performance was carried out under the cover of our top-blankets. We automatically fell into the way of acknowledging the meaning of only half-spelt words and found signals both for repeats and warnings of impending danger. This nocturnal companionship to which we both looked forward all day was an unexpected boon that was to lighten our burden through thousands of crawling hours. Had it not been for the war, Marzelle and I would never have met, nor would we have searched each other out as companions, but had it not been for Marzelle's presence and the joy of these conversations I do not know how I should have borne the horror of these lonely days.

Marzelle's plight was even worse than mine, for in the women's section was his entire family, consisting of his wife and two daughters, aged twenty and twenty-one. A native of Le Grand Fougeray in Normandy, he had belonged to a Resistance circuit run by a British officer and had been captured with the rest of a reception committee whilst attending a night parachute drop.

Marzelle's case was serious, for he had been armed at the time. His modest home had been ransacked and his wife and daughters collected as suspects. It was some consolation for him to learn that my "wife" was also in the women's division, though he never managed to meet any of his family.

Through the wall he was able to tell me his whole life's history; his experience of trench warfare in the Great War, the way he had given a false age so as to join up and be in the same regiment as his brothers, how two of them had been killed and what had impelled him to join the Resistance. Marzelle's main grievance— apart from the constant gnawing agony at the injustice that made his wife and daughters share a fate he was perfectly prepared to face alone—was his suspicion that the British officer in charge of the Normandy group was not British at all and that besides, everything led him to believe that they had been betrayed by him.

He gave me the date of this man's arrival in France, his full description and every other detail he could remember about him. I racked my brains in an attempt to remember anyone of this description who might have been in the Training Schools with me or whom I might conceivably have met either at the London Office or in Gibraltar. But I could not pin this man down and told Marzelle that whilst most of the men in the "racket" were unknown to me it was also on the cards that his man might belong to de Gaulle's volunteers.

Marzelle was entitled to moments of grief and depression with all that preyed on his mind. I was glad that he was not shy in communicating his occasional fits of "cafard" to me. Who could be better qualified to restore his morale than his partner in the Valley of the Shadow? The only moral victories I ever won in cell No. 220 were those isolated occasions when the good Lord kept back my tears of compassion and withheld my own yearning for consolation whilst giving me the strength and the words that were required to bring back peace of mind to my invisible friend.

Shortly after my first interrogation I was fetched down for another interview with Henri.

"Well, you certainly played the fool at your interrogation," he began. "Lucky for you that your name is Churchill."

"You've all got enough on me already to have me hanged," I said.

"You mustn't talk like that, Pierre," said Henri. "They're convinced that you're a close relation of Winston. Can't you understand now that I hate the Gestapo? I'm not going to help them; nor am I going to try to get anything out of you myself. It's sufficient for me to have captured you, and now that you're here I can't bear to see you slowly starving to death in this lousy hole. I know all about the meagre rations of Fresnes. Why don't you tell me the name of some friend of yours in Paris who could provide you with food parcels? Just give me the name and address and I'll call and arrange the whole thing."

"My dear Henri," I said. "If I were to give you anyone's name and address, you'd immediately suspect that they were implicated in Resistance activities and put them under arrest."

"You do me a grave injustice, Pierre," said Henri, in all seriousness. "I have often been able to help people in this way, nor do I stoop to such low tricks in order to capture people."

"Well, you certainly stooped in a big way to pick me up," I said.

"That was different. Marsac was a fool and played right into my hands. After all, you were a big fish and I certainly wouldn't have picked you up if the bomber had been sent for me."

"Do you really expect me to believe that, Henri?"

"I do. Marsac told the Gestapo about the bomber business and they began to smell a rat. If the bomber had come I should have vanished from the scene. As it didn't I had to pick you up or I should have found myself inside in your place."

"It's all a little difficult for me to comprehend," I said.

"But surely everyone in England knows about the rift between the Abwehr and the Gestapo?"

"Maybe they do," I said, still mystified, "but I've never heard of it."

"More's the pity," said Henri. "Nonetheless, since the beginning of hostilities a small percentage of good Germans have been doing everything in their power to put out peace-feelers to the Allies in the hopes of putting an end to this crazy war."

"It's all news to me," I said, quite perplexed and rather suspecting a trap.

"Never mind, Pierre. As far as you're concerned I give you my word of honour that I would not arrest the man or woman whose name you gave me for the purpose of these food parcels."

"I'll think about it, Henri. Just give me a little time to digest the idea that you and the Gestapo don't work hand in glove. In the meantime, if you want to give me a treat, have Odette brought here."

Henri got up, went to the door and gave the order. A swirling of happy anticipation set itself going inside me so that our conversation in the interval became meaningless.

When the door finally opened Odette and I fell into each other's arms. She had gone much thinner and the cavernous grey that comes from rotting inside a cell had taken away the little colour she ever had. As I held her close to me the prison smell of carbolic came to my nostrils from her hair. Deprived of powder, cream and scent, she—like everyone else—had taken on the scrubbed odour of the living vault in which we were entombed.

But Odette, like many of her women companions—as I was to learn later—was an immortal amongst the living-dead. After shaking hands with Henri she insisted on being taken back to her cell in order to fetch something she had kept for me. Henri complied with her wish and, although I hated to see her go off in the hands of her disagreeable wardress, I felt that Henri could not afford anything to go wrong at this stage.

Presently the door was reopened and there stood Odette holding two half-loaves and some gingerbreads in her arms.

She held them out to me and said, "These are for you, Pierre. I know how hungry you must be. Little by little I managed to put them aside, only eating the stale bread so as to keep you the fresh ones. I knew I should get the opportunity one day of passing them to you."

A lump came in my throat at this sacrifice so that my trembling words were strangled into silence.

Seeing me hesitate, she pushed the food into my arms, saying, "You know I'm never very hungry."

In our ensuing conversation Odette reiterated her certainty that I should survive this experience and added, perhaps for my sake, that her intuition told her we should both one day breathe the air of freedom. I suggested rather pessimistically that it would be at least eighteen months before we should get the first sniff of a possible end to the war.

We could not say very much about our interrogations, for we were not certain how we stood with Henri.

The glorious moments were over all too soon and once again I returned to my cell with my batteries of hope recharged. Twice

E

in a month I had seen Odette and I gave thanks to God for this rich blessing.

All day I went over every word Odette had spoken and re-captured every look and every move she had made. In my mind I implanted each feature of this face, now more dear to me under her present coiffure than ever it had been on returning, all per-fumed, from a visit to the hairdresser. That night, without telling Marzelle the source of my fortune, I was able to transmit very special waves of hope and encouragement to him through the wall.

The question of the food parcels now began to revolve slowly in my mind. Of course I had a friend in Paris who could provide them; several friends, in fact. There was Loulou Chevalier, for instance, and the entire Fol family—all of whom I had known for years. Perhaps the best bet was Charles Fol, at whose flat I had spent two nights in March on my way to the Lysander pick-up operation near Compiegne. He and his wife were probably better placed than any for this sort of thing. However, there was always the snag that they were technically as well as literally guilty of the charge of knowingly harbouring a British officer. If I was to give Henri their name and address I simply must get a message through to them somehow to inform them that I had sworn blind that the last time we had met was just before the war in London, but never during the war.

Although I never considered Henri to be the kind of amateur bungler or over-keen police officer who would pick up entire families in order to increase his record of arrests, nevertheless I was not prepared to take the slightest risk where other people's freedom was at stake. The idea of the tall, handsome and elegant Charles Fol—banker, broker and gentleman farmer—being hauled into this depressing backwater simply because I had suggested him as a possible provider of extra food was something my conscience would have been unable to bear.

My opportunity to tip him off came sooner than I could have imagined possible. One morning a team of French prisoners was cleaning the walls along the cat-walk outside my cell. I opened the spy-hole slot and got into conversation with a very humorous and crafty member of this gang. Whilst pretending to take great pains in scrubbing the outside of my door, this 'Titi' Parisien—the exact counterpart of the London Cockney—was talking twenty to the dozen through the hole. Close by stood their guard, but since these Frenchmen never stopped talking, it was quite impossible for him to know that one of them was talking to me. They could not linger eternally outside my cell, so, after we had exchanged a fair number of pleasantries, my good Samaritan said:

"Fooling apart, Louis, how's the food market in there?"

"Take away the bread and there would be no market at all," I said.

"Don't you get parcels?"

"No. I daren't give my friend's name until I can get a message through to him."

"Give me the message. My wife's visiting on Friday. She'll get it through to him."

"Good for her. Listen carefully, then. Ask your wife to call on Monsieur Fol, F . . . O . . . L . . . at 8 bis Chaussée de la Muette in the 16th '*arrondissement*'—top floor. She's to tell him that his friend Churchill is in Fresnes and warn him that one day a German officer will call to discuss the possibility of food parcels. The important thing she simply must remember is to tell him that our very last meeting was in London, before the war. That's all."

"It's in the bag," winked my gay friend, and began recapitulating, "Fol, 8 bis Chaussée de la Muette, 16th, top floor. Friend Churchill in Fresnes. German officer may call to discuss food parcels. Your last meeting in London before the war. . . . The old girl will fix it. Good luck. I'll tip you off when she reports back."

"Bless you, chum!" I said, giving him the thumbs up sign as far as the little aperture would permit.

They moved on, chattering like magpies. I closed the slot and walked away, chortling to myself and rubbing my hands together with glee at this short, merry, lucky encounter. When I reached the crucifix I laced my fingers together tightly and looked up at the tiny emblem of hope and promise.

"Let it work," I said. "Please let it work."

And now time began to stand still with a vengeance. May had somehow passed and the great ship of Fresnes with its 3,000 stunned and half-starved passengers had floundered unsteadily into the second week of June.

I had now got the hang of prison life and could distinguish the meaning of the faintest sounds. Though Henri had made it perfectly plain that any privileges he might obtain for me were strictly against Gestapo orders, I was confident that he would do his best. His first success was in getting me onto the library list, after I had spent a month without books. This meant that the weekly trolley bearing a miscellaneous heap of books now stopped outside my cell. When the door opened I was not allowed to take my pick, but had a 47-page screed of rubbish on the romance of a chamber-maid thrust into my hand. Half an hour's reading brought me to the end of this empty drivel and my reading for that week was over. I could see that my apprenticeship in this Institution was to be a long one before I should graduate to the elevated position of being allowed to pick my own choice off the pile, as I saw others do.

Having rehearsed my first interrogation until it was word perfect my mind became a vacuum in which was bottled the obsessing thought of food closely followed by the almost constant fear and uncertainty as to my ultimate fate. When taken out of my cell for any motive I could not identify, fear got the upper hand and hunger took second place. But no sooner had the fear passed than the hunger returned. It is true to some extent that he who sleeps dines; but, within an hour of waking, the digestive organs began their endless gnawing work, grinding away at what was not there.

The hopeless search for some thought that would take the mind off the chronic dream of food was an added torment in these wasted hours. One day, by mistake perhaps—although

I prefer to think it was due to the kind intention of one of the older guards—a small Red Cross parcel was brought into my cell. It weighed perhaps two pounds. Feverishly I unwrapped the outside paper which revealed a solid mass of unbroken biscuits. I laid them out in rows on the bed and counted them. There were seventy-two. I placed them in twelve rows of six, then six rows of twelve. Then I tried out other formations. Whichever way I faced them they looked and smelt just as good. And now the question was as to how many I should eat now and how many I should keep for later on. I walked up and down and deliberated on the problem. As in any case I was bound to eat some of them now I started off with the first dozen. Their sugar content answered a need my stomach had been complaining about these last forty days. Why not give it a treat, I thought; one gigantic feast was the way to accept this unexpected gift out of the blue. No sooner thought than done. In a matter of moments the seventy-two had disappeared. I walked for a while awaiting the feel of repletion, but no such thing resulted. Clearly it required more than this to attain satiety. I simply had to put an end to this hunger—just for once. When my bread arrived a short while afterwards, I ate it all at one fell swoop. My litre of vegetable liquid vanished in the same way. With all this food inside me, weighing about four pounds, I was conscious of having the feeling one normally gets after a long morning's work that I was ready for a square meal.

This feast had been like a drop in the ocean and before long I was back in the old groove of starvation and mental torment.

I used to think how much easier it must be for someone condemned to a definite term of imprisonment to stretch out his patience in the certain knowledge that, at a given date, this patience would reap its reward. Even if condemned to death, one would know—in England, at least—that one had three weeks in which to make one's peace with God and approach the end with firmness. But in Fresnes the vast majority of prisoners had no idea how long they would be kept there or what to expect if they were sent to Germany, into the unknown terrors of the Concentration Camps.

Like myself, therefore, they probably prepared themselves for the worst and then, when they had worked themselves into a state of almost happy acceptance of the thought that death would put an end to all their miseries, the sun would shine against their windows bringing back the passionate desire for life and the urgent hope that the cup of death was not for them. So came and went the resignation, the hope and the despair of the inmates of Fresnes, following each other round, hand in hand, like the four seasons, in a regular cycle.

On week-days all this could be faced more easily because of the type of existence each man had fashioned for himself: his conversations with his neighbours, the frequent opening of his door for a monthly haircut, ten-day shave, the occasional walk, the odd snap-control of his modest possessions or the occasional visit of an interpreter or prison Chaplain which entailed seeing another face.

But on Sundays none of these things could happen. The regular guards were off and a silent gang of old soldiers crept silently around the cat-walk in bedroom slippers. Then Fresnes went dead and only the R.A.F. could save the day. If the sirens went and thirty or forty bombers flew overhead, howls of delight would rise from 3,000 tortured souls. Those pilots, navigators, bomb-aimers and rear-gunners, who would gaily return to lunch in the Mess, who would be awaited by the adoring arms of wives and families and who, even if their days were numbered—as indeed they were—would meet their end in the heat of action, clean, shaved and honoured—how little they knew of the joy they brought to the aching hearts of their compatriots and allies. If only they would drop some bombs onto the prison and give the living-dead a chance to escape, or die in a moment of exultation!

But alas, if, as so often happened, they did not come on a Sunday, despair would fill the hearts of these poor wretches. Some, who could not stand it any longer, would put an end to it all by hanging themselves from the electric light bracket against the wall, and then the same trolley that brought the life-giving soup would rumble to the suicide's cell and take away his dead body.

Men and woman were deported, others taken to Mont Valerien and shot and a handful who could wangle it and afford the 300,000 franc bribe were released. They might or might not be recaptured. It just depended on how well they covered up their tracks and hid themselves away. These were the three numbers that lay in the hat holding the fate of the inmates of Fresnes. The address or mere existence of a place at which one might deposit a healthy bribe was not blazoned abroad; thus many who could have afforded it, never knew how to go about it. So far as British agents were concerned this loophole could never arise, for we were all warned before leaving England that in the event of capture nothing could be done for us by the War Office.

It was after one of these appalling Sundays that I awoke to the sound of torrential summer rain clattering onto the glass roof of the second division. Gusts of it were sweeping across the unroofed exercise enclosures in the yard below. I watched it for a while through my broken pane of glass.

Starving and with a six-day's growth of beard I was not in the best of spirits. As I ploughed up and down my beat, repeating to myself over and over again the half-crazed chant: "Surely this can't have happened to me," the door was quietly opened and in stepped a Wehrmacht Padre. He was in uniform and bore the insignia of a Major. Half-way down his jacket was the ribbon of the Eastern Front. Slim and below average height, the unmistakable light of goodness and faith shone on his ascetic face. He could not have been more than thirty-five.

Closing the door behind him he came up to me and shook my hand, saying in French, "I've just come from your wife's cell in the third division. She asked me to call on you and give you her love and to say that she was well. If I may be permitted to say so, she is a very fine woman. She hopes you are being patient in these difficult times."

"Thank you, Father," I said. "You are the first German

who has spoken to me as though I were a human being in seven weeks."

"My profession has no frontiers, Monsieur. We are all God's children and answerable only to him. If we have acted with loyalty to our friends or for a cause, there is no shame in that."

"Tell me, Father," I said, returning to my favourite subject. "How is my wife, really?"

"She is well and serene. She behaves with great dignity and has already earned the respect of many people, including myself."

"Yes," I smiled. "I knew she would be like that. Adversity is only a challenge to her. Perhaps, one day when this madness is over, we shall be able to start afresh and I shall be able to make up to her for all this."

"No doubt, Monsieur. In the meantime be patient, for she is anxious about you. I know you are a Protestant, but if you would like me to I will visit you as often as possible."

He opened his brief-case, saying: "Here is an amusing book which will teach you German. I gave it to your wife, but she said you would benefit more from it since you found pleasure in studying languages."

"Thank you very much, *mon Père*. Please give my love to my wife and tell her that I am well, that I think of her all day and especially at our meeting hour, and I pray for her every night. And . . . *mon Père*, please come again."

"I will," he replied.

We shook hands, then the Padre gathered up his leather bag, bulging with treasures for other people, and left me. He had his own key and turned it gently in the lock.

The storm still raged outside and the rain fell in cataracts against the ledge of my window, but its depressing effect had gone. Gone, too, was the darkness within my cell. A flashing ray of light shone in my mind. This conversation would last me for days.

I now turned my attention to my new treasure—a book all to myself. I could hardly contain myself for joy. On the cover

I read the title: *Deutsch ohne Mühe*. What the dickens could that mean?

Inside I slowly digested every word of the introduction. It explained the simple process of learning German by this new method of assimilation. Here, it said, the student would not have to begin with a list of tiresome words, but would start in, straight away, from chapter one, with current expressions of the German language. Only half-way through the book would he be required to delve more seriously into the various tenses of the verbs. On each left hand page he would find the German text and on the right hand page the French translation and phonetic pronunciation. A matter of some twenty minutes per day was suggested as the time required to learn each lesson.

I turned to chapter one and began my study of the German language. Before the rain had stopped that day I had the first six lessons off by heart.

So great was my thirst for anything that would take my mind off the horror of being left to its own feeble resources that I saw in this book the turning point that was to save my reason. Every ten days or so before the Chaplain's first visit, when the realisation of my plight burned itself into my mind, I had been subject to fits of near-madness and bursting into tears of despair. Despite my best endeavours and my most earnest prayers, my new faith and control would slip through my fingers with exasperating ease. I could see that the battle of faith required many scars before it was won. It was only excellent health that pulled me out of these fits and as like as not I would be singing on the very next day.

A feature of this portion of the prison at about this time was the beautiful singing that wafted along the wall from one of the communal cells on the fourth or fifth floor. These cells were exactly the same size as mine and palliasses were placed on the floor as beds for the occupants. During the day these were stacked on the iron bedstead occupied by one of the quartet, thus leaving some space for movement. On the whole, as far as my ears could observe from the sounds that reached me through the central heating vent, this arrangement had quite harmonious results. Certainly the harmonious singing that emanated from above, so rich and strong as to suggest the combined efforts of more than one cell, showed that this particular group at least was in accord. It was as though these men had been specially placed together to form a choir for the general delight of all who were close enough to hear.

Every single night for weeks on end we were treated to at least two hours of all the popular songs of the past thirty years. As time went by the choir developed its own style and harmonies so that I came to look for and share in the pianissimo passages that only prisoners could render with such pathos, just as I was carried away by their full-throated crescendos. At the final long-held chord in harmony a shiver would run down my back and I would wait in ecstasy for the next song. The discriminating audience handed out the applause it thought fit for each number and the equally discerning artistes rearranged their programme accordingly, excluding certain items and keeping the plums for the end. A hot favourite at all times was the Song of the Partisans with 'Le Clocher de mon Coeur' a close second. It was a blessing that these men were allowed to open their window and bring so much joy to so many who had suffered the privation that comes from the absence of music. As it was against all rules to sing in this manner, I began by supposing that the guards condoned this healing infringement. But when the concert closed, as it always did, with our National Anthem and the Marseillaise, I quickly changed that view and came to the conclusion that their system of keeping "cave" up there included picking a moment for these treasonable highlights when the guard was on the opposite cat-walk.

As for me, I was touched beyond words that they should include the National Anthem and I have no shame in confessing that as soon as I heard the opening notes I would spring off my bed and stand to attention in the middle of the cell. My emotions may be imagined as I stood there alone in the failing light and thought of our beloved Royal Family and all that they meant to Britons wherever they might be. I was eternally grateful to my unseen French comrades for bringing me these sublime moments when I could also strengthen my resolve to merit the prayers, devotion and sacrifice of the woman I saluted when they sang the Marseillaise.

CHAPTER

VI

THROUGH June and July my French neighbours along this part of the wall were, with one exception, a splendid bunch. The exception inhabited the cell immediately below my own and, during part of every day, he bemoaned his fate out loud and for another part his sobbing could be heard by one and all. His name, like that of all who used his cell, was Porthos. If ever a name should have endowed its bearer with the qualities of a gay swashbuckler it was this; but its present bearer—an intellectual of twenty-five—behaved in a manner that would have surprised the Three Musketeers (who were, of course, four)— Athos, Aramis and d'Artagnan. I noted with interest that at no time during his three months' occupation of this cell did he receive an unkind word from any of his neighbours. I once overheard Michel trying to console him by comparing his lot with mine, but Porthos was unaffected by anything outside the orbit of his own private misery. When he finally left, a groan of relief was exhaled along the wall.

Within a matter of hours his place was taken by a fresh tenant to whom the usual questions were put. They were answered by a beautiful alto voice from a lad of fifteen who explained that he was a Communist who had been arrested after a roof-top chase. He said that his chances of survival were non-existent because, like his brother, he had shot a German officer. In his sing-song tones he related that his brother's clothes had already been returned to his mother by the Red Cross and that very soon she would be receiving his.

When the question of his name arose, Michel voiced everybody's opinion when he said:

"We'll call you Alfred. The last chap who stayed in your cell was called Porthos, but he disgraced the name so that we've become sick of it."

It was not long before Alfred became the centre of attraction to his invisible companions along this sector of the grim walls. His personality entered every cell. Everyone built a picture of him in his own imagination. Alfred was a youth of one piece who had played his short tragic role of life with a singleness of purpose only matched by his philosophy in facing the inevitable consequences. True to himself, his only regret was that he had been caught before he could murder any more Germans. When he knew that he was to be transferred to a condemned cell, he was quite unshaken. He did not make light of it as though to cover up fear through a show of bravado, but simply announced the fact as one might say one was going to the Bank. If Alfred was admired for his courage and philosophy he was loved for his beautiful voice. The news of his impending departure to the death cells was a sore blow to all. Within a few weeks he had won a place in everyone's heart and the realisation that this boy must shortly die before his sixteenth birthday gave me much food for thought.

Being one floor below me meant that I had been in constant touch with Alfred through the heating vent and although I would gladly have shared any extra trifle that might have come my way, alas, I was still scraping along on an empty stomach myself. However, my string and loop now came in very useful, for not only could I share my books with him, but owing to my position with regard to gravity I could fish him up anything that Michel could afford to spare from his cell below.

Alfred had no board to cover up the shaft and consequently I often caught the drift of what passed in his cell if the rest of the prison was quiet. The truth of the phrase that walls have ears was never more clearly demonstrated to me than at this particular time. One's behaviour in solitary confinement is generally known to someone, however much one may imagine the contrary. I am fairly certain that Alfred, who was new to it all, could have no notion that anyone overheard his penultimate conversation with the Catholic Chaplain of Fresnes, Father Paul Steinert, as I discovered he was named.

Alive to every sound, like all highly sensitized prisoners of long standing, I soon picked up the alto tones from Alfred's cell, during a quiet lull, as he welcomed Father Steinert.

"*Bonjour, mon Père,*" came the voice, rich and clear. "Have you noticed how sweetly the birds sing when it is going to be a fine day? Through this broken pane of glass I can see the leaves shining in the morning sun."

"Yes, my son, it is indeed a fine sight. But are you not afraid of going without soup for several days if they catch you looking out?"

"I am already caught, Monsieur, and very soon I shall pay the supreme penalty. What should I care if I finished up a little hungrier than I already am?"

"True enough, my son," said Father Steinert. There was a moment's pause before I heard his voice again, saying: "Take these bars of chocolate"—and Alfred's reply, "You are very kind, Monsieur."

"Is there anything I can do for you, *mon petit?*"

"Yes," replied the lovely voice. "I promised I would get a letter through to my mother. Would you take it to her?"

"Would you like a pencil and some paper?" asked the Padre.

"No, thank you, *mon Père.* I have already managed to procure them. In fact the letter is already written." There was another short pause, before, "Here it is. The address is on the envelope. *Mon Père*, thank you for all the kindness you have shown me. If only there were more people like you in this world there would be fewer in my position."

"I thank you, my son. Later on, when you have been moved from this room I will come and see you again and we will pursue this conversation. *A bientôt, mon petit.*"

"*Au revoir, mon Père.*"

I walked over to my crucifix and stood looking at it for a long time in silent thought.

Though Alfred was an atheist as I had been, Alfred would die an atheist. Nothing would change him, not even Paul Steinert. Of that I was sure. Alfred was the perfect material for Communism. Won over whilst very young, and all the more simply because his elder brother had passed that way before him, he would go down as he had lived, denying God. If he worshipped anything it was the power of man and by his exemplary behaviour he would have everybody saying, as he did me, "The Communists behaved magnificently in prison and they went to their deaths like heroes."

As I looked up at the Cross it came to me that so great was the Unknown that everyone would be accepted, irrespective of his creed or lack of it; our struttings on the earth were about as important as the movement of one grain of sand over the centuries in relation to eternity. But I still admired Alfred, for I was but a grain of sand myself.

It was not long before they fetched him and for the last time his gentle voice came to us through the broken pane.

"Raymond, Athos, Louis, Emile and all my other friends, come to your windows."

When he could hear our answering calls, he continued, simply, "They're taking me across the way in a few moments. I knew it would come sooner or later, but don't grieve over me. Keep your chins up and good luck to you all. . . . *Adieu, mes amis.*"

There was a moment's deathly hush before voices, made deep so as to control the choking pain of men saying farewell to a beloved companion without being able to embrace him—let alone see him, came back with,

"Courage, Alfred. . . . *Adieu, petit.* . . ."

I sat on my bed and wept.

*   *   *

That night another light was switched on in the first division. It was kept burning throughout the hours of darkness so that

Alfred, who was helping to make up the numbers necessary to trouble a firing squad, could not cheat the Third and last Reich of one of its victims by committing suicide.

That night, it seemed as though the choir's singing rolled across the yard like a Requiem Mass.

*   *   *

There was still another method of communicating between one cell and another; this was through the tube where the flush-rod connected with the cistern outside. Adjacent cells had their cisterns side by side within a cupboard which could only be opened from the cat-walk. Consequently, if you put your mouth to the tube and your neighbour put his ear to his, the result was a very passable telephone service. Of course, if a passing guard placed his ear against the cupboard doors, you very soon learned that the Exchange had been listening in to your conversation.

This system connected me with the cell adjoining the wall on the opposite side to that which I shared with Marzelle. Until this moment, there had been no cause to use it very much, for the patient in No. 219 was strictly a clod. So much so, in fact, that I was quite unaware of his departure date.

I met his successor at about this time when we were on our way to what was so luxuriously termed a "promenade". Jo Venot was a man of some six feet in height, weighing in the region of sixteen stone. His smart overcoat and Trilby hat made him a distinctive figure amidst the heterogeneously garbed crocodile that shuffled noisily towards the central staircase. Due to my anxiety to share these precious moments with my friend Marzelle, I could only spare sufficient time to tell Jo Venot, who had introduced himself from behind, how to use the telephone through which, I explained, we could talk to our heart's content.

Once inside my open cage the first thing I did was to look up to the open windows of the fourth and fifth floors to wave at any faces that might appear. On this particular walk I was astonished to see peering down at me a man who had been one of the three candidates of my class to pass out of the Training Schools at home.

I waved up to my old friend, George Abbott*, and signalled up the question as to how long he had been there. As I ran round the cloister I was appalled to see his hands indicate the sum of twenty months. No sooner had I gasped my amazement than my door was thrown open and a wasp of a guard came raving up to me.

"*Fous barlez, doujours barlez! Afec qui?*" he screamed, pointing skywards to a mass of now empty windows.

"I signal anyone I happen to see," I said.

"Oh no, you don't. This was a particular friend. Which cell was it? Come on, now!"

"You don't imagine I'm going to tell you that and get some innocent fellow into trouble, do you?"

"I'll find him, all right. Another of your gang of filthy saboteurs, I'll warrant."

I was saved from any more of this tirade since our time was now up and the doors were beginning to be opened. The guard kept close to me and as we passed into the building he pointed me out to the sergeant controlling this point, saying: "*Der Englander sprach mit einem Kameraden oben*"—before running off up the stairs to try and trap my friend. Without any help from my book *Deutsch ohne Mühe* I easily got the hang of this lot and began to wonder how many days I should now have to go without soup. The fear that this Fritz would connect Abbott with me, or even find him, did not give me a qualm. You do not fall for that sort of thing after twenty months in prison.

Luckily the sergeant to whom I was reported was quite a pleasant young man who had been transferred to Fresnes after getting frostbite on the Eastern Front. He followed me to my cell and, before locking me up, waggled an admonishing finger at me and said, simply: "*Böser Engländer!*"

I was now able to get onto the "phone" to Jo. He soon got

* Survived.

the hang of this business and before long we were at it hammer and tongs. I could not help smiling at the idea of Jo's benign face and portly frame leaning over the w.c., now putting his mouth to the tube and now his ear. I was sure he kept his hat on during this performance.

"What did they get you for, Jo?" I asked.

"A mistake," he said.

I thought of the man who had been in this place two years for buying a gallon of petrol on the Black Market, but I held my peace.

"What do you do in 'Civvy Street' ?" I asked.

"I run a pub opposite the Gare St. Lazare."

"What's it called?"

"The Fox Bar. . . . What are *you* in for?"

I explained.

"How long have you been here?"

"Only ten weeks."

"*Mon Dieu*, and you say *only*. . . . How d'you feel?"

"Distinctly peckish. They give you practically nothing to eat in this restaurant."

"I know. I've been in here two days already and I don't think much of the menus. But that doesn't worry me. I'm not hungry and when I get back, my wife'll fix me a steak as big as a manhole cover. Would you like me to pass you my bread?"

"Don't be a chump. You'll starve to death."

"Heavens no. Anyway I'll be out of here in a few days."

At this juncture I asked Jo if he would do me the great service of calling on my friend Charles Fol as soon as he got out. Without telling him that someone else was also warning him of the possible visit of a German officer, I thus doubled my precautions with regard to Fol's safety before setting the ball rolling over the food parcels.

Jo repeated every detail of these instructions and promised faithfully to carry them out. At no time during our long and pleasant telephone conversations did it cross my mind that Jo might be a stooge, nor did I ever doubt that, once free, he would

F

fail to keep his promise; Jo's face was not that of either a stooge or a man who broke his promises.

Day after day Jo got the soup Kalfaktor to pass me his bread. Day after day I asked Jo how he could possibly keep his large frame going without this precious bread and Jo's replies were always the same.

"I don't need the stuff, Louis. The thought of the smell of that steak and those chips my wife'll prepare for me when I get back is quite enough to put me off the local fare."

Jo was right, after all. His vision of liberty was not an empty mirage, as such visions generally turned out to be. Within ten days of his arrival he was on his way back to the steak which his wife would prepare for him and watch him eat whilst smiling at him through tears of relief.

My pleasure at Jo's release was devoid of envy. I knew nothing of his real story or to what extent he was involved with the group who used his café as a "*boîte aux lettres*". Jo was the embodiment of all that is implied by the French word "*sympathique*"—a good fellow—and I simply rejoiced in his good fortune.

My first two and a half months of semi-starvation in Fresnes had now been mitigated by three well-spaced additions to my daily fare. There had been Odette's gift of two half-loaves and the gingerbreads, followed by the Red Cross parcel containing the seventy-two biscuits and, finally, some half-dozen extra rations of bread from Jo. . . . Although the pangs of hunger soon returned after each of these benefits had been disposed of, the net result was that I was that much better off than those who had not had such good fortune.

I now fell into the habit of cutting up my bread into so many lumps of equal weight and eating these every two hours or so with plenty of water. Thanks to my astonishing powers of sleep, my regular exercises, the delight which I found in learning my German lessons by heart, my daily communion with Odette, my prayers, the long nightly talks with Marzelle and the final treat from the invisible choir, I realized that the Lord was doing everything possible to help me pass the time with patience.

But despite these benefits I never became resigned to my fate of powerless waiting, and the uncertainty of its duration and outcome never ceased to prey on my mind. When I felt the groans of anguish rumbling up inside me, like Vesuvius before an eruption, I would stave off many a crisis by saying to myself— "I'll think about this tomorrow." Then I would dive blindly into a new chapter of my German book.

At about this time a Catholic tract was brought into my cell. It contained a message to prisoners from a Bishop, the gist of which was: "You, whose mind is often tormented with anguish, take heart. You are not forgotten by your brothers outside and you are never forgotten by the Lord of eternal freedom. The shackles that bind the limbs cannot imprison the soul. Some day all this will come to an end and you will be free. When that day comes you will, once again, find yourself prone to fret because you are not so well off as your neighbour. If you wish to benefit from this experience, remember these black days and let them serve as a yard-stick of comparison to your new lot. Only by doing this will you avoid discontent."

There seemed to be a great deal of truth in this and I supposed that the longer one's imprisonment the easier it would be to apply the comparison. I swore that if ever I survived this mess I would never complain about anything as long as I lived.

My blessings were added to a few days later by a second visit from Paul Steinert. He brought me a copy of Goethe's *Mignon* to add to my library. It had the German text on the left-hand page and a French translation opposite. I put this treasure on my bed so as not to lose the precious minutes of my guest's society.

When my mind had been put at ease as to Odette's state of health—and here Father Steinert wisely thought fit to tell me a white lie but for which I think the longing for survival would have died within me—we began to talk of other things.

"How is it, *mon Père*," I asked, "that you manage to leave something of yourself behind you in every cell you enter? There must be many cells and many difficult and painful encounters." (I was thinking of Alfred.)

"Mine is a rather long day, Monsieur, but I have been blessed with faith that helps to conquer the fatigue of the body. My prayers for guidance are always answered and I sometimes find words are put into my mouth."

"Do you prefer this to the Eastern Front?" I asked.

"Man's needs are much the same everywhere, Monsieur. Whether I am sent back to the East or remain here is entirely the same to me. I am at God's disposal to be called wherever He may command."

"What does your day consist of?"

"I get up at 5 o'clock and my first call is at one of the big Paris hospitals where some of our wounded are treated. I then take Mass in a nearby church. Afterwards I come here and call on those who appear on this daily list, and after lunch I sometimes visit the parents of those who are to be deported. Finally I get to bed around midnight. Before going to sleep I pray for strength to fulfil my duties on the following day and this strength is always given me."

Father Steinert had left out two things which I was fairly certain also belonged to the credit side of his balance-sheet. One of these things, which shone out of his remarks, was that to him the gates of death were but the entrance to the real life, and the other, that his visits to parents—unknown to the Gestapo and contrary to their security regulations—were not merely to speak of the deported, but to advise relatives that a son or husband was in Fresnes as well as sometimes having to be the bearer of the painful news of executions.

When he left me with my thanks for his gift and visit, and bearing my affectionate messages to Odette, I thought long about Father Steinert. What a superb representative of God he was. His tact and sensitiveness in not showing off the full extent of his faith and duties indicated that he was not suffering from the sin of pride. Surely this man was even more than a magnificent Catholic Priest; he was a veritable Saint on earth. I gave thanks that the scales of selfishness had been sufficiently removed from my eyes for me to have recognized this fact.

My present level in the German language now made it possible for me to follow Goethe's tragic story of the life and early death of the angelic Mignon. Despite the French translation it required much time and concentration before I could master the finer points of this great poet's work. It was natural that this should be so and a fortunate thing into the bargain, as this treasure would have to last me for a long time. However much I read on and however much I sought its meaning from the crib, it was only by dint of constant rereading that the fullness and wealth of Goethe's language finally reached my untrained powers of comprehension.

Each day I learned a new verse of its lovely poems. In time my modest record was to reach the dizzy heights—for me—of 120 lines by heart. It was curious how, in the end, I came to understand, or think I understood, every shade of thought and meaning in these poems and yet could never find suitable translations for them in either French or English. It was also somewhat incongruous that the only verses I ever recited in prison should be German, due to my complete inability to remember anything else.

There was much in *Mignon* that found a poignant echo in the prisoner's plight; sometimes the echo was far too clear, such as in the first verse of the very first poem, which ran:

Wer nie sein Brot mit Tränen ass,
Wer nie die kummervollen Nächte auf seinem Bette weinend sass,
Der kennt Euch nicht,
Ihr himmlischen Mächte.

Months of thought and repetition of this great truth never brought me a better translation than:

He who has not eaten his bread in tears,
He who has not sat up weeping upon his bed throughout the
    night of despair,
He knows you not, Oh Heavenly Father.

If *Deutsch ohne Mühe* had been the turning point in saving my reason, then Goethe's *Mignon* so raised my status as to make me aware that as long as it remained in my possession I could have no further cause for complaint in regard to stagnation of the mind.

When I had spent three months in Fresnes it became difficult to believe that I had ever had a previous life. The distant hum of cars hurtling along highway 20 between Paris and Etampes was the sound of things happening in a world of unreality. *This* was the real thing; this and what was happening in the thousands of other prisons throughout the Occupied Countries and in the Concentration Camps. Even at this stage of the war, towards the end of July 1943, we sensed that when the bells of victory tolled for the Allies—as we knew they inevitably would—the power of might would merely change hands from Nazi Germany to Communist Russia, equally ambitious for world domination. There could therefore be no whole-hearted jubilation at the thought of final victory, only the feeling that if one should survive so long, the clear skies of hard-earned liberty would soon be overcast with further threatening clouds. And long before those clouds poured forth their venom, more millions would be facing the same reality as ours in Russian camps; the reality of separation, death and bitter tears.

Unshaven, unrecognised and half-starved, it seemed from here that the millions of living-dead who would go on lifting their joined and trembling hands to the Light that struggled through their opaque windows, represented the real world of the mid-twentieth century and that the thousands of golf courses, cricket grounds, greyhound tracks and happy families sitting around tea tables or setting off on an excursion of their own choice in a land of freedom belonged to a world of dreams. Through my own misfortune and that which had overtaken so many millions of Poles, Czechs, Belgians, Norwegians, Finns, Dutchmen, Latvians, Lithuanians, Greeks, Bulgarians, Hungarians, Roumanians, anti-Fascist Italians, anti-Nazi Germans and innumerable other people with the same longings as myself, I came to fear desperately for those who lived in that world of dreams, lest they allowed those dreams to fade.

It used to be thought along my sector of the wall that Winston Churchill would somehow guide us through the dangerous waters we should enter after the defeat of Germany. We were convinced, likewise, that he was aware that every day he could ✳ shorten the war would save thousands of prisoners' as well as soldiers' lives. We were sure that he would not forget us. He was the prisoners' one great hope and inspiration. But what we did not know was that Mr. Roosevelt was to hold out for unconditional surrender, thus giving Hitler time to wreak his vengeance on another million souls trapped in the scores of extermination camps. Nor did we know that Roosevelt thought himself able to handle Stalin singlehanded. In this way, turning down the wise guidance of the greatest statesman of all times, and keeping the Anglo-American troops waiting for the Russian advance into the very heart of Germany—in accordance with Stalin's wishes—Poland was to fall behind the Iron Curtain and Germany be split as she was.

It is one thing to sit over a pint of beer and discuss wars as being natural recurring phenomena brought on for the reduction of an over-populated world. It is quite another to be caught up in the process of being reduced.

It can be seen that the immobility of prison life imbues the smallest event with a significance proportionate to its static background. All movement or conversation puts a term to a period where neither of these things has existed. Though I had now reached the exalted state of a monk studying quietly in his cell, the occasional ten-minute breaks in the cloisters were like platinum milestones to me because of their rarity. I would bring back a wild flower and spend hours analysing its formation, its pistil, its petals and the veins in its curved velvety substance. The limitless time at one's disposal meant that one could study so small a trifle with a minuteness of care and attention that no flower-lover ever gave or could afford to give even to a pet orchid. The idea of suddenly finding oneself transplanted into the wealth of Kew Gardens was almost overwhelming.

In every way but one the prisoner is slowed down to a stand-

✳ not according to John Grigg. "1943. The Victory that never was."

still. The one exception is his mind. This keeps travelling at the same rate, if not faster, than it did in freedom. Unhampered by interruptions and outside influences, it grasps more quickly and penetrates more deeply than it can when moving continuously from place to place at the speed of modern transport. It is as easy to travel for twenty minutes in the Underground and think of practically nothing as it is impossible to spend the same amount of time in a cell and do likewise. Glancing at the faces of the travellers on the opposite bench, letting one's eyes roam over the advertisements, being distracted by the smell of dirty clothes, or listening to the indistinct hum of a nearby conversation—and the time has gone.

If movement is life, then stagnation is a kind of death that seems very real to the prisoner. The only life in this death being the life of the mind it stands to reason that the molehills of our variety were magnified into mountains of spice by the legions of the living-dead.

A few days later Henri paid me a flying visit in my cell.

"Have you thought any more about those food parcels?" he asked.

"If I give you the name of a friend, do you still swear you won't arrest him?" I said.

"I swear it on the bones of all those I hold most dear."

I then gave Henri Fol's name and address and assured him that he had had nothing whatsoever to do with my war activities and that our last meeting had been in London before the war.

"I shall arrange for you and Odette to have food parcels as soon as it can be done," he assured me.

"Can I see Odette?" I asked.

"I'm afraid I haven't got time today."

"Have you seen her?"

"Yes."

"How is she?"

"Perfectly all right."

"I'm glad she's in a communal cell."

"How did you know that?"

"You know how it is in prison, Henri. . . ."

"Yes, only too well. I suppose they required her cell for some-one else. We're always overcrowded. . . . I'm sorry I must rush now, but I'll call on Monsieur Fol personally."

After Henri had gone I felt that the usual pleasant atmosphere between us had been missing. I could not make it out.

Ten days later, on my hundredth day in Fresnes, I heard my cell number being called out by the sergeant on the ground floor. As the second floor guard stumped along the cat-walk in my direction I thought to myself, "This must be for Henri; he's done the trick."

My door opened and I was led downstairs. In the office, left empty by the sergeant, stood Henri and beside him the elegant, smiling Charles Fol. At sight of me he raised two well-stuffed hold-alls and then set them down to come over and embrace me.

"My dear Peter," he began, winking at me to show that he had been tipped off. "I had no idea you were in France until our friend here called the other day and bowled me over with the news of your goings-on. I hear you're married into the bargain and that your poor wife is in here too. That's why I brought two parcels. I do hope I shall be allowed to see the young lady, Monsieur Henri."

"So do I," I said, to back up this excellent move.

"Of course," said Henri, and walked through the door leaving us together for a few moments.

"You were tipped off all right, then?" I asked hurriedly.

"Yes. A delightful man called and saw me at my Bank. I'm glad you had me warned, as Henri tried me out jokingly on the question of our having met since the war. . . . Now tell me, what's all this nonsense about your being married?"

"It's not nonsense, I assure you," I lied, determined that there should be no slip-up through confessing our ruse even to an intimate friend.

Henri came back at that moment and put an end to our privacy.

"I'm afraid I can't arrange for Odette to come today, but I'll see that you meet before long, Monsieur," he said. Then he turned towards me, changing the subject rapidly:

"Monsieur Fol has very kindly agreed to arrange for fortnightly parcels to reach you and Odette. They will come in small suitcases and when these are empty you will be able to place your dirty laundry inside them. This will be washed and returned to you with the subsequent parcel."

It was also agreed that books and cigarettes would be included as well as a wick-lighter.

My friend and benefactor appeared entirely at ease in the poky room where the three of us were gathered. As for Henri, he was so favourably disposed towards him that he accepted his suggestion of bringing Odette and me, separately, to his house for lunch at future dates to be arranged.

Back in my cell I was torn between gratitude to Charles Fol and disappointment at not having seen Odette. How long should I have to content myself with the few tantalising moments I had spent with her? How could I know if she would ever receive these life-saving parcels? How long must we exist so near and yet so far apart? Would I ever know what pain was tormenting the mind of this beloved creature? These agonising thoughts must be my lot for hundreds, maybe thousands, of hours. I wondered just how much the human mind could bear.

And now I discovered that it was easier to stand mental torment on a full stomach than when half starved, and that it was still easier with a cigarette in one's mouth. The blessed relief of tobacco! I chain-smoked ten Gauloises on end. After three and a half months of hell during which I knew that others had had parcels I nevertheless felt almost ashamed of my advantage over those who must still do without them. My great consolation was that this nourishing food was being shared by Odette who so desperately needed it. If only Alfred could have been below just now. Even Michel had left and their successors took no part in local affairs.

Since my experiment with the seventy-two biscuits had failed

I was not going to try it out on ten pounds of food. This had got to last for a fortnight or back would come the pains of hunger. In point of fact this extra food only lasted me for two days, but I went slowly on my forty cigarettes, keeping the butts and rolling them into ever thinner shadows of their former selves with the cigarette papers that had been so thoughtfully provided.

The two most nourishing items of my parcel were butter and sugar, the very things which the stomach was crying out for most.

As the weeks crawled by I got into the habit of rationing out these extra delicacies so that they lasted until the next parcel arrived and in this manner my solitary existence took on a new and less frugal outlook.

Whenever I was struck down by despondency in these new circumstances I would think of the advice I had read in the Catholic tract which I had sworn never to forget. These words were to do me a great service.

CHAPTER

VII

August was now drawing to an end and I began to think that the incredible lunch outing that had been suggested must have fallen through. But not a bit of it. One fine morning at about ten o'clock I was fetched from my cell and taken downstairs, through the underground passages and up the main doors of the prison. After a short wait Henri appeared in the company of several other Germans, all looking as though they had come from an important board meeting. Henri led me off, intimating to the others that he was taking me away for interrogation.

Once inside his Citroën and through the outer gates, he said:

"Now, Pierre, it would be a simple matter for you to bash me over the head whilst my hands are on this wheel, so I must ask you for your parole for the whole period of the outing. If you were to do the dirty on me, I should probably have to pay for it with my neck."

I gave my parole.

My eyes were not large enough to take in all the loveliness of this impossible drive. The sun shining down through the trees along the streets where life seemed to be going on as in a past dream was quite beyond me. Henri was once more his usual agreeable self—the counter-espionage agent with panache. Driving through Paris, the eternal City of elegance, was like bathing in champagne. We talked of this and that and Henri warned me that I should eventually be called for a second interrogation as they had got nothing to send to Berlin from the first. He said I should not have to worry particularly about this visit since the man who would be handling it was not a very bright spark.

We pulled up outside a house and mounted the stairs to his flat. Inside I was introduced to his French mistress, a pleasant and unaffected woman, sensitive and yet not embarrassed by the queer situation that brought her German lover into contact with a British agent in her presence and under the roof of a confiscated flat in Paris. No doubt she must have experienced similar situations before.

The furnishings in the flat were like a film set. The large living-room was a dark symphony of brown and gold and some forty cushions were neatly arranged side by side, with corners pointing upwards, along the wall seats that ran round most of the room.

Next door was a tiny salon containing a set of flimsy golden-legged chairs and a sofa of a type too elegant to be sat on. I was taken through here on my way to the bathroom where Henri filled the bath and set out his shaving tackle so that I could make myself presentable for lunch.

Shaved and refreshed I looked with heart-burning at the drain pipes joining all the bathroom wastes running down into the area below, for the call of freedom is ever at the top of human longings.

The strange but friendly car-load bearing a Frenchwoman, a German and an Englishman now wended its way to the Chaussée de la Muette where Charles Fol, his wife and American mother-in-law were no doubt waiting with mixed feelings to receive the queerest assortment of guests that can ever have entered their home.

I was warmly embraced by the two ladies who yet managed to control their natural emotions at seeing the prison pallor on the face of their old family friend whose last visit had left behind the memory of sun-tanned health and vigour.

A tie was produced for my open shirt and we all sat down for lunch. Everyone was determined to be gay and the conversation never lagged. Joining in with the spirit of this incongruous gathering I gave the best rendering I could of the person who is accustomed to leaving his penitentiary from time to time in order to lunch out in this manner. I was even unconscious of the fact that I had no shoelaces.

Behind all this banter Charles' undetectable nervousness was betrayed by his breaking two glasses during the course of the meal.

We took coffee in their large studio where the two grand pianos stood as a reminder of happier days. These did not stand silent for long, since my request that Charles' wife, Biche—pronounced Beesh and meaning doe—should play some of her most recent favourites was unanimously seconded and presently the studio filled with the music of this first-class concert pianist.

When she had finished playing two pieces, she turned to me and said:

"Your turn now, Pierre."

I sat down and vaguely ran over the keys to see if anything would come back. It did. It was just the same as ever; nothing brilliant, but accurate harmonies and enough to give me pleasure.

Aided by the encouragingly light touch of the Steinbeck I ran through one or two tunes. Presently I heard the second piano joining in. Biche was obviously helping to recreate some of the happy memories of the past.

I turned to smile at her only to find Henri's face looking at me over the top of the second "grand". His enigmatic smile might have been the reflex of his enjoyment at this improbable situation. He played beautifully. Neither of us knew that the other played and I could never have imagined that such thick fingers could produce such melody. He could play a descant to anything I knew, and in any key.

Soon spotting his superior talent I left him to it and he gave us half an hour of Viennese waltzes that delighted the whole assembly. The scene reminded me strangely of Captain von Rintelen's courteous reception by Admiral Hall after this supreme German saboteur had been picked up by British Naval Intelligence in the previous war. Von Rintelen had been treated to a first class dinner in a private flat, after which an expert had played Bach for him until midnight, when he was led off to prison.

With the one great difference that I was not a supreme saboteur, this was a kind of repetition of history with the roles reversed. Cinderella's hour must inevitably strike for me, too, and I decided to call a halt myself rather than wait for the sad bells of midnight to remind me that the party was over.

During the afternoon Charles said to me in front of Henri,

"This lunch and Henri's visits to this house have certainly been noticed by the *concierge*, if by nobody else. When the war is over I have a feeling that there may be a wild period of settling of accounts during which I may be accused of having collaborated with the enemy. Would you, therefore, mind writing and signing a note explaining all this?"

I said I would gladly oblige and wrote, roughly, as follows:

"This is to certify that my friend, Charles Fol, received me to lunch at his flat on August 29th 1943 in the presence and through the goodwill of Hugo Bleicher—the counter-espionage agent who captured me—and that the latter's visits to his flat at 8 bis, Chaussée de la Muette, have been for the sole purpose of arranging for the delivery of food parcels to myself and my wife in Fresnes prison.

Signed

PETER CHURCHILL,

Capt. I.C. 162707."

At about 5.30 p.m. I called it a day. The Fols had put up a magnificent and unforgettable show. They would now prepare themselves for a repeat performance in Odette's favour.

Charles' mother-in-law gave me two small packs of patience cards and Suzanne, who had left the flat a few moments before Henri and myself, saw us off in the car and handed me two big bunches of grapes.

On the way back to Fresnes Henri returned to the charge on his pet subject of going back to England. He said,

"I've got a secret transmitter tucked away somewhere. Why don't you come out with me one day and send a message to London asking for a Lysander to come and pick us up on any field you like? If you consent to do this, I can get you out on some pretext or another and we'll return to London together."

"My dear Henri," I said, "I've told you already that if I were to be responsible for the capture of a Lysander and its pilot I simply couldn't live with my own conscience. If you really want to get back to England so badly, drive me down to the Pyrenees and I'll get you across the frontier. I know the Consul General in Barcelona and can promise you a 'Safe Conduct' from him through Spain and good treatment in England."

"I'd do it like a shot," said Henri, "but we'd never get through all these military traffic controls. We've been stopped twice already, as you've seen."

"A pity, Henri. Then I must simply sweat it out inside."

Returning to the still backwater of Fresnes, now doubly charged with silent deadliness, was one of the grimmer experiences of my life. The film of grease that had formed itself on the top

of my cold soup was a mocking reminder of what went on outside. The grisly walls, the gaping lavatory pan and the hard bed
all joined forces to smite me between the eyes.

In a moment of privacy Charles had promised to write to
friends in Switzerland who would pass on news to the War Office
that would be transmitted to our parents. Soon, hope would be
kindled in the anxious minds of our relatives; hope that had
little reason to be inspired by a single excursion of this nature,
but nevertheless hope that would be clung to with the same
avidity as a drowning man will clutch at a straw.

I had not gone out on this trip of self-indulgence with that
idea in view. I merely consoled myself now with the fortunate
effect of what I had done without any motive whatsoever.

Before turning in I gave thanks for this wonderful day and
for the rich blessing of friends who knew how to launch out the
boat.

That night I had great difficulty in finding words to carry
on my nightly conversation with Marzelle and after we had grown
silent I remained awake for the rest of the night.

*   *   *

As I could not study German every single minute of the day,
the great problem was to find a subject for the mind to work
on. Owing to the simplicity of my mental faculties I was unable
to resort to philosophy or enter a state of contemplation. Consequently I was obliged to draw on memories of my past life and,
whilst these did not yield a particularly rich harvest, I derived
a certain amusement from imaginary conversations with friends
of highly varied personalities. So vivid was my memory of their
voices and mannerisms that I found myself laughing at my own
imitations of the pompous or humorous remarks I put into their
mouths and spoke out loud for my own entertainment. Some I
listened to in earnest and actually obtained great comfort from
the thoughts and words I knew must be theirs.

Amongst such memories I also had a very consoling thought.

This was the time and love that I had given to my parents in return for all their goodness to me. My thoughts were centred principally around memories shared with my mother, a sweet and humane woman who dispensed nothing but warmth and goodness to all around. Added to her natural charm, she was a Shakespeare scholar, a master of the English language and a natural linguist.

I had been given the knack of being able to make her laugh and had profited shamelessly from this advantage in wheedling everything I wanted out of her, from an early age. Intelligent and astute, she knew very well when she was being taken for a ride. But realising that behind all this gay nonsense there lay a deep filial love, she gave way without much show of resistance. I was glad, now, of all the time I had spent with her and for all the happy laughter we had shared.

Whilst my father was the strong, silent type, slow of speech and movement, but proud of his three sons in the Forces, my mother, quick of mind, word and bearing, abhorred the war that took away the three main reasons for her existence. She knew very well that one had to fight to defend freedom and be prepared to make sacrifices for an ideal, but this did not prevent her, like most mothers, from hating all the futile carnage that came ever closer to her home.

My last memory of her was the tragic, suddenly-aged vision of a dried-up old lady who had held me at arm's length at the end of my final leave to give me her blessing. The two veins in her neck were throbbing out the dying beats of her broken heart. She had fair reason to have reached this pass, for she had lost her only daughter—aged eighteen—after a major operation, her eldest son had been killed in the war, her third son was a leader of Italian Partisans and now her second son was off again behind the enemy lines. As she looked at me out of the deep hollows where once gay eyes had shone, I knew that I should never see her again.

And now as the last days of September were slowly dwindling from my calendar, I had the only telepathic premonition of my

G

whole life. Suddenly I heard my mother calling out my name. I stopped in my pacing and held my breath in case I should hear more. In the empty silence that followed I knew that she had died.

My impotence in the face of this unbearable blow sent me sliding back dangerously down the slopes of my hard-earned climb towards patience. But once again the increasing fits of despair were checked by my growing faith, and comfort came to me as I stood below the crucifix. I felt that I simply must bear the seemingly inconsolable grief and that my mother's death was a blessed release that would take her at the speed of thought to those others whom she loved and who had gone before her. With these confirmed thoughts I dried my tears and took a step forward in the endless struggle to live with myself.

Throughout all these days I had constantly run over the questions and answers of my first interrogation and it was a lucky thing I had done so, for when my second trial took place I was not caught napping. More than five months had now passed since our capture and I realised that the gates were now legitimately open for me to admit connivance with a certain number of people who had, by now, had plenty of time to vanish from the scene. But thanks to the gratuitous information that Henri had passed me regarding the style of the man who was to question me this time, I determined to continue the village idiot act and only give away the barest minimum.

When I returned to my cell after this second experience, I was satisfied that I had done the best I could and that no one, not already in the bag, had been implicated.

*　　*　　*

One night in mid-October a false alarm spread through the second division like wild fire, raising hopes to a pitch of mass hysteria.

It all started at midnight with a great commotion of marching feet coming from the ground floor. Never before had so much activity been heard at so late an hour. It seemed as though the entire division was being evacuated.

Suddenly the cry went up, "They've landed! The Allies have landed!" In a flash the news was picked up and bellowed along the wall, through doors and across the yard to the first division where German deserters and condemned allies alike shrieked their relief at this eleventh-hour miracle that might alter their doom.

Within half a minute the place was in an uproar, people were dressing so as to be prepared for the move and the first strains of the Marseillaise were picked up by a thousand pulsing throats until its thunder crammed the hollow nave of our mausoleum.

Whatever caution one's private reasoning might advise it was impossible not to be affected by the surging spirit that pervaded the air. I lay in bed with my heart thumping and said nothing. Presently I heard Emile's board being removed from the heating shaft. Then his voice came down, saying,

"Did you hear that news, Louis?"

"Yes, I heard it," I said rather flatly.

"What do you think of it?"

"I can't believe it's true, Emile. I've crossed the Channel too often in October to believe they'd risk it at this time of year. Personally I'm waiting for confirmation before working myself into a lather about it."

There was a moment's silence during which I dimly overheard Emile relaying the gist of this cold douche to his cell-mates, then his voice came back with,

"There's something in what you say, Louis, but I hope you're wrong."

"So do I, Emile," I replied fervently.

The plank was returned to its position and I composed myself uneasily for sleep.

Next day, by pure coincidence, I had a visit from the German interpreter, a most agreeable young man by the name of Boucher. His family had lived for years in Brussels where he had received part of his education; he had been to England and through his interest in Association Football knew many of our professional sides. Boucher did not resemble the shouting German guards—as they were known to millions of prisoners—in any respect. He had a cultured tenor voice and his manners were those of a gentleman in any country. I considered each of his four visits to my cell as a treat.

His first call had been in an official capacity to make enquiries into a mystery that was never solved. It appeared that he had found a note that seemed to have been inspired by a Canadian woman, whose name I believe was Betty, and which revealed a plot to spring me out of Fresnes with outside help. Since I knew nothing about all this I was unable to shed any light on the matter.

His second visit came as a result of my own request and he was able to persuade the German Guard Commander to take off the handcuffs which I had worn for six hours for an offence I had not committed.

Boucher's third visit was a social call during which he informed me that he was off to Lyon for a "battle course" prior to being transferred to the eastern front. He promised to come and see me again when the course was over. He kept this promise. Boucher's personality was such that I sincerely hoped he would survive the war. If his simple explanation of the previous night's pandemonium—that a large convoy of fresh prisoners had arrived to take up residence on the ground floor—was an expected disappointment, his expression of surprise at my constant patience in solitary confinement was a pleasure to hear, even if I knew it to be a trifle inaccurate, for a little encouragement goes a long way in any walk of life.

I purposely avoided sharing the "landing" disappointment with my neighbours through the window; it was bad enough if the error became apparent with time. That night, however, I confided the news to Marzelle, softening the blow as much as possible.

In early October my friend Marzelle was taken off to Germany. Having been warned of his imminent departure on the previous evening, he was able to tell me about it during our final session through the wall. We had a long night of friendly conversation and I assured him, without any grounds for doing so, that life in the open camp would be streets ahead of our dreadful existence.

During October, Emile and his crowd were also deported, as was the choir. With their departure silence fell upon this sector of the wall. I wondered how many of them would turn up at the Café du Rond Point des Champs Elysées where we agreed to meet one month after the armistice was signed. We were still a long way from the end of term and from the gaping loop in my life line which gave no indications of wanting to close, I did not give much for my chances of attending this old lags reunion.

During October I heard from Paul Steinert that Odette was still in a communal cell. As the weather grew colder she had a grey dressing-gown delivered to my cell with my initials on the breast pocket. I wondered if she was warm enough herself. Father Steinert also brought me his third gift—a Bible in French. With these three treasures plus my patience cards I was well set up with a rich variety of ways to help me pass the winter.

One of the greatest strokes of good fortune that ever came my way—as though in answer to my prayers—was a ten-minute exercise period which occurred after a solid month inside my cell. Because the cloisters on our side were full, we were taken through the building to those situated at the foot of the other wall, facing the third division. This wall, like all the others, was nearly 200 yards in length with an overhead tunnel connecting the two divisions and blocking out a large portion of visibility owing to its central position.

Through some happy coincidence I found myself opposite the women's section. Those who had their windows open waved and entered into animated exchanges with the men opposite and about seventy yards away. Some recognised husbands, others simply joined in to exhort their compatriots, so that cries of defiance were mingled with those of encouragement, and refined voices struggled to make themselves heard through the superior din of the fish wives. To all this noise was added that of the guards shouting, *"Fermez le bouche!"*—their ungrammatical and, to us, ridiculous way of saying, "*ta gueule!*"—whilst they situated the guilty windows for later attention.

Amidst this cacophony my heart was beating fast and my ears were wide open, registering at once the moans of the inconsolable and the crossed lines of a dozen conversations, for amongst those women there was a fifty-fifty chance of my finding Odette.

I knew she had not the voice to pierce this pandemonium and my anxiety increased with the growing fear that the moment would pass and I should never know if she had seen me and vainly tried to make herself heard.

Presently a mighty shout of, "*Pierre, Pierre, votre Odette est ici!*"—your Odette is here—topped the rest and in one frantic second I caught sight of a square of paper being moved from side to side through a pane of glass that seemed to open by a sliding device. Now I could see the dim figure of a woman standing on the back of her chair and shouting at me through the small top window.

"Can you see her waving the paper?" asked the voice. "She sends you her love and says 'courage'."

I shouted back in French, "Tell her to listen and I will sing her my reply." Then I broke into a French version of the song Richard Tauber had made so famous—"You are my Heart's Delight"—and inventing my own words I serenaded her whilst the paper waved continuously to show that she was listening.

When time was up I shouted, "*Au revoir, chérie Odette.*" The paper fluttered wildly and it was over.

I now began to receive fortnightly gifts of food from Odette which she succeeded in having delivered by one of the wardresses. I tried to shunt these unselfish gifts back to her but the wardress assured me that she had quite sufficient in her communal cell. The principal satisfaction I had from these deliveries was the knowledge that her parcels were coming through all right.

One day in early November I was severely shaken out of my ascetic torpor by the unexpected shout of "Tribunal!" Taken out of my cell I found myself once more amid a group of men and women on the ground floor. In the midst of the women I quickly spotted the smiling grey face of Odette. She seemed in great form and rightly imagining that I expected a further interrogation she fearlessly announced across the gap that separated our two ranks,

"We're going to have our finger-prints taken. We shall be together: I've fixed it."

True enough, our convoy deposited us at the Rue des Saussaies and I found myself in a large open pen where the whole group was herded together under the eye of a guard whilst waiting for the next move. I slipped up close to Odette and as she spoke to me with her back to the sentry, a girl I had never seen before, but who was patently English to her finger tips, stood between me and the guard so that he could not see my mouth moving. Despite my anxiety not to miss a second of this golden opportunity to speak with Odette, I was nevertheless instinctively conscious of this girl's unselfish act which included a delicacy of feeling that made her turn about and face the German so as not to butt in on our privacy. I could not imagine what this refined creature with reddish hair was doing in our midst.

"Who is she?" I asked Odette.

"Diana Rowden*," she replied. ". . . . One of us."

Presently we were led up some narrow stairs and kept waiting in a passage. This fortunate delay enabled Odette and me to speak to each other for a whole hour. In all my days I never knew time to pass so rapidly.

She told me how she had arranged this visit through the Captain of the prison, how one of the wardresses showed her various kindnesses that included bringing me a portion of her spare food, how she had contrived to get into the sewing-room and only worked there on the understanding that she did nothing for the Germans, but only made children's toys such as rabbits and dolls.

Seeing the new style of Afrika Korps caps affected by some of the guards she had converted them all to this style and on each piece of cardboard that stiffened the peak she had written the words, "Made in England". She related how she had blown the

* Executed.

fuses of the power point by jamming her scissors into the holes and how she cut the wires and then got the guards to fetch in the most hungry prisoners on the pretext that they were electricians so that she could slip them some extra food. She spoke of my friend Roger Renaudie's* unquenchable spirit in the third division with high praise.

This was the Odette I had known in Arles when, as my courier, Lise, she had made a German General fork out for a "winter-relief" coupon to which only the French were obliged to subscribe when paying for a meal. This was the Lise who had put the cat among the canaries by placing a broom-stick against a German Colonel's door in an occupied hotel where we had once stayed. How she had chuckled when he had opened the door and it had struck him in the face.

Odette's morale was sky-high. It was where she had put it and maintained it through her own optimistic personality, and it had devolved on other prisoners and guards alike. I began to understand what Paul Steinert meant by the regard in which he said she was held. But what I did not and could not understand was the principal reason for these words, since neither he, nor Odette, nor Henri ever told me of the sufferings she had undergone, for it was her intention that I should never know and she had sworn those who knew to silence.

We talked of the dozens of matters that concerned us so closely, but only after first reassuring ourselves that the other had not been tortured.

"Did they ill-treat you in your interrogations, Pierre?"

"No." I said. "In any case I only had two visits to the Avenue Foch. Did they ill-treat you?"

"Never," said Odette. "But they've had me up fourteen times."

"What on earth for?" I asked.

"They seem to think I know more than I do."

"How's that?"

"Well, it all started by my having a dreadfully near shave

* See Appendix.

at my first interrogation," she said. "The man who heard you
in the morning took me on in the afternoon and began by chal-
lenging me about our marriage. After I had flobred him on that
point he said that you weren't the brains of the south-east zone
but the dumbest nincompoop he had ever met. I was just going
to set about him and fall into the trap of violently denying this
lying insult, when it dawned on my stupid impetuous mind that
this was the dream defence."

"What do you mean?" I said, nonplussed.

"Why, if I grudgingly admitted that you were a numb-skull
I could make out that I was the grey eminence behind our movement, of course."

"Oh God!" I said. "You did that! . . . No wonder they left
me alone. . . . Oh, Odette, you sweet, crazy fathead!"

Later I asked her if she had been out to lunch with the Fols
and here she gave me some distressing news. Charles Fol had
been introduced to her one day in her cell, but knowing nothing
about him she had been very cagy. He had promised to send her
parcels but they had never been delivered. He had told her that
she, like myself, would be invited to lunch at his house with his
wife and she had vaguely accepted, but on the day that Henri
came to fetch her she had refused to go on the grounds that
she distrusted Henri, she did not wish to go to the house of
people she did not know and was not sure she could trust; that
even if she could trust them, her association could only endanger
them. Finally she could see no point in leaving the prison only
to return after tasting a few hours of freedom.

I asked her how, in the circumstances, she had managed to
send me all the food I had received. She explained that since
the Gestapo had allowed her no privileges, her long semi-
starvation had made her so weak that the prison Captain had had
her transferred, against her own wishes, to a communal cell where
he hoped her new companions would restore her to better health.
She had only just arrived in this cell, with a gland on her neck
swollen up to the size of an orange, when I had appeared in one
of the cloisters below. It was thanks to her friends that my

attention had been drawn in her direction. It was also entirely thanks to them—Simone Hérail* in particular—that she was able to send me the extra food.

I told Odette about my missing wallet and of my fears that Henri had picked it up when he captured us. With a twinkle in her eye, Odette reminded me of how she had come into my room and then explained how, under the barrage of vituperation against Louis le Belge, she had slipped it out of my inside pocket and hidden it on her person. She went on to relate how she had tucked it under the seat of the car that had taken us to Annecy barracks, and of her certainty that any soldier who found it would be only too glad to return it to an officer after collecting the 70,000 francs and burning the radio messages he would find inside. I looked at Odette with sheer admiration as she unfolded this tale; her quick-witted act, that no one had seen, had averted a host of questions entailing the lives of agents probably still at large.

She told me that Henri had tried out a series of tempting proposals on her, offering freedom on conditions that had made her smile; her constant refusals had resulted in putting a full stop to his visits. She said that he had hinted strongly that I did not love her in the least and I began to see that Henri's suave manner included more tricks than exuding his charm on me.

Odette was still convinced that we should both survive, but it was not until much later that I was to discover the sound reason that provoked this conviction in regard to myself. We compared notes on our interrogations, but she seemed loath to pursue this topic and led me off onto other matters each time it came up.

I could not agree with Odette's certainty that we had been betrayed by Roger Bardet, nor would I believe that he was working for the Germans. Though I had heard that he had been captured and subsequently escaped from the Black Maria that was taking him to an interrogation I was still sceptical when she claimed the door had been opened for him by pre-arrangement just outside a "métro" station. My inability to understand this and my counter-claim that Marsac's letter introducing Henri to her had

* Survived.

not exactly helped matters, used up much of our time. However, the simple fact of being so close together and for so long brought us immeasurable joy at the time, for such joy is not always dependent on constant accord.

Odette suggested that in future she could write me little notes on cigarette paper and slip these inside the cardboard top of the jam container she would send me every fortnight. She told me I could send my replies in books which I could send her by way of the wardress who delivered her parcels to me. All I had to do was mark the letters forming my words by impressing a pin below each letter, beginning on page fifty of each book. I was full of admiration at this ingenious scheme.

Eventually our finger-prints were taken and we were photographed for the criminal records. After this somewhat debasing process, a small price to pay for our happy reunion, I had the joy of Odette's proximity all the way back to Fresnes in the central passage of our crowded Black Maria, all the way through the dark underground passages and up to the second division where our roads parted.

As I saw her beloved form vanishing down the next tunnel I did not suspect the torment that lay ahead of her, any more than I did the dreadful tortures that lay behind and which she had so valiantly concealed from me behind her gay smile and bubbling talk.

Christmas came and went. The Fols included a little Christmas tree in my fortnightly parcel, and below my crucifix I pinned a poem called "Espérance," a gift from a Catholic Society. With these touching emblems and a free Red Cross parcel for all, the prisoners in solitary confinement ate their delicacies in silent loneliness, thanking God for the thoughts of those outside and praying through their tears that in His great mercy He would bring comfort, hope and courage to absent parents and children bravely facing empty chairs in this war-time travesty of the family reunion.

*   *   *

January crept by on leaden feet. On my birthday I received

an embroidered handkerchief from Odette on which she had sewn the words, "To Peter, with all my love. Odette"—and the date. Added to this treasure I had by now received three of her private messages by means of the jam-pot cover and a regular exchange of love letters was under way between us, thanks to this brilliant system. It pained me to have to burn these words after reading them.

When it looked as though we had at last got ourselves organised to face the intolerable siege of time, the blow fell.

My door was opened on February 13th by a new guard who said,

"*Schnell, schnell*, pack up your belongings. You're off to Germany."

I looked up with a start from the book in which I was only half-way through "pointing" a letter to Odette and, staring vacantly at the man over my shoulder, I said,

"I've been here almost 300 days. What's the sudden hurry?"

"Come on, *los*! They're waiting for you downstairs."

He closed the door and left me to my packing.

Thanks to a large kit-bag which Odette had made for me in the workroom I had no difficulty in finding space for the possessions I had gathered in the course of time. I made up a large parcel of sugar and other luxuries, including the latest book Charles Fol had sent me, called *La Grande Meute*—an international masterpiece on fox and stag-hunting—which contained my unfinished letter.

Before I had time to look for odds and ends around this cell where I had become 500 years old and where I had learned so much the guard was back to fetch me.

I gave him some cigarettes and, holding out the parcel for Odette, said,

"Will you kindly arrange for this to be delivered to my wife in the third division?"

It never occurred to me that she might be coming to Germany as well, sharing this part of the journey, just as we had shared every other step so far. Nothing occurred to me and my mind was a blank as I walked along the second-floor cat-walk for the last time.

Down below, two guards grabbed my possessions and violently emptied everything onto the floor. One of them shook out my tobacco pouch and let the contents fall into some butter, which then rolled into the gap of the trolley rails. As I tried to save some of the precious tobacco that represented the small victory of months of control, I looked at the dumb ape who had committed this unnecessary waste and said, scathingly,

"Thank you very much!"

As I gathered up what I could of the remains of the prisoner's "gold dust," the wardress who had so often acted as the bearer of Odette's gifts to me, came up and joined her loathsome compatriots.

"Where are you going?" she asked.

I looked up and tried to distract my numb and furious mind from its futile purpose. I glanced at this strange woman who, according to Odette, was as capable of cruelty towards some of the prisoners as she was ready to kow-tow to her favourites. Normally, she was a woman who talked so much that I could hardly get a word in edgewise. Now I realised that she was asking me a question and actually waiting for a reply. Truly Odette had this woman eating out of her hand and the name of Churchill was having precisely the effect that she had foreseen.

Here was a gift from the gods to compensate me for the lost tobacco.

"I'm going to Germany, apparently," I said.

She looked at me aghast and said, "Frau Churchill won't like this thought. Am I to tell her this news?"

"Of course you must tell her. And please make sure that the parcel I gave to the guard who just brought me down from my cell is safely delivered to her."

"I will see to it all."

She rushed off, only too glad to be the authorised bearer of such news.

In a moment my things were repacked and I was led off through the underground passages and up to the desk where the articles that had been taken from me on arrival had been ticketed and stored. I rethreaded my shoelaces, tied my tie round the attached collar of my open shirt and after receiving a hundred-franc note I had forgotten all about and signed for a small parcel I had never seen before, I was ushered into a private car and driven off to Paris at break-neck speed. This sudden swift movement after the still-ness of my long imprisonment was a terrifying experience which I managed to overcome by the happy thought that we might capsize.

At Gestapo headquarters I was led upstairs and locked up in a box-room until I should be required. When I heard the door lock behind me I lit a cigarette and began to test all the sensitive currents of my intuition in search of the meaning of this move. Germany could mean imprisonment in a German jail, internment in a Concentration Camp, the one-in-a-thousand chance of a P.O.W. camp, or execution from either of the first two.

I opened the little parcel I had signed for in Fresnes and, to my amazement, there was my wallet—the one Odette had so cunningly hidden in the car on our first grim ride to captivity. I hastily opened it and examined each compartment. The money had gone and there was no trace of Arnaud's last five messages. Odette had been absolutely right. What an ace she was! I slipped my hand into the special compartment with the flap, felt the Sainte Thérèse medal she had sewn in by its ring near the corner, and pulled out the contents; a small photograph of my mother and one of Odette. Well, well, well, what a find! I examined the photographs carefully and smiled wistfully at the two faces that smiled up at me. Was it really possible that in captivity I should be looking at snaps that had been taken so long ago as in the days of peace? I raised my mother's face to my lips and then put her image away.

Looking again at Odette's image I wondered what sad thoughts were now running through her mind, what the future held for her, for us. I remembered her telling me during our glorious hour together at the finger-print department that a cell-mate of hers had frequently told her fortune from the cards and that each time they had foretold that we should both survive after much hardship. I would cling onto this hopeful prognostic with all my strength, however flimsy it might seem.

My thoughts were interrupted by the opening of the door and in swept the Chief of the Paris Gestapo in full uniform. He walked about the tiny room for a while, prodded my kit-bag and inspected my coats; then he stared at me in silence for a while. Finally he said,

"*Sprechen Sie Deutsch?*"

I said that I did.

"I've got some good news for you," he began, in the tones of a Judge who has just donned the black cap and is about to pronounce the death sentence. I prepared myself for whatever might come.

"You are being sent back to England."

My heart started to pound at these incredible words, spoken in all apparent seriousness. I was sure it was a trap and gaped at him in silent amazement.

"It's true," he said and repeated the words, "*nach Hause.*"

"You're pulling my leg," I said, with a wry smile, using one of the 5,000 German expressions I had learned by heart.

"Not at all. You and a British major are being exchanged for a German lieutenant now in British hands. We are offering two of you to get him back. Your colleague is already in Berlin where you will also be held until you go home via Switzerland or Sweden. Would you like your wife to travel with you?"

Now I was sure it was a hoax. Why had he mooched around the room instead of bringing this out in the first place? In a tired voice I said,

"What do *you* think?"

"I'll ring up Fresnes and make the arrangements."

He turned on his heel and was gone.

The door was immediately reopened and a steaming dish of meat balls, boiled potatoes and cabbage was brought in with a knife and fork. I could no more believe my eyes than I could the turmoil inside my mind.

What was the point of telling me all he had if it was not true? Surely Gestapo officials of his exalted rank had no time to think up romances of this wild nature just for fun; or had they? The butterflies of hope began their wild fluttering inside me and I entered into rash flights of fancy extending to visions of Odette and myself leaning over the rail of a Swedish ship and watching the Aurora Borealis. I worked myself up into such a state of excitement that my feet were hardly touching the ground and the hours of waiting passed by in a flash. I was beginning to think of all the things I would say to Odette once she was brought into my presence, when footsteps in the passage warned me that something was about to take place. I stood back expectantly and heard the key turn in my lock.

The Gestapo Chief entered with two men in civilian clothes. Paying no attention to me he addressed the two others in a dialect entirely beyond my comprehension. Then he walked round behind me, suddenly threw an overcoat over my shoulders, grabbed my arms by the elbows and when the others closed in I thought some serious trouble was about to be served up. Nothing of the sort. Letting go my elbows just as suddenly as he had pinned them, he stalked out of the room followed by his henchmen. The door was locked behind him by a guard who had watched the whole mysterious scene.

In the ensuing silence the castles I had built in the air came tumbling to the ground, transforming themselves into misgivings as the rubble of my dreams crashed louder and louder about my ears. Whichever way I looked at it this astonishing performance could not possibly augur anything good.

The hours of waiting now dragged by interminably and the only good thing that came out of them was my increasing determination to call for an interpreter at my next meeting with the Head of the Gestapo. It was getting late and I began to wonder if he would make another appearance.

Towards eight o'clock in the evening I was told to gather my belongings. I was then led into the hall on the second floor where the same three men awaited me.

At sight of the Gestapo Chief I said,

"I want an interpreter, please."

A Frenchman was brought in. He said,

"What can I do for you?"

"I want you to ask the Chief two questions. The first is, why is my wife not here, and the second, what was the idea of the pantomime that took place three hours ago during which he pinned my arms together behind my back?"

The man translated these questions into fluent German and I heard and understood the replies. However, I waited for them to be turned into French.

"With regard to your wife, Berlin was telephoned and they said that she was not to travel with you. As for the other question the Gestapo Commander has to make certain that you don't escape in transit and he was explaining to the two men who are to escort you to Berlin the best method of hand-cuffing you so that you can still wear one coat and carry the other."

I looked at the Gestapo Chief and said in German.

"Why should I want to escape after what you told me about the exchange plan?"

He gave me a knowing look and said,

"Englishmen are crazy enough to escape on the last day of war and it is my duty to see that you reach Berlin. If you would care to give me your parole we need not go in for these indignities."

"I give it," I said.

"Very well then, bon voyage."

H

PART TWO

PART TWO

CHAPTER

I

THE two others now led me downstairs to a waiting car and we drove off to the Gare de L'Est. On the platform I bought half a bottle of red wine with my hundred-franc note and we boarded the train.

Entering an already occupied second-class compartment one of my escorts produced his Gestapo badge and we quickly had the place to ourselves. This was the first time I had actually bene-fitted from the Secret Police of Nazi Germany.

My two civilian guards turned out to be a couple of per-fectly agreeable German citizens; one was over-age for military service and the other, a young man, belonged to a reserved occupa-tion. Both had been enrolled as part-time agents and this trip to Berlin was a lucky break that enabled them to pay a flying visit to the coveted capital as well as doing a job of work.

As I had overheard them telling the German R.T.O. the importance of their captive, I laid on the Winston business fairly heavily.

After we had travelled all night, daylight found us well into Germany. I looked out at the dismal wintry countryside, noted the effects of bombing on factories, houses and marshalling yards and took in the German railway motto plastered on the walls of buildings and the sides of locomotives:

"*Alle Räder müssen rollen für den Sieg.*"—All wheels must roll for victory. Sometimes the word "*müssen*" was left out. I thought of our motto: "Is your journey really necessary?"

Such had been the recent bombing that it took the entire day and two changes to reach the Anhalter station. It was dark when we got there.

I had spoken a great deal of German during the trip and was glad to see that *Deutsche ohne Mühe*, whose 365 pages I had almost learned off by heart, could produce such practical results.

By the time I was fetched by an officer from Gestapo head-quarters my two escorts and I were only a few jumps away from exchanging cards. In their courteous treatment of me, which was merely obeying orders, they had discovered that their "terrorist" captive was a human being after all.

As we approached the entrance to Gestapo H.Q. in the Albrecht-strasse, their manner grew more aloof in the presence of the uniformed officer. The car pulled up outside some high wooden gates and a few peeps on the horn soon had them opened by an S.S. soldier from within. We drove in and came to a halt in the yard. I saw that there had been considerable bomb-damage already.

It was 11 p.m. before I was led through the long passages of this ghastly building, clocked in and then led still further.

The younger man had gone home and I was led along the final corridor by the driver and the older man. We stopped outside a pair of massive oak doors on which the officer knocked timidly. The door opened and my escort and I entered, whilst the officer remained outside, closing the door behind us.

I was now proudly exhibited by my train "companion" who pushed me into the centre of the room. Puffing out his chest, he announced, in a voice of which I did not think him capable,

"Erik Hoffmeyer reporting with his prisoner from Paris."

"All right, all right," said the senior officer, an elderly thick-set man, in a quiet voice. He beckoned Hoffmeyer up to the large table on a dais beside which he was seated and they entered into a long conversation whilst I was left as the central theme in the tableau of still life.

I took it all in as I stood there with a five days' growth of beard and a look of surly indifference on my face.

So this was the holy of holies. On the raised double-desks stood a battery of telephones. Seated at the opposite end of the table was an even older man than the one who was talking to Hoffmeyer. He was in uniform. In the centre of the far wall hung a large framed picture of Himmler. Hitler's picture was not in evidence. On a table close to the desks a radio set was switched on and, for the first time I heard the words, *"Wir geben die Nachrichten. Das Oberkommando der Wehrmacht gibt bekannt. . . ."*

To my left sat half a dozen uniformed officers drinking tea and, seated by herself near the centre of the right hand wall, was a young girl with pencil and pad at the ready on her knee. As I glanced at her pretty down-turned face, I felt the eyes of all the officers on my left burning into me. I switched my glance across at them only to find their gaze averted.

The whole picture reminded me of a scene from the film "Confessions of a Nazi Spy," the great difference being in the drab uniforms I now beheld and in the atmosphere created by the sullen fanaticism in the grey faces of the men around me. This was no longer the bright hopeful élite of Hitler's private thugs, but a dishevelled handful of men, tired of the constant inter-rogations, the endless executions which, in the light of the gloomy war news, was taking them further and further from their dreams of "The New Order" and nearer and nearer to the day of reckoning!

The older Gestapo Chief now rose from his chair and started walking in my direction with the slow movements of a chameleon. He waved me to the seat which the secretary had vacated for some reason.

Here it comes, I thought. A midnight interrogation in the heart of the spider's web.

Seeing me hesitate, he said quietly, in German,

"Do be seated." And I complied.

He returned to his chair and sat down.

A major now rose from amongst the tea drinkers and made his way with slow deliberate steps onto the dais. Picking up one of the telephones he drawled out, "Is that the chief receptionist of the Ritz?" After a moment's pause, he continued in the same vein, "I want you to prepare your very best room with a private bath, of course, for a most important new guest." His raucous laughter at his own rich jest was accompanied by a diabolical sneer in my direction. Then, wiping this look off his face to make way for what I felt sure was his natural expression—one of chronic hatred—he came past me and walked over to my kit-bag. Simultaneously a young S.S. sergeant entered the room, hatless.

The major turned to me and said,

"Can you speak German?"

"A little," I answered.

"Good. Then we don't have to waste time with interpreters."

He turned his full attention to the bag, prodding it, then looking back at me,

"What's in here?"

"Spare clothes and so forth," I said. "They've been checked before I came in."

"And they'll be checked again!" he snarled. "I wouldn't put it past you to have kept a small charge of explosive for our benefit."

I felt like saying how very much I regretted not having thought of such a splendid idea, but was certain that silence was the wiser course.

Turning to the guard, he said,

"You make a thorough search of his things."

I was glad to get out of this room. The young N.C.O. took me down some steps into the basement block and up to the checking-in desk where he and another man went through my belongings. They confiscated all my books but allowed me to keep my remaining food and tobacco.

I was now taken along the corridor of the cell block and told to read the notice board on the wall, with all its regulations; then I was locked up in a cell.

One glance at this place showed it to be the cleanest cell I had ever inhabited. It was more like a sleeping-car compartment than anything I had yet experienced. Somewhat smaller than the cells in Fresnes, this had a smooth rubber floor with the rounded edges of a hospital room. The bed had adequate springs, two sheets and plenty of blankets—the top one being marked rather ominously *"Geheime Staats Polizei"*—the table and chair were solid pieces of furniture and the hooks and shelves were not dilapidated. A piece of cardboard acted as a black-out over the tiny high-set window.

When I was in bed the light was put out and I slept soundly.

At 6 a.m. it was switched on again, my door was opened and a broom put inside by a prison worker. He said, "You must get dressed now and sweep the floor. I'll be back in ten minutes to collect your sweepings."

There was no w.c. in this cell and we were taken out for this purpose later in the morning—six at a time—when there was also an opportunity to wash.

On my first visit to the washhouse I noticed a very distinguished-looking man of maybe fifty-two, walking ahead of me. Though not tall, his bearing was so striking that my eyes were automatically drawn towards him. An air of just but undisputed proprietorship was the essence of his aura. His studied pace, the perfect cut of his grey suit, matching his iron-grey hair, proclaimed the descendant of a long line of châtelains, or maybe Vikings, who through centuries of traditional authority was master of all he surveyed. Beside him the guards looked like mere hirelings in his pay.

When I caught his eye I gave him a big smile which he acknowledged.

By chance we found ourselves in neighbouring w.c.'s and it was not long before a sheet of toilet paper was passed to me below the partition on which I read these words, in English,

ARE YOU A BRITISH OFFICER?

Using the pencil he had thoughtfully glided through with his message, I wrote below his question,

YES, AND YOU?

Back it came with DANISH SECRET SERVICE. MY NAME IS VON LUNDING. WHAT'S YOURS?

As fast as possible we passed the paper back and forth exchanging the following information:

PETER CHURCHILL—SABOTEUR.

v.L.—ANY CHANCE YOU GETTING HOME?

me.—VERY SLIGHT. WHY?

v.L.—IF YOU DO, INFORM DANISH H.Q. LONDON MY PRESENCE HERE. I WAS PICKED UP BY U-BOAT ON WAY TO LONDON BY DANISH SHIP. SUSPECTED OF REVEALING V.1 LAUNCHING SIGHTS. MY WIFE ANXIOUS NO NEWS.

me.—I WON'T FORGET BUT DON'T COUNT ON ME GETTING BACK.

This was the end of our rapid exchange, but not the last time I was to meet this aristocratic officer of the Danish General Staff.

The slow routine of prison life now began once more and here, despite my long apprenticeship, I was a new-boy all over again; nothing to read, no parcels and no exercise whatsoever. I was left strictly alone and my crêpe-soled pacing on the rubber floor was ghostly in its silence. Here there was no talking through the window, knocking on walls or telephoning. All was silent as the tomb.

I wondered when or if I should be called for further interrogation and began to consider the question of the exchange as viewed from here and in the new light of the sarcastic fiend I had encountered in the lions' den. I was fairly certain—albeit without any proof—that the Germans would make serious efforts to save their captured agent in London, if such an agent really existed. British reactions to the proposed exchange, however, were a totally different matter. In my mind I followed each move in the game with only the prisoner's intuition to guide me. I saw the Wilhelmstrasse's cable being handed to the German Ambassador in Stockholm; his visit to the British Minister and the latter's promise to deal with the matter urgently. I was sure that this had been carried out and that somewhere in the honeycomb of the Foreign Office was an IN-tray in which this cable was maturing. A telephone call on a private line to M.I.5. would elicit the information that Standartenfuehrer Hans Wolfgang was, in effect, a captive of the Security Branch but that he had been found guilty of espionage and by the implacable laws of the country had been condemned to death. I could almost hear the voice at the other end, saying:

"I'll tell the Chief what you say and you might as well send a copy of the cable by D.R. to back me up, but he's due for the firing squad in four days and, well . . . you know how it is. . . . We've had these exchange proposals before, so, in the circs, you may as well forget it."

"What about our two chaps in Germany?"

" 'Fraid they'll have to take pot luck."

I wondered if I should ever meet anyone in the Foreign Office who would tell me what had really happened, if anything, or if my pot luck would put paid to me altogether.

Almost every night we were treated to the most majestic raids by the R.A.F., but on February 27th came a performance that reduced its forerunners to mere pin-pricks. This visitation lasted for over an hour throughout which the twin-noted sirens of the Berlin fire engines were dwarfed by the constant roar of tight-packed squadrons and the bark of anti-aircraft guns. Having witnessed the "Fires of London" in May and December 1941, I thought it was about time for Berliners to wipe the smirk off their faces and realise that Goering's proud claim that our bombers would never get through was nothing but the hollow boast of one of their bombastic war-lords, intoxicated by his own power to the point of insane hysteria.

As the bombs crashed all round the prison, I thought to myself, "Let them all come, and if some happen to drop on the prison, all the better. If the lights must go out for good I should never blame a British pilot. This is as good a way of going as any. Who cares!"

I looked at the scratches on my door where my predecessor had been thrown headlong by the blast of a bomb that had shattered all the windows, smashed the central-heating plant and caused the wreckage of this loathsome building that I had already seen on my arrival. I had learned that my predecessor and eleven others in the basement cells had been removed to hospital and that four had died. I wondered when my turn would come.

All through the raid the guards patrolled the passage, whistling quietly to themselves and for the benefit of those inside—an action that could only be put to their credit. They had unlocked the doors and we were only kept in by the bolt.

At the end of this giant attack the wailing sirens came as an anti-climax. My door was opened and a tough guard peered in. Perhaps he expected to find me cringing under the bed. To his question, "How goes it?" I replied slowly, looking him square in the eye:

"First class."

And now in the silence that followed, two things occurred to me. The first was that these raids must be destroying many prisoners' files, so that in the end our captors would not know what half their political prisoners were there for.

The second thing was that if London did not play on the exchange, the two "poor chaps" in Germany would be done in out of sheer vengeance.

The days dragged on in eternal uncertainty.

On March 2nd my door was opened and the duty guard said:

"Get your things ready. You're off."

I was taken up to the desk where my belongings were returned to me. Two thugs—one with a scar on his face—in civilian clothes, stood by and watched the proceedings. When I was ready the uglier of the two planted himself in front of me and said:

"Do you understand German?"

"Yes," I replied.

"Well, if you try any funny business, you'll get this." He opened his jacket to reveal a Luger tucked into a shoulder-holster.

"Good," I said. "Where are we going?"

Taken aback that a prisoner should have the nerve to ask such a leading question, he fobbed me off with:

"To your new residence."

"Where is it?" I asked.

"You'll soon see!" he spat out.

"Why all the mystery?" I enquired.

He growled and led me off into the yard where a small Opel was ticking over with a soldier behind the wheel.

We drove off through the gates and headed north. Yellow signs at every cross-roads, bearing the dreaded indication of Oranienburg, soon told me what to expect. Just before the war I had read Louis Golding's *Dr. Emanuel* which unfolded the doubtful pleasures in store for anyone who entered the gates of Sachsenhausen Concentration Camp. So that was it. I should now experience the terrors that Golding had so vividly described as to make the reader feel he was sharing them with the unhappy Dr. Emanuel. I braced myself to bear the blow of what now seemed my certain fate.

As the kilometres dwindled so the town of Oranienburg came closer into view until finally the signposts changed to Sachsenhausen. Soon we were slowing up under the machine-gun-turreted and electrically-wired walls, then the car turned in at the entrance and stopped at the barrier. Beyond this I saw the entrance arch over which was written in large letters:

SCHUTZHAFTLAGER

which, as far as my German went, indicated Protective Custody Camp.

Through the gap I saw a large squad of prisoners in striped jackets staggering by with huge rucksacks on their backs, over what appeared to be broken stones. Later I discovered that these starving wrecks of humanity had thirty kilos of bricks on their backs and that they were being marched over this rough ground in order to test the wearing power of some new boots.

The barrier was raised and the car drove through and pulled up, after doing a wide circle to the right, beside a wall.

I looked at "Scarface" who had never opened his mouth to me during the thirty kilometre drive and said:

"Is this my new residence?"

"What if it is? All you foreigners misrepresent these camps. Just look at those flowers over there. . . . And every Sunday the loudspeakers relay the best music in the world. Why, they even hold football matches here."

I refrained from comment.

Presently a dapper little officer came up to the car, put his head through the window and looking at me, said, all in one word,

"*Sindsielaüsig?*"

I gaped at him uncomprehendingly. The question was repeated by "Scarface" in a threatening shout. I knew the word *lausbube*, but never connected the two.

With a grunt that sounded like "*Kvatch*" the officer moved off, adding something else to the others that was also beyond my comprehension. I got the jitters wondering what would happen now.

The officer got into a small car and drove up to the barrier. Ours followed suit. Could we possibly be going elsewhere? We now passed under the barrier and followed the camp walls, first north, then west, finally stopping, after less than half a mile, outside a tiny gate.

The regularly spaced machine-gun turrets warned me that this must be a special entrance to the camp where they probably kept the cell block.

The camp Adjutant—for that was the officer's designation—knocked at the gate and it was opened by a tall powerfully-built Guard Commander. Tipped off by the eternal shout of "*raus*!"—the last farewell from "Scarface"—I picked up my things and followed the others.

On passing through the gate the first thing I saw was a pine-tree-studded enclosure of some eighty yards in length by perhaps thirty in width in which stood two low wooden huts. Below the trees half a dozen men in allied uniforms—some with decorations—were strolling up and down. This haven could not possibly be for me; I was certainly by-passing this "playground" to enter the main camp by another side door.

But no! The guard turned left along a path leading to a wired gate. Inserting a large key he opened it and beckoned me through. Marching ahead, he led me into the first hut, turned right and opened a door. Smiling at my incredulous look he said:

"Your room," and then left me.

CHAPTER II

II

STANDING on a chair, cleaning the large clear glass windows was an orderly. He turned at the sound of my entry and, beaming from ear to ear, enquired:

"*Russki?*"

"*Nein. Engländer,*" I said.

He jumped off the chair and rushed out of the room.

I stood there trying to take it in; the iron bedstead, the chairs, the table, the stove; but, above all, the great open windows and the companionship awaiting outside.

It wasn't true. It couldn't be true. I walked up to the windows and looked up into the clear blue sky. I felt weak after my long solitude and was sorely tempted to collapse on the bed and give way to the sudden reaction. But footsteps behind me disclosed that I was not alone. I turned to see a khaki-clad soldier with a sergeant's stripes on his battle-jacket sleeves.

The man sprang to attention and, with a smiling face, said:

"Sergeant Cushing at your service, Sorr, and welcome to Sonderlager 'A' ".

I thought I should collapse entirely at the sound of this wonderful Irish brogue, but realising that I could not afford to do so in front of an N.C.O., I somehow managed a smile and then heard myself automatically uttering the right words:

"Stand easy, Sergeant."

I held out my hand which was caught in his strong grip.

Still smiling and still standing to attention—for Sergeant Cushing was not only sensitive to my feelings, but had also guessed that I was an officer—he said:

"Which would you prefer, an English cigarette or a cup of tea?"

"Both, Sergeant," I replied, and laughed with him, glad that the ice was broken.

He turned smartly and left the room.

I could see that I should have to be very much on parade in this place and would have no time to indulge in sloppiness. Something told me that I was probably the only British officer in the camp. If this was so I had better pull myself together right away. I therefore unpacked my things and pinned Odette's picture over the head of my bed, placing the crucifix just below it.

I had no sooner put out my three books and the patience cards before the Guard Commander was back with a pair of khaki slacks and a battle-jacket. He took all my civilian clothes away.

When I had changed into this new outfit Sergeant Cushing returned with a mug full of tea and a cigarette which he had begged, borrowed or stolen from somewhere. He was accompanied by a tall dark compatriot with large, rather tragic brown eyes, whom he introduced as Corporal Walsh.

I told them not to stand on ceremony and as I sipped the exquisite tea I gave them a very rapid résumé of the reasons leading up to my presence here.

Cushing lighted my cigarette and watched me blowing out the smoke of my first Virginia cigarette since an eternity, with the pleasure that comes from being able to give pleasure.

I did not have to enquire how many thousands of these cigarettes were still tucked away in the canteen, for I was pretty sure there was no canteen and that this particular cigarette, brought in loose, was the last one in the camp. Therefore, after taking two good pulls I handed it to Cushing and said:

"Take a drag and pass it round."

They now gave me the set-up of the camp. There were eight rooms in each hut, four on either side of the washhouse. The end room, nearest the gate to the compound, was theirs. In it was a loudspeaker controlled from the guard hut and everyone was welcome to listen to the German music whenever they liked; the rush-hours, in principal, being when the German news was on. They also had their daily dose of Lord Haw-Haw's insidious propaganda.

The next room to theirs was occupied by their compatriots Lance-Bombardier Spence and Private O'Brien. I was given to understand that all four had been captured in the early stages of the war, that they had met in a P.O.W. camp where the Senior British Officer, Lt.-Col. McGrath, had selected them as likely candidates to enrol themselves in the German recruiting drive for Irishmen prepared to strike a blow against the hated British. They would then be taken out of camp and given a course of sabotage prior to being dropped over England for their respective tasks. The idea behind this apparently traitorous rôle was that each man should immediately report to the first British officer he could contact on arrival in the U.K., insert the pre-arranged notice, which would indicate their safe arrival, in the advertisement columns of some newspaper and, since these papers reached the German Ambassador in Dublin, who would be on the lookout for these very announcements so as to cable them forthwith to Berlin, more men would be dropped over England and by this means an escape route would be established in which the Germans would be providing the transport, besides wasting precious time training men to no purpose whatsoever.

Despite the excellence of this idea, on paper, there was always the human element to be considered and, as far as I could gather, for reasons too long, too intricate and not concerned with this story, the four Irishmen found themselves in this camp, cut off from all communication with the outside world because they had been shown too much and the Germans suspected that they had no intention of carrying out the tasks over which so much time and money had been spent.

The third room from the end was mine and between me and the washhouse were two Polish airmen, Pilot-Officer Jan Buchowski

I

and Sergeant-Pilot Leshek Komorowski. (False names since their families are alive in Poland.)

Beyond the washhouse the next four rooms were occupied by Russians; the first being Fiodr Ceridilin, the orderly whom I had seen cleaning my windows and who had hoped I might possibly swell the Russian contingent. He, apparently, was always smiling and had reason to be happy for, out of thousands of Russians over the wall in the main camp, he had been picked as the cleanest and most suitable candidate to be the private servant of Major-General Jan Bessonov, late Kommissar to a Russian Division and late Second-in-Command of the 800,000 N.K.V.D. Frontier Troops, who inhabited the end room. Fiodr, who now lived on the fat of the land, being treated—like everyone else in this camp—to S.S. food, had forgotten all about the evil days over the wall when he had stolen coal, not for heating purposes, but so as to eat it.

The room beyond Fiodr's was occupied by Colonel Brodnikow, followed by that of Lieutenant-General Privalov, hero of Stalingrad.

Strengthened by my cup of tea I gave myself up to the delight of hearing my own language spoken at last and enhanced by the rich phraseology of these Irishmen. I learned something of the astounding tale surrounding these three high-ranking Russian officers and the reasons that had brought them into this special camp of political prisoners, sometimes called Sonderhäftling or Prominenten.

After their early advances into the Soviet Union the Germans had, in their inhumanity, killed thousands upon thousands of Russian prisoners by jamming them into horse trucks which, at the slow pace of goods' trains, had taken over three weeks to reach Germany. When the sealed doors were opened the wagons contained nothing but corpses. But as always happens in these cases the odd escapee had survived to tell the tale, with the consequence that Russian troops preferred to be killed in action rather than to be taken prisoner, only to be massacred in like fashion.

Having observed the adverse results of what they probably put down to a foolish policy rather than criminal barbarity, they had quickly changed their tune and now kept their prisoners very much alive.

When they captured officers they asked them one leading question beyond the standard three of name, rank and number; namely, "What do you think of Stalin?"

If the man showed approval of the Soviet's Supreme Marshal, the man was interned. If, however, the officer intimated that he considered him a tyrant of the first water, he was then asked if he would consider joining the Staff of his compatriot General Wlassow who was forming an army of Russian prisoners of war which was ultimately to join the German divisions on the eastern front and help put an end to Communism. The price of this provisional liberty for Russian officers was their agreement to cede the Ukraine to Germany at the successful conclusion of this enterprise.

Having given the second reply to the query as to their views on Stalin, Bessonov, Privalov and Brodnikow had lived in style at the Adlon Hotel, Berlin, where the Russian Staff was billeted.

A slight indiscretion of Bessonov's at an evening party given by their German hosts was the cause of this trio's presence in the camp. Under the happy but truth-compelling influence of much vodka he had been overheard to say to the others: "As if I'd give these baskets the Ukraine!"

The second hut housed the Italian Army, Naval and Air-Attachés of Mussolini's Staff in Berlin, as well as their two Italian batmen.

At the time when Marshal Badoglio had joined forces with the Allies these senior officers had been exchanged for their German opposite numbers in Rome; but whereas the latter had safely reached their German terminus, the former had been flagrantly arrested at Munich and now found themselves here.

The timely arrival of a huge bowl of thick pea soup and a ration of bread, butter and honey, gave me the chance of some privacy of which I was very glad to avail myself.

As I ate my soup I turned all this rich information over in my mind and, for once, eating alone was not the sad affair that it had been and always must be for the man or woman in solitary confinement of whom Goethe might almost have been thinking when he wrote:

> *"Nur wer die Sehnsucht kennt,*
> *Weiss wass ich leide,*
> *Allein und abgetrennt von alle Freude. . . ."*

From time to time I looked at the unaccustomed sight of the glorious sky through my large windows and my mind clouded at the thought of Odette. In what hole was she languishing at this moment? I had not been very clever at Gestapo H.Q. in Paris. I wondered if anything I could have said would have improved her lot. I wished I could know what that lot actually was and was likely to be. But, in particular, I wished I could have that interview in Paris all over again. But there it was. Some are born to do and say the right thing at all times, some only do it sometimes by mistake, some never do it at all and others just plough through life and never consider the matter either way.

After lunch I went for my first walk and was glad to find the compound empty. 318 days in cells had made no noticeable difference to my walking and I took in great gulps of the fresh March air as though to rid myself of the poison of my past confinement. The knowledge that I could come out here whenever I chose gave me the sensation of having taken as large a step towards freedom as I could manage at one stride.

But was this a step towards freedom or were we not merely sixteen hostages living in comparative comfort whilst waiting for the toss of a coin? The two Italian batmen and Fiodr would naturally not enter into this category, but it stood out a mile that there must be many more "Prominenten" in other similar camps or tucked away elsewhere out of sight whom Hitler must certainly be keeping as valuable pawns with which to barter for his own and his satellites' lives in case he could not turn the swift and relentless tide of defeat already staring the nation in the face.

A guard mooched up and down the alley formed by the electrified wire on one side and the wall beyond, his thumbs tucked through his rifle sling. Seeing the new man of whose arrival he had probably heard in the guard hut, he hailed me politely enough. I gave him a wave and he proceeded along his beat, bored and bent.

The two Poles were now coming towards me from the hut's entrance. Both were in uniform, and just as both were young, so the one was as dark as the other was fair. They stopped in front of me and introduced themselves. Jan was the dark one. A giant "Father Christmas" beard smothered most of his friend's face, the upper half of which was terribly burnt up to a line where his helmet had saved an inch of his forehead as well as his hair.

With undisguised admiration, Jan told me how his companion, an ace pilot, had brought down their burning bomber and landed it on a pitch dark night somewhere in France, how they had climbed out of the wreckage and escaped, how, due to the excruciating agony from his burnt hands and face they had to stop after three days to get him medical attention. He related how this had been their undoing and how, after their capture, the Germans had beaten Leshek's bandaged hands in Frankfurt jail in an attempt to extract information they had no right to seek—the number of his squadron.

From the two Poles I learned of the age-old hatred between Russia and Poland and their fears that the end of the war would find their whole country under Soviet domination, just as that country had grabbed half of it after Hitler's early advance on the capital in 1939. If they got back to England, it looked as if they would never be able to return to their own homeland.

Jan and Leshek agreed with me that we should probably be used as hostages, and now that someone with my name had joined their ranks they were all the more convinced of this. Their view was that Hitler would stage a final show of resistance in the Dolomites and that we should not find ourselves very far from there when the war was over.

Our threesome was now increased to six by the advent of the Italian officers to whom I was introduced. Sticking rigidly to protocol the first one to shake my hand was the Military Attaché, Colonel-General de Marras. With great courtesy and a friendly smile that wrinkled up his eyes behind his pince-nez, he welcomed me to their midst in English. Next came the tall aristocratic Naval Attaché, Admiral de Angelis, whose English was simply perfect. Last on the list, but by no means the least of this distinguished trio, was the tough Air-Attaché, Colonel Teucci. He had formerly been second-in-command of General Balbo's famous squadron of seaplanes which had accomplished the first mass flight around half the world.

As we walked up and down, talking easily, I could see at a glance with whom I should be spending most of my time—if they would let me. What struck me most about these three delightful Italians was not so much that they treated each other with easy courtesy, nor that they spoke both German and English so well and, with natural good manners, never broke into their own language in our presence, but that they were interested and knowledgeable in all topics and in no way bound by the limitations of their profession. These men were international diplomats of the highest order.

After strolling into the end room to hear some afternoon news I was invited by General Marras to join his party in the second hut. Bottles of beer and packets of cigarettes were produced by their two orderlies with the decorum of a well run officers' mess. When the orderlies had closed the door I learned that their names were Bartoli and Amici and that the latter was a cousin of the Hollywood actor Don Ameche, to whom his resemblance was striking.

My Italian hosts were rather sick at having been arrested on their way to Italy, and they showed some surprise when I told them I had a strong hunch that their wives would kick up such a fuss over the matter with Mussolini that I felt that a compromise would be made with Hitler to have them transferred to an Italian Fortress to which their wives would be allowed access.

Our acquaintanceship strengthened when they discovered I could speak some Italian and had once acted as Secretary to the Villa d'Este golf course during a long vacation from Cambridge. I left them after gladly agreeing to give English lessons to General Marras and Colonel Teucci.

In the late afternoon I met Spence and O'Brien and I accepted the former's offer of his services as my batman.

During the evening news period I shook hands with the remaining three Russians in the N.C.O.'s room. The boss of this group was clearly Bessonov, a short powerfully-built Georgian with black teeth, close-cropped hair, a strong determined jowl and eyes that were a mixture of devilry and merriment. Added to these features he had a soft creamy skin and on hearing his deep voice and husky wicked laugh, one had a fair picture of the generally accepted notion of a Mongol bandit. Still, thirty-eight-year-old Jan Bessonov struck me as being an attractive character. I was soon to learn that he was much more.

Compared to the picturesque N.K.V.D. man, the hero of Stalingrad was diffidence and simplicity personified. Wounded eleven times and decorated with the Star of Lenin, fifty-two-year-old General Privalov spoke so little German that I feared I should never discover what was going on behind his kindly eyes and well-shaped forehead.

The tall, bearded and stooping Colonel Brodnikow was a refined career-officer of some forty-five years of age. He had somehow escaped the purges that had decimated the Soviet Army between the years of 1933 and 1937, when 68,000 officers of the rank of Colonel and upwards had been liquidated on suspicion of not being loyal Communists. Despite his stoop Brodnikow was definitely a charmer due to his handsome eyes, beautiful voice and well-tended shapely hands.

My mind was in a whirl by the time I got into bed that night.

Though gregarious by nature the sudden transition from dead silence into the vortex of this international settlement where almost every member was a star in his own firmament, had been a little tiring, to say the least of it.

I had managed to keep my private tryst with Odette, which I was determined to do every day against all comers, but when the lights went out and I was just settling down to an extension of our distant communion and the door opened, silhouetting two figures in the flood-lighting from the compound, I felt that things were going too far.

Closing the door behind them Sergeant Cushing and Corporal Walsh stole silently up to my bed. With Irish charm and in a voice calculated to make even St. Peter put his key back in the lock, Cushing said:

"We know you must be flogged, Sorr, but it's a matter of great importance that we're after telling you. D'ye moind if we park on yer bed so's not to wak op the naborrs?"

Walsh held up the unattached edge of a cigarette paper surrounding a concoction of tobacco dust, Russian Mahorrka and other sweepings from his pocket for me to lick. I let him light it and drew my first taste of hot splinters before saying:

"Well, Sergeant, I'm listening."

The tale that was now unfolded in the dark by these two pastmasters of wordcraft would have kept me awake, despite the lull of their voices, through the sheer wealth of their phraseology, even if the subject that lay tucked away behind it all had not its own elusive charm. Relaying one another in their anxiety to unburden their minds to an officer, and afraid to lose a second while the other stopped to light another cigarette of Russian tobacco stalks, they spun out a masterpiece of verbiage that would have kept a large audience of paying customers spellbound. Who was I to turn down a free show given for my own special benefit?

They began their story with a long preamble on the situation in the Soviet Union combined with vivid descriptions of life inside the Slave Labour and Concentration Camps, as described to them by Fiodr who had spent two years in one of these

Institutions and General Bessonov who knew more about them than anyone in Russia. Against this grim back-cloth they painted the picture of Bessonov; sketching his early life as a Cossack Squadron Commander leading charges in frontier skirmishes, taking part in the white-uniformed Guard of Honour that had received Anthony Eden on his 1934 visit to Moscow, and running through to the position he had held before the war.

At 11.30 the tale was interrupted by the wailing of the sirens and before long my room was lit up by the distant searchlights picking out the vanguard of the night raiders over Berlin. Looking through the window we watched the lights handing on their well-held targets to their neighbours along the line. Presently a series of flashes on the ground and others in the air showed that bombs were landing and the flak was engaging the R.A.F.

Our comfortable ringside seat felt very safe after the sensations I had experienced in the Albrechtstrasse up till the previous night. This was brought home still more when Cushing said: "The poor bleeders of Berlin are copping another packet," and I wondered how the powerless inmates of the Gestapo cellars were faring that night.

The flak seemed very strong and for an hour their shells burst in the sky in their thousands. The whine of German nightfighters joined in the din as they came and went, now passing overhead to join the battle and now returning to base for more ammunition.

Several of the bombers were hit, to be followed by a search-light as they fell helplessly over the fires they had themselves started. Others with an engine on fire limped slowly away whilst their wide-eyed gunners stared frantically around for night-fighters who could not possibly miss the sitting target pointed out to them by another moving finger of light.

When the barking and droning had passed and the "all-clear" sirens had indicated that that was all for the night, my two gate-crashers proceeded with their tale.

They told me that notwithstanding the purges there was constant unrest in Russia which not even the power of that totalitarian state could quell. They gave me the gist of what they had heard from Bessonov day after day for months on end, and this reduced itself to his comparison of Leninism with Stalinism and his comments on their respective views on Communism. Lenin had said: "If it should take 500 or 1,000 years, Communism will spread over the entire world as surely as a stone that is thrown into the air must reach its highest point." Stalin had changed this to "Communism must be spread throughout the world during my lifetime."

They went on to explain how this would affect the peace terms and how, when the war was over, we should see Stalin swallow one neighbouring country after the other, just as the Germans had done before the war and, little by little, by means of peaceful penetration interspersed with judicious retreats when too much alarm had been caused, we should finally see them occupying every base from Algeciras to the Baltic.

Cushing handed on Bessenov's claim that Russia was so rich in raw materials, including gold, that she had no need to look beyond her frontiers for a place in the sun, and that this mad plan to force the spread of Communism was like turning the pages of history before you had come to them. Having been shown over Berlin and Paris during his liberty at the Adlon Hotel he had realised how backward was his own country and how much wiser it would be to improve conditions there than force their doctrines onto other people whose countries were far better run than Russia.

At no point in this fascinating exposé of things as they were and as they might become did I interrupt my able lecturers for, in my ignorance of these vital matters, it was all news to me. And now, as they approached the point of their visit, Cushing took over the helm.

Bessonov had been curious to know my story and when they had outlined it to him he had said:

"This man may have been led here by the hand of destiny. Related to the British Prime Minister and a parachutist into the bargain, he is the very man I want. The Germans will do anything to stop the further advance of our Armies onto their soil and if Captain Churchill is willing to be dropped by them over England, he can expose my plan to Winston Churchill for flying out British paratroops to a few dozen scattered points I can mark on the map, namely the Concentration Camps of the Soviet Union where all those who think as I do are interned. By picking the fittest survivors of these ten million haters of Stalin they would have a ready-made army of people crying out for vengeance. I also know all the roads that lead to Moscow and since we should meet with little resistance because all the troops are at the front, this is the way to put an end to the fanatics of the Kremlin and bring about a lasting peace."

A deathly silence followed this climax and I could almost feel the eyes of Bessonov's messengers watching my reply form in my brain.

I knew from the first that my answer would be "no" and this for the simple reason that I was tired of adventure and worn out by the fears and anxieties that had mounted up over the past months and whose demoralising effect I could not possibly wipe out in a flash. Yet, whilst reason told me that Winston Churchill must know all this and would not be prepared to strike his dangerous ally in the back, I was nevertheless fully aware that in ordinary circumstances I would have leaped at this opportunity of being an instrument in a Crusade that might have changed the course of history.

"I'm sorry to disappoint you," I said. "But you can be sure that Winston knows anything that we know. Anyway he would never play on this wicket and as far as I'm concerned, I'm tired, very tired and I don't feel up to it."

That they were disappointed there was no doubt, but they seemed to understand my reasoning and were silenced by my frank admission of unwillingness to entertain the plan.

It was 3 a.m. when they left me and without giving the matter further thought I fell fast asleep.

The days rolled by easily and swiftly and there was plenty to do all the time; books, walks, music, bridge, drafts and above all, the fascination of hearing eye-witness accounts of the doings and sayings of Hitler, Mussolini and life inside the Soviet Union. To me it seemed like Paradise after what I had known. Odette and the stifling pain of prison seemed very far away and as the days swept past and my activities increased so they grew farther and were harder to recapture.

In this small camp the Poles and the Irish and myself received one third of a Red Cross parcel per week. Considering that we were on S.S. food, the situation was quite tolerable, though most unfair to the Russians. However, they made no complaint, for the Soviet Union has nothing to do with the Red Cross and this merely served to draw another odious comparison, which they made, not we. No letters were ever exchanged by Russian or German prisoners of war with their folk at home. Russia does not recognise her own men when they are captured, not even a pilot who climbs out of a burning 'plane when there is nothing else he can do. All this and plenty more was told to me by the Russian officers, and when I heard that after their war with Finland all prisoners were court-martialled when they got home and many put to death I began to agree with Bessonov and Brodnikov when they used to say:

"What beats us is how anyone in your civilised countries can work themselves up about Communism when the worst conditions you can get are streets ahead of life in our police State where even ballet dancers, playwrights and authors must betray their own souls."

German was the common language of our community and though the guards rated me the best exponent of their tongue after the Italians, I never reached the ease and speed of the Irish quartet. Ignoring all grammar they simply strung their words together with neither hesitation nor care for gender, throwing in an occasional infinitive or present indicative to tie up the bundle, which served equally well for the imperfect, the future or the past.

Fiodr, who had never heard of Jesus Christ and whose only superiority to a good-natured sheep dog was the faculty of speech, managed to convey his thoughts on a vocabulary of some fifty German words. But even this limitation placed him above General Privalov who seemed tied to a couple of dozen.

The erudite Brodnikov was the best German scholar among the Russians with Bessonov a close second. To hear Bessonov conversing with one of the Irishmen was to attend the most excrutiating sabotage of the language that can be imagined; and yet they understood each other perfectly.

It was a fortunate arrangement that the Italians had the second hut to themselves, for although Admiral de Angelis found pleasure in Brodnikov's society, none of them could quite hit it off with Bessonov whose crude manners included spitting on the floor.

The personalities, friendships and enmities of the camp were not long in revealing themselves to me. The Irish boys, true to their fighting reputation, rowed occasionally amongst themselves. Bessonov, reputed to have either killed or frightened a Russian Colonel to death—his body had been carried out of Privalov's room a few months before my arrival—ran his group with a rod of iron. The Poles stuck to themselves and were courteous to all who entered their room. They got on very well with Privalov and Brodnikov and conversed with them in Polish whilst the others spoke in Russian; the similarity of the two languages having some resemblance to that obtaining between Spanish and Italian.

To all of them I told the same tale, namely that Odette and I were married. It was a fortunate thing that I did so, for in this camp there was a stool pigeon who reported everything to the Sachsenhausen Camp Commandant, Colonel Keindl. A slip-up here, in a moment of confidence, would have reached Gestapo Headquarters within twenty-four hours; so, for what it was worth in not aggravating her position still further, this lie was carried through to the very end. As always happens in these cases, the camp traitor did not wear an armband bearing the name Judas Iscariot. But we shall come to him presently.

In the third week of March a giant Englishman was brought

into my room, dressed in a rough suit which had clearly been fashioned from an airman's uniform. Slinging a bag off his shoulder he placed it apologetically on a chair, like a hiker entering a private room in a country pub who does not want to upset the person who may be snoozing beside the fire.

He held out his hand, saying:

"My name's Dodge, Johnny Dodge. I'm awfully sorry to break in on your privacy, but it looks as if we're to be room-mates."

I shook his hand and noticed that his middle finger was folded inside my grip. Wondering if this was a secret sign, I said:

"I'm Peter Churchill and you're most welcome, I assure you. What's your rank?"

"Major," he said, leaving out the facts which I was to learn from others that he had been a Lieutenant-Colonel in the Great War and had received the D.S.O. and D.S.C. for gallantry in the Dardanelles, where both his hands had been pierced by machine-gun bullets as he dragged a boatful of wounded men singlehanded through the water. It was due to these wounds that his handshake was a little unconventional.

"Then you're the Senior British Officer," I said, "as I'm only a Captain."

Telling me his story as though relating the brighter features of an average country ramble I gleaned the fact that my new room-mate who was one of seventy-eight who had crawled out of Sagan camp—Luft IIID—by means of a tunnel. Johnny Dodge could not know how many had got away but figured that we should shortly be joined by some of his old friends who, like himself, had failed to make the 'home' run.

I was frankly delighted with my new companion and whatever he may have thought of me he certainly made the best of it and we got on extremely well together.

I was also most fortunate in his timely arrival, for only a few days later my Italian friends were marched out of the camp. Standing beside their disconsolate orderlies by an open window in the passage of our hut into which they had also been locked so as to avoid any demonstrations, conversation or dramatic farewells, I smiled at the outgoing trio with mixed feelings. Whilst I was deeply sorry to see them go I felt certain that my forecast for their future was to prove correct. In my conviction I found it easy to console Bartoli and Amici in their own language.

The strange affinity which I had felt for these high-ranking Italian officers had never been marred by any thought that up till September 1943 they had been our enemies; in fact, at no time during the war could I quite grasp this was or had been so.

As Spence had soon tired of being my batman, I gladly took on the Italian boys who were only too happy to fall into a vacant job where they would continue to be appreciated and hear their own language spoken.

Bartoli was six feet tall and had been through the Abyssinian campaign. By trade a pastry-cook and waiter he could make a cake out of porridge, condensed milk and cocoa. He was brave, loyal and an asset to the community; besides this he was a natural comic.

Amici was the shy product of a small Italian farmstead. Strong as a bull, he was gentleness itself.

One day when Johnny Dodge was just about getting the feel of the camp our door was opened and in swept three more customers from Sagan. It was like a family reunion to see him welcome his oddly-clad cronies.

I was first introduced to 'Wings' Day, Senior British Officer of many an R.A.F. Oflag and ace aerobatic pilot of Hendon days; next, to Flight-Lieutenant Sydney Dowse and lastly to Jimmy James of the same rank.

Although they were all disgusted at having been caught and wondered what sort of a hole this could be, I felt that things would liven up with their presence in the camp. They were lodged in the second hut and joined Johnny and me for meals. Once again 'Wings' Day found himself in his old job as S.B.O., though this time of a very small British contingent.

Sonderlager "A" now transformed itself rapidly into the

next best thing to an R.A.F. camp. A large wall map was prepared from several sheets of paper in our room and the daily Allied advances were marked up by Sergeant Cushing.

A long-jump pit was prepared in the compound, early-morning runs round the perimeter became a daily institution, net-ball, with a ball made from paper crammed inside a piece of felt which was then sewn up, rapidly became the most popular game and, thanks to 'Wings' demands, we were provided with a set of parallel bars.

As spring turned into early summer the younger elements of the camp became transformed into a team of healthy bronzed athletes.

We were always very conscious of the hardships and misery in the main camp from which we were merely separated by a common wall. An occasional burst of machine-gun fire in the night told us that some poor wretch had been caught in the search-lights outside his hut. When smoke rose from the crematorium—the evil monuments of these living Hells—it was best to think that another soul was out of its misery.

Whilst life had to go on in our camp as it always must and certainly does in freedom where laughter and song are not very far removed from others who are dying a violent death, yet to those who believe in the sanctity of human life, something is lost forever by the sound and smell of bestiality and sadness comes to eyes that see what the mind can never forget.

Towards the end of April a young Russian Lieutenant came to swell out numbers (for many good reasons I shall simply call him Stefanov). He recognised me immediately as someone he had seen in the basement passages of the Berlin Gestapo Head-quarters, and he told me the sobering news that on the very day of my departure the underground cells in the Albrechtstrasse had received the effects of a direct hit on the yard outside and that every prisoner had been killed. This was the raid I had watched through my window on the night of my arrival.

Stefanov was in poor shape when he joined us, but a few days of kindness and companionship soon put him right. He was

given a room in the second hut and within a short space of time
became the most popular man in the camp.

III

Soon after the arrival of 'Wings' Dowse and Jimmy James a
leading article in the *Deutsche Allgemeine Zeitung* confirmed the
rumour that about fifty of the seventy-eight men with whom
they had escaped from Sagan had been shot after capture. The
article, needless to say, did not give this information in so many
words, but dealt sarcastically with the British Government's
strong protest about these assassinations.

Instead of thanking their lucky stars that the mad rage of
Hitler had somehow passed them by, it was precisely at this
moment that they unanimously decided to show their captors
to what extent they were cowed by this vile inhuman butchery,
by escaping.

All three and Johnny Dodge had been told by the S.S. officer
who had escorted them to the camp that from Sonderlager "A"
there was simply no hope of escape. The soil was sandy and would
fall in on tunnellers; the twenty odd inmates were guarded by
thirty-two guards, plus dogs; the wire stretched well below
ground surface and the Guard Commander's hut was fitted with
coloured electric light bulbs that would light up if the wire was
tampered with.

Armed with this interesting information they planned to
make a tunnel from their hut which should come out on the grass
verge just outside the wall.

Apart from myself, the secret of this project was kept from
everyone. Although I was invited to join them, I declined, and my
view that as a political prisoner, whose story was too well known
in Berlin, it would be highly inadvisable to do so, was accepted.

K

Dowse and James soon unscrewed one of the floor-boards in their room and the heavy preliminaries began. As the hut was slightly raised above the ground, here was the answer to their main problem—the dispersal of the earth.

It was the longest and dirtiest job of the lot and was to take them nearly three months out of the four necessary for the complete job. They had to work with handkerchiefs tied around their faces owing to the clouds of fine sand flying about.

They took turns during the day so as not to attract the dogs through noise that would be more easily heard at night.

The tunnel slowly grew in length and depth. A small saw was smuggled into the camp by blackmail and with this the wainscoting of several rooms in the chosen hut was sawn up and served to shore their warren. Two chairs also helped for this purpose.

The months passed by and despite the increasingly heavy raids of the R.A.F. now added to by massed daylight bombing by the Americans, the tunnel stood up to all earth tremors.

Camp life went on as before. By day I gave German lessons to 'Wings' and Johnny Dodge who were determined to know and pronounce certain phrases correctly.

When the lights were switched off at 10 o'clock every night we would take down the black-out boards so as to get all the fresh air we could. This was done likewise in the many-windowed corridor, through which our small compound lay clearly defined under the shaded flood-lights.

Most of the inmates of Sonderlager "A" were only conscious of the electric wire beyond which the guards patrolled all night with their Alsatians. Most of them only saw the skulls and cross bones which appeared at regular intervals along the warning wire, the over-stepping of which was an invitation for a bullet. But to me after what I had known, this place was still like a fore-court of Paradise which, at night, turned into a fairyland with the lights shining through the tall pine trees onto our stadium and the low-built not unattractive huts.

Lying on my bed and letting the varied influences of the camp and the ever-improving war situation filter into my brain like a keleton key searching out the tumblers of any given lock, I could see some of it through the passage window.

In the next hut Dowse and James would be discussing the chnicalities of their ambitious and daring plan whilst 'Wings', who had been shot down on the very first day of the war, would be lying awake, chafed by the eternal bug of freedom on the one hand and impelled towards yet another escape, by the highest traditions of a Regular Officer's duty, on the other. Thinking also of his family and the happy days of freedom that he had known centuries ago he would be wondering how many more birthdays he must pass in captivity. So often, when he had thought it was the last, the war had ground on for yet another. Surely the way things were proceeding now it must end before Christmas. But time was getting on. At forty-seven one began to ask how many more years the system could stand before it was past caring for the joys of freedom. He would be thinking of the strange new revelations that had come from his talks with Bessonov and wondering what it all spelt for the years after the Armistice. God, how tired he was of it all! Wasn't it about time someone else took the world's burden off his shoulders? Why should he meddle in high politics? Why interfere? Why was Peter Churchill so keen that he should listen to Jan Bessonov's eternal political song? Bessonov was a bandit and no better than Stalin whose power he merely hoped to usurp. These Russians thrived on intrigue. It was the breath of their life; they even dreamed intrigue. And yet Bessonov had written two large books on Communism in captivity. He had translated certain passages to them when he and Johnny Dodge had dutifully gone to his room for these regular and strangely fascinating discourses on the changing face of the Soviet Union. His exposition of Lenin's Ten Points and the way Stalin had changed them was an able piece of writing, to say the least of it. And then the man's handwriting itself belied the ruffian one saw. It was regular in its slope, round and full of character. Possibly there was something in it after all, blast it!

In the next room Stefanov would be sound asleep after a

long day of laughter and athletics. His natural, friendly personality brought him the high dividends that were reflected by those with whom he came in contact. Totally ignorant of the fact that a tunnel was forging ahead from an entrance not four yards from his head and blessed with the faculty of being able to lay aside all thoughts of the past he would be sleeping soundly with a look of innocence on his face.

And yet behind that look what frantic memories he had to lay aside. At twenty-three, Stefanov had been the youngest professor at the University of K and now, aged twenty-seven, he had already lived more fully than most men who reach a hundred. He had known the deadly cold of the Finnish Campaign and had there witnessed the farce whereby Russian troops were entitled to question their superiors' orders and complain to the Kommissar in attendance. This was the state of chaos that had caused the failure of the Russian Goliath to swallow the David of Finland any sooner, and it was only thanks to Timoshenko's courage in daring to tell Stalin the effects of his foolish policy that Russian Army discipline had been restored. During the war with Germany Stefanov had been a partisan, wearing German uniform. He had been captured and the lorry that was transporting him and other Russian partisans had had to stop for a puncture. They had got out to lessen the strain on the jacks and then an air-raid had interrupted the proceedings. Falling down flat under the low-flying aircraft he had seen his chance. The officer's open holster was within easy reach of his hand. In one swift movement he had the Luger in his grasp and shot the officer in the back. Then he had attended to the rest of them, thus rescuing the entire Russian convoy. Another year of adventures behind the lines and Stefanov was captured again. The Gestapo had spent months trying to connect him with the murder of a German officer and several guards who had been found dead beside their burnt-out lorry and Stefanov had known what it was like to sweat it out in the tombs of the Albrechtstrasse.

Such mental ramblings did not take long to pass through my mind and, jumping from room to room, a review of the small group was soon made. Sometimes I thought of the men over the wall; always I thought of Odette.

The unfairness with which the Hand of Destiny was kind to some and struck down others constantly baffled me. But, of course, there is no fairness; any more than there is in a family where one child is blessed with all that pleases and another is stricken with chronic illness. What matters is what you do with what you have got. Odette had shown me what could be done with practically nothing.

I knew that just as I shuddered over her fate, so her state—if she was still alive—would have improved in the knowledge that things were well with me. Something told me that she *was* alive, for our daily thoughts seemed to come into contact as before and if anything dreadful had happened I felt sure that I should have sensed it somehow.

Odette was not a person who ever wished others to be as badly off as herself. Hers had been a fight for freedom, the freedom of those she had left at home, the freedom of France and the land of her adoption. In captivity she hoped that by playing her part to the best of her ability, she was paying a small price towards that same end. To me Odette was a kind of counterpart of Sainte Thérèse, for as against being willing to sacrifice her place in Heaven so as to do good on earth, she was prepared to face Hell on earth so that others might avoid it.

One June evening when my room-mate and I were feeling in particularly good fettle we had started a sing-song which had been joined by some of the Irish boys. When the session was over and we lay talking on our beds, a new prisoner was brought in through the gates. It must have been eleven o'clock and as he passed through the flood-lit compound we caught a glimpse of his very fair hair and saw that he was dressed in an open shirt and khaki shorts. Having read an article in the *Voelkisher Beobachter* some days before, reporting the capture of a Colonel Churchill after a raid on the mainland from the Island of Lissa in the Dalmatians, we were pretty sure who this new customer must be, especially as the article had boasted that the German

Reich was doing well in its collection of Churchillian prisoners

The following day proved that our guess had been right Jack Churchill—no relation of mine or Winston's, but always known as my cousin to our captors—simply leapt at the invitation to join in the escape. He also helped in the digging. This now made three diggers and, whereas Johnny Dodge would have been perfectly willing to help, he lived in the wrong hut and his absences might have been noticed. As for 'Wings', he suffered constantly from water on the knee and, as S.B.O., he was more conspicuous, so he was exempted from such work.

The would-be escapees made themselves satchels large enough to carry three weeks' quantity of food and one or two other odds and ends. Their vast experience in these matters was of great benefit to Jack Churchill.

Throughout these preparations the five men laid their plans for the immediate route they would take once outside the wall. The general direction for home would then depend very much on luck.

They decided to go in couples and this meant that one of them would have to go alone. This lot fell to Major Dodge. 'Wings' was to go with Dowse and Jack Churchill with James. Johnny decided that he would either walk west in the general direction of the Anglo-American advance or lie low somewhere until the end of the war.

'Wings' and Dowse planned to contact a German Black-marketeer who was reputed, according to Andy Walsh, to run lorries for the Todt Organisation and who cordially disliked the Nazi régime. The idea was that they hoped he would hide them away in one of his lorries and have them sent in the right direction. Although this contact had, in the past, been a member of the Kreisau Circle—a German Resistance group—that was so long ago that almost anything might have happened to the man in the meantime. However, his address on the outskirts of Berlin was known and they would simply go there by "S" Bahn—a suburban electric train—and trust to luck. The Oranienburg station was not far from the camp and they hoped to catch the last train, due out around midnight, which would get them to their destination well before the hue and cry had been raised. They hoped that the fact that their German was not fluent would not arouse any undue suspicion owing to the millions of foreign workers in the country.

Jack Churchill and Jimmy James decided to head north for Denmark and try to board a vessel bound for Sweden. They would walk and jump goods trains.

The tunnel was now proceeding apace and the only snag was to get the Major transferred to the other hut. Every night the officers who slept there were accompanied back immediately after supper in our communal mess before the complement of each hut was counted and the two huts locked for the night. He could not possibly accompany his fellow-conspirators to their hut without being seen, arousing suspicion and spoiling the whole show.

It was therefore decided that he should make a written application to the Camp Commandant explaining that as he was a man of fifty years of age who liked quiet in the evening it seemed a reasonable request that he should have a room to himself in the other hut where there was plenty of free space.

It was now September 1944 and the war was going extremely well for the Allies. The advances in the west and the east were so rapid that to the allied "barbed wire" Generals—as camp strategists were known—it seemed impossible for the Germans to hold out much longer.

The vast daylight raids now followed upon night raids in closer and closer succession and our optimistic little band of prisoners, like our less fortunate but increasingly hopeful hordes of colleagues "over the wall", were never disappointed of their daily or nightly giant raids.

The usual bets were made that the war would be over by Christmas and it really seemed as though it might. It was a debateable point as to whether the escape was now even worth while undertaking.

After some days the Camp Commandant's permission was granted for the Major to move into the other hut and so his die was cast.

The tunnel was almost complete. Dug tirelessly in pitch darkness the entire length was now ready for crawling through. The wire, if it went below the earth's surface, had not been touched and by all calculations they should be out on the grass verge after half an hour's further scraping.

Only two things were now required. To begin with, the night of the break had to coincide with "Jim" being Guard Commander. If there was anything that could add flavour to this already spicy enterprise it was the idea of Jim—as he had been nicknamed—being court-martialled for negligence while on duty. Jim was a loud-mouthed sergeant, a typical product of the Nazi régime, whereas "George"—the other Guard Commander—was a pleasant-spoken man who spent his time on duty seeing that the prisoners were given every comfort to which they were entitled. George did not crow over their captivity as did Jim, nor did he ram Hitler and the Third and last Reich down their throats.

The second necessity was that it should rain fairly hard on "the night" so that the noise they made breaking out of the tunnel and crossing the road should not be audible to the dogs.

If things went against them it might be a long time before these two conditions coincided. And, as evil luck would have it, the weather kept fine for three weeks after the tunnel was ready. It was not until the 23rd September that everything was in their favour.

As they sat down for supper the rain began to pour down. It was Jack Churchill's birthday and the Italians had laid on a special feast in the honour of the occasion. It was a gay party and sharing in the natural excitement of my friends prevented me from thinking of the loneliness to come.

When Jim turned up to take his charges away he must have put down any noticeable difference in the atmosphere to the Colonel's birthday.

The five men said good night and left.

Meanwhile the unsuspecting inmates of my hut were carrying on their usual evening activities before settling down to sleep. I alone lay wide awake in the knowledge that at any moment my five companions would be making their dangerous bid for freedom.

Between 11 p.m. and midnight I hardly dared to breathe. Towards one o'clock I felt better and by 2 a.m. I managed to doze off, convinced that the break had been successful.

At 7 a.m. there was the usual round of the Guard Commander, but five minutes later both Guard Commanders began crashing through the hut in the hopeless attempt to discover the whereabouts of the five missing men. The balloon had gone up.

Pandemonium now broke loose. The compound was filled with shouting and recrimination. The new guard stood around and thanked their lucky stars they had no responsibility in the matter. The old guard looked like condemned men.

After telephoning the incredible news to the Camp Commandant the two huts were locked and now everyone knew that something was wrong.

The Irish boys—as bright as they make them and always first to sense the least thing wrong in the camp—were wise enough to lie in and pretend to be asleep (which was their daily routine in any case) until 11 a.m. This would presumably help to clear them of any complicity, if such a thing were ever suspected.

General Privalov, on hearing the news, showed his delight by dancing a little ballet. He was heard to say, "Brave chaps! If only I had known I should have joined them. And if they didn't want me, at least I could have given them my civilian suit."

Amongst the others the news was received either with chortling satisfaction or selfish fear of reprisals. If ever the real characters of the individuals in Sonderlager "A" required putting to the test, this occasion provided that opportunity.

As soon as the Gestapo arrived on the scene the interrogations got under way. The first to be called in was Stefanov who had to confess he had never even heard of the tunnel until the night of the break when his friends had told him about it and asked if he would care to use it. When he was asked why he had not availed himself of this opportunity he had replied that one could not leave for such an excursion without a certain amount of preparation. Asked what kind of preparation, he had said, "Food," and left it at that.

For some reason my turn did not come until the very end and when I entered the guard-room at about five o'clock in the afternoon there were six strange men in civilian clothes besides the uniformed Commandant, Keindl, seated about a long table.

Waving me up to the vacant seat at the very top, the President, seated on my right, opened the proceedings.

At the end of a long and frustrating day of repeated denials of connivance or knowledge of the tunnel's existence, the President's air of patience, fairness and impartiality, was nothing short of admirable. He said,

"Captain Churchill, do you understand German?"

"Yes," I replied.

"Have you any idea why you have been called here?"

"Certainly."

"Why, then?"

"Because of my friends' escape."

"You knew about it then?"

"From the very beginning?"

"Did they ask you to go with them?"

"Yes."

"Why did you not go?"

"Because I am not a prisoner of war, captured in uniform, whose escape is recognised by the Geneva Conventions."

"I see," said the President, scratching his chin. Then looking at me sideways, he said.

"If the gate was left open, would you go then?"

"The gate would not improve my chances of not being re-captured."

At this point a rather dull man at the far end of the table interrupted with,

"But, Captain Churchill, supposing the gate were opened and all the guards went away, would you go then?"

Failing to understand what was in his mind, I smiled and said,

"If the gate was opened and there was a rose arbour leading all the way to England with a pub at every milestone, I'd be out like a shot."

The President stopped this nonsense with a point in my favour, by saying,

"Captain Churchill has already answered that question."

He now changed the subject with a deference that showed that the war news was even worse than the newspapers and radio admitted.

"Captain, although of course we quite understand that these escapes are considered very sporting events amongst your compatriots, and we fully realise that you are not the kind of person who is going to give anything away that will help us recapture your friends, nevertheless there are one or two simple points we should like to clear up and perhaps you will help us with these.

The first is, why did they go?"

"Because escaping is in their blood and it is the duty of every British officer to escape."

"Yes, yes. I know all about that, but was there not some special reason? Were they badly treated here?"

I could see that this was a Gestapo shot at Keindl and the Adjutant and although I had little time for either of these men, I had still less for the Gestapo, so I answered,

"They were treated perfectly well here. It was the classic escape, for the reasons I have already given."

"How is it that a man like Wing-Commander Day could join in such an escapade when only two days before he had a litre of water syphoned out of his knee in the hospital?"

"He timed the removal of the water so as to join the escape."

"He is a very brave man."

I looked around the table and replied slowly, for the benefit of all,

"He is braver than you think. His knee developed another litre of water on the day before he left."

"Indeed," said the President, at last getting a lead. "In the circumstances do you think it possible that he may have aimed at a nearby aerodrome with a view to stealing an aircraft?"

"If it weren't for the fact that he has been a prisoner of war for five solid years and has therefore got a little rusty on German aircraft controls, I am quite sure that that is what he would have done."

"How were they dressed, Captain Churchill?"

"I'm sorry," I shrugged.

"Very well. What provisions did they take with them?"

"Red Cross articles which they had saved up."

"Did any of them speak German?"

"Some of them. I used to give lessons to Wing-Commander Day and Major Dodge every day."

"Did they learn anything?"

"Wing-Commander Day was an excellent student, but I'm afraid my friend Dodge was a great disappointment to me."

"How about the others?"

"James speaks good German but Dowse and Colonel Churchill hardly a word."

"Did they all go together?" he tried.

"Yes," I lied.

"Did they have any money with them?"

"You can't save much on five marks a month, which is our *canteen* allowance."

"How much do you think they had between them?"

"Not enough to spend their nights in riotous living."

"Captain Churchill, one last question. Did anyone else in the camp, apart from yourself, know anything about this escape?"

"As far as I know, nobody."

Seeing that all this was not leading them very far, the President said,

"Well, I think that is all we wish to ask you. Of course, we shall recapture your friends very soon. They haven't a chance."

Looking round at the dead-pan faces, I said somewhat quiz-zically,

"I wonder."

I returned to my room highly delighted at the Gestapo's com-plete mystification over what was probably the only tunnel escape from an S.S. camp.

CHAPTER

IV

IF this event was a slap in the face to the Gestapo someone else's ears were burning badly after the slapping down they had received that day. This man had had a long session in the guard-hut and I would have given a great deal to have attended that interview. How could a tunnel possibly be built without his knowledge of it? True, Stefanov had never suspected its presence or heard any sounds of subterranean scratching, but Stefanov was not on the look-out for this sort of thing: he was minding his own busi-ness. The tunnel was the traitor's business, and he had missed it.

All the morning I had sat in my room with the door wide open watching events over a game of double patience which served as a cover for my chortling satisfaction at the plight of Jim and his guards who were kept on duty all day. As they tore off the wainscoting in every room and placed square wooden spy-holes in all the doors so that the extra guards, who were now to patrol the corridors, could keep an eye on the remaining horses still left in the stable after the door had been left open by the "favourites", I could not help smiling at their discomfiture. It was quite on the cards that the entire guard would be executed if this scandal ever reached Hitler's ears, and whilst they might still get the last laugh on us, it was impossible for me not to enjoy the present situation to the full.

I had look-outs posted for the traitor's return to the camp.

As soon as the word was given I took up my position in the corridor so that I could watch him come through the compound gate and see his face all the way past the hut as he was escorted back to his room. The look of shame and baffled rage at having missed this plum of his long and grisly career was just the look I was expecting. No doubt he had not found favour in the eyes of his masters. How was it possible that he, who had given away secret camp radio sets and had had to be rescued by the enemy from the natural wrath and murderous intentions of his own compatriots by being shifted from camp to camp, could have missed such a monumental scoop?

I was determined to get this man. And yet, despite my loathing for his despicable trade, my observation of him over the past months showed that betrayal was ingrained in his soul. The only way he could justify his ego and overcome his inferiority was by betrayal, and as he slid down the slimy slopes of his own degradation his sole relief came from yet another betrayal, just as the drink addict finds solace for his morning shame in the fumes of just another drink.

As the only British officer left in the camp he was now my responsibility. I would try out an experiment I had in mind and give the traitor a chance.

Now, for reasons that will be clarified later, I shall not give this man's name, nor his nationality. Though Odette and I were betrayed in the French Resistance by a Frenchman aided by a Belgian—both condemned to death and both reprieved— this has in no way altered my love for France, and when I think of Belgium my thoughts are not of Louis le Belge but of my friend Doctor A. Gérisse, hero of the R.A.F. "escape route" and only holder of the George Cross in that country.

So, for the sake of argument and with apologies to all bearers of the same name and the entire population of England, I shall call him Judd and say that he was English.

Long before my arrival in the camp Lance-Corporal Judd had rowed with everyone to such an extent that no one would have him as a room-mate. Cursed by a loathing for humanity only equalled by his incapacity to live on his own, Judd's life was a misery to himself and a plague to the entire camp. He had boasted of the fact that he had broadcast for the Germans in English at a special Radio Station that catered for the dissemination of propaganda calculated to sow despondency in the United Kingdom. But this was mere chicken-feed in the scale of his treachery. His best effort had been when he had accepted the post of being infiltrated by the Gestapo, under a false flag, into a certain milieu in Berlin where, after being received with kindness, he had repaid that kindness by putting the finger on surviving Berlin Jews— the victims of this particular operation—and these unfortunate people had been dragged off to the extermination camps.

'Such had been the hatred for Judd in number one hut that, after one or two skirmishes and several more threats against his life, Keindl, fearing a repetition of the Russian Colonel's death followed by the end of Stalin's son, Dshugashwilly, who had mysteriously jumped out of his window at 5 a.m. and run screaming over the warning wire to die the combined deaths of electrocution and several shots from a guard, had had him removed to the safety of the second hut where he carried on his evil machinations to the prejudice of guards and inmates alike.

This briefly, was the electric atmosphere that I inherited on 'Wings' ' departure. Whilst the British officers had been there our sheer numbers and principle of ignoring Judd as far as possible, except when he was blatantly rude or insulting to us—as he was to each of us in turn—had kept the pot from boiling over. But now, and especially in view of his prodigious failure to spot the tunnel, I felt that he might do anything to re-establish his slipping prestige in the Kommandantur.

My defensive plan contained something of an attack, but the main idea was to hoist him with his own petard by condemning him out of his own mouth.

Before I could put my project in motion, Judd made the first move. Slinking around the camp one day he overheard a young S.S. guard telling Andy Walsh that when he was on duty alone in the guard-hut at 4 a.m. he would move the selector control on the radio one millimetre to the right where he had previously noted an emission of news in English.

No sooner was Judd in possession of this news than he asked to see the Camp Commandant. Fortunately "George" got wind of the subject of this private interview and got another of his guards to approach me the day before Keindl was due to make his enquiries amongst the inmates of our camp. A single admission that any such news had been turned on for our benefit and the now imprisoned guard would be shot out of hand. I promised the messenger that all would be well and told him to tell his friend that even if we were enemies I would not let him suffer through our traitor. Then I went from room to room warning everyone of Keindl's visit and getting them to agree to put on a look of complete amazement when questioned and to deny flatly that they had ever heard any news in English apart from Haw-Haw's programme. This step was essential, for Cushing and Walsh who had kept awake that night had spread the war news around.

The enquiry that took place resulted in the guard being exonerated and, at the same time, making an even bigger fool out of Judd.

Raging with frustration, the traitor now began seriously to make his loathsome presence felt in the camp. As soon as the rations arrived in the orderlies' room for dividing up, Judd would be there, elbowing his way in first and grabbing the lion's share. He would sit all morning on the steps of the hut sharpening a knife on the stone and scowling at the passers-by. He never saluted any officer and soon had the whole camp on edge.

When Bessonov told me politely one day that if Fiodr refused to salute me I should not think much of Russian discipline, I knew it was time to act.

Getting out a razor blade and putting it on the table I sent Sergeant Cushing and Corporal Walsh to fetch Judd. I told them that they were on parade, that this was no fooling and that they were to come in with Judd and act as witnesses to what would take place.

Delighted at the signs of a battle they went off in search of the traitor. Presently there was a knock on the door and they were back, empty-handed. Judd had flatly refused to obey my orders.

"Is that so!" I said. "You come with me. I'm going to give Judd a big surprise."

Putting the razor blade inside a breast pocket of my jacket I stalked out, closely followed by the two N.C.O.'s.

Kicking in Judd's door I walked up to him. He remained seated at his table, pretending to read, a cigarette stuck out of the corner of his mouth.

"What's the idea of refusing to obey my order?" I barked.

Judd ignored me.

I got a hold of the front of his battle-dress with one hand and lifted him off his chair, saying,

"Stand up when an officer speaks to you!"

Judd leered at me, sure that he could get away with it, as usual. I smacked the cigarette out of his mouth, and gave him a stinging blow that sent him spinning into the corner of the room.

Before he had time to make up his mind what to do I was in front of him with a look on my face that told him clearly that if he so much as raised his hand I should probably kill him.

"Stand to attention when an officer addresses you!" I shouted.

He remained as he was, his feet apart.

I now gave him a blow in the face that set his eyes squinting, but I kept him from sagging into a heap with my left hand. As he recovered, his heels came slowly together and Mr. Judd began to look at me through new eyes.

Standing within a foot of him I glowered into his treacherous face and said,

"You scum! You filthy rotten bastard! This is where you pipe down for good. In future you'll salute every officer you meet, first thing in the morning and last thing at night. You'll address all Russian officers by their correct titles. You will cease sitting on the step sharpening that god-damn knife, and in fact you will either stay in your room or walk in the compound as others do. You are not to enter anyone's room unless specifically invited and henceforth you'll wait for your food to be brought to you

L

and you'll be served last. As a mild punishment for your bloody awful behaviour in this camp you'll give your next Red Cross parcel to the Russians and finally, Judd, I'm degrading you as from today to the rank of private."

Still keeping my eyes on his I slowly withdrew the razor blade. Then, feeling for his sleeve, I said threateningly.

"Be careful, Judd. This thing might slip. Accidents happen so easily."

With that I tore his badges of rank off his sleeves and threw them into the stove, adding,

"You disgracer of the King's uniform, I suppose you'll go whining to the Camp Commandant now instead of taking your punishment like a man."

He spoke for the first time:

"Oh no, I won't, Sir. I know when I'm beat and I'll obey your orders."

I put my hand into another pocket and drew out a piece of paper. Handing this to Judd, I said,

"In case you should forget what those orders are, I've made it simple for you and written them down, Any infringement of these orders, Judd, and I'll beat the daylights out of you. Do you understand?"

"Yes, Sir."

I left the room, signalling to Cushing and Walsh to follow me.

The afternoon now dragged on and I waited for the inevitable which was not long in coming. A knock on my door and there was George. He placed a note in Judd's hand-writing on my table and said,

"Herr, Hauptmann, I think this may interest you."

I looked at it and read:

"To the Camp Commandant,   Sept. 29th, 1944.
Sachsenhausen.

 Sir,

  This afternoon Captain Churchill entered my room with two other men and they beat me up.

Captain Churchill has ordered me in future to remain in my room.

He has also ordered me to give up all my Red Cross parcels to the Russians.

I am, Sir,

Yours etc.,

C. JUDD."

I smiled up at George and said,

"Why did you bother to tip me off?"

"It is a small thing. You saved the life of one of my men."

I looked at George, acknowledging our bond.

"Do you mind if I take a copy of this?"

"That's why I brought it."

I quickly jotted down the three whopping lies and handed back the original.

As we stood by the door George shrugged his shoulders hopelessly.

Keindl wasted no time over this episode and I was fetched into his presence the very next day. Keindl started off.

"Is it true that you struck Judd yesterday?"

"Yes."

"A German officer is not allowed to strike a private and therefore you are not allowed to strike one either. If you have any complaint against any member of the British contingent you can complain to me and I will attend to the matter."

"Wing-Commander Day complained to you about Judd on more than one occasion and as nothing was done I took the matter into my own hands."

"In future you will refrain from doing so, or placing anyone under any restraint whatsoever. I run this place and I hereby cancel your orders to Judd."

There was nothing to be said. I had already seen Keindl in one of his tearing rages and since there was no hope of co-operation from this quarter, that was the end of that.

Judd crowed all over the camp. He swaggered around as though he owned the place and all but cocked a snoot at me as he passed.

I was now ripe for my plan. In my determination to break Judd by using the few brains that I possessed, I could understand how people with even less of this element could resort to murder. In the Resistance a man like Judd would have been attended to a long time ago without bothering any court of law, and although this kind of thing is highly illegal it is curious at times how little one is exercised by such a consideration.

Going from room to room I arranged with every single member of the camp to put Judd in Coventry. Most of them agreed with alacrity. The two Italians and Fiodr could not have been more pleased, but I had to put on some pressure here and there so as not to spoil the whole effect by any weakening. When this was tied up I sat back and waited. Knowing Judd I gave him three weeks.

In the interval a French fighter-pilot was brought in to share my room. Van Wymeersch was in very poor shape, for he had had a rotten time. After a first-class train escape with forged camp papers he had been captured whilst waiting for his connection at Strasbourg. After a beating-up he was left, chained, in a dungeon for three weeks. After this he was crammed into a cell, half the size of the Fresnes cells, with three other men. We soon brought him round and his beaming happy face could be seen all over the camp.

I was sorry to have to bother him with the Judd business, but I wanted him as a witness to what I hoped would take place.

In the meantime I had prepared a written confession which I intended Judd to sign. I was all set for the big day.

Before the three weeks had fully expired Sergeant Cushing came in to announce the news.

"Judd would like to see you, Skipper."

"Where is he?"

"He's gone back to his room to wait. He's all shiny and dolled up."

"Very well, Sergeant Cushing. Go along with Andy and bring him in style and stay here when you come back. I want you both as witnesses."

"Right, Sir."

He swung round and left the room with military correctness, getting himself into the right mood for a Company Office session.

"Here we go," I said to Van Wymeersch.

A knock on the door was followed by the entry of Judd, correctly dressed, closely followed by his escort—a visit I had not been successful in arranging in any other way.

Judd stood rigidly to attention in the centre of the room, his eyes just above my head, in proper Guards' manner. I sat behind the table and Van Wymeersch sat on his bed.

"Permission to speak, Sir?" said Judd, continuing along the lines of his complete metamorphosis.

"Fire away, Judd," I said.

"I can't stand this silence any more, Sir."

"Well, you brought it on your own head, didn't you?"

"Yes, Sir. I've behaved very badly, Sir. And when I think of all your past kindness in talking to me, playing drafts with me and taking me out of myself, if you see what I mean, Sir. . . . Well, Sir, I've had time to think and . . ."

"All right, Judd." I cut him short. "In other words you want me to turn off the screw, is that it?"

"Yes, Sir. And I give you my word I'll behave if you do."

I looked at him for a moment and I was glad of the presence of the three witnesses or I might have been tempted to let it go at that. But I hardened my heart and went on with it.

"That's where the whole trouble lies, Judd. The last time you gave me your word was when you said you wouldn't write to the Camp Commandant, and what did you do? As soon as my back was turned you sat down and did that very thing, and told him a pack of lies into the bargain."

"What makes you say that, Sir?" asked Judd, his cunning mind getting the upper hand.

"Damn it, man, Keindl showed me your letter!"

"I'm sorry, Sir. . . . I don't understand why I do it. . . . Something seems to come over me."

"Well, Judd, just because of that and since the only thing you recognise is force I am going to apply two conditions to letting you share in any fun that's going on in this camp, and here they are. You can take them or leave them."

"The first is that you give up your next Red Cross parcel to the Russians and you write a letter to the Camp Commandant saying that you do so voluntarily. You will show me that letter and hand it to George in my presence. Secondly you will sign the confession I have here all ready for you. On my part I promise you in front of Mr. Van Wymeersch, Sgt. Cushing and Corporal Walsh that if you behave until the end of the war I will burn it in front of you and the same witnesses. But, Judd, if you should slip back into your old ways, I will hand this to the proper Authority and you will be shot as a traitor."

"May I read the confession, Sir?"

"Naturally. But as you may have some difficulty with my writing, I'll read it for you."

I picked up the paper and read out:

"I the undersigned, Corporal C. Judd, down-graded to Private by Captain Peter Churchill on September 29th, 1944, hereby declare that in 1942 I agreed to be released from Stalag No. X in order to work for the Germans. This I did, and for a period of Y months I broadcast seditious propaganda designed to be harmful to my country.

"After this I worked for the Gestapo and betrayed the faith of people in whose houses I allowed myself to be introduced under false colours, by indicating the presence of Jews in those houses. I am therefore guilty of having been willingly instrumental in the apprehension and subsequent detention of over a dozen Jews, who in all probability have been murdered in the Extermination Camps to which I know and knew they would be sent.

"I continued to act as traitor to my country by accepting the job of snooper in Stalag Z, and when my compatriots discovered my betrayal of their secret radio set I had to be rescued from their righteous wrath by the Germans and placed in another camp.

"The same thing happened here.

"Since my entry into Sonderlager 'A' I admit having stirred up continuous trouble with everyone. I have been insubordinate to all the officers and have flatly refused to obey their orders, knowing I could get away with it, since I worked hand in glove with the German Commandant to whom I have written on every possible occasion when I saw anything that could interest him and increase his regard for me.

"On one occasion I even tried to betray one of the guards who, out of friendliness, turned on the English news one night. Thanks to the intervention of the entire camp, his life, at least, is not on my guilty conscience.

"I have disgraced the uniform of my country, lost all honour, and fully understand that any court-martial handling my case after the war must, in the knowledge that I sign this voluntarily and under no strain or duress, condemn me to a traitor's death."

At the end of this reading I looked up at Judd. He had listened to it all in silence and his look was not the look of someone who wished to deny anything he had heard, but rather that of someone weighing up the price for his peace of mind.

Finally he spoke.

"It's a bit hard, Sir."

"You know it's all true, Judd. Which is it to be, good behaviour and your rotten past consigned to the flames, or silence till the end of the war?"

"I'll sign it, Sir," he said and picked up the pen I held in my hand.

When all the witnesses had signed, I said,

"Well, that's all, Judd. See and keep your part of the bargain and I'll keep mine."

Judd saluted, turned smartly and marched out.

*   *   *

At last peace settled over the camp; and it was to prove a lasting peace. With the sword of Damocles hanging over his head Judd seemed determined to fulfil his part of the contract. Officers were saluted morning, noon and night and they, in turn, responded to the transfigured being who now could be seen walking up and down in their society or that of the orderlies with a brisk stride, denoting the return of his self respect.

Judd's battle with himself was not an easy one. His infamous acts had been too numerous and gone on too long for him to be purged overnight.

Sometimes during our regular games of drafts he confided his torments to me. One day his eyes would give away the thought that officers were easy meat who could be twisted any way his cunning mind desired, and the next, judging others by himself, he would doubt my word about burning the confession if he behaved. Then again there were days when he was quite normal and received me with utmost courtesy: then he would offer me half a cigarette, cut through with a pair of scissors, and I would accept his hospitality as the most natural thing in the world. I did everything I could to assist him in regaining a measure of equilibrium and, just as I had been prepared to beat his brains out if he had not come into line, so, now that he was under control, I pursued the long task of helping him to warrant the burning of his own death sentence. Legal minds may well ask if I had the intention of withholding information against the traitor after the war, always supposing he fulfilled his role in our agreement. The answer is that if Judd behaved himself I should not volunteer a charge against him as I intended to do if he failed, but would merely add my testimony, if asked, whilst stressing the attenuating circumstances.

So our camp life pursued the even tenor of its new way. Once or twice a week we were treated to the spectacle of gigantic daylight raids by the American Air Force, whose precision instruments permitted them to bomb with uncanny accuracy, even through cloud. In the main, however, their visits were on cloudless days.

The most outstanding performance we ever saw was their raid on the Heinkel works, one Sunday morning. This factory bordered on the far wall of the main camp, less than 1,000 yards away.

Squadrons of sixty silvery four-engined planes in bunched formations of twelve roared through the blue sky at a time, leaving behind 240 trails of vapour around which the succeeding and neighbouring hordes filled in the sky until a solid white cloud blanketed out the sun.

The great formations could be seen as far as the eye could reach and all came straight towards us out of the western sky, having purposely circled the principal Berlin defences. "Mosquito" outriders from advanced bases in Europe wove their own private patterns in their constant search for German fighter planes; but none sallied forth to break up the attack, for they were already fully occupied on the eastern front.

As the first sixty came directly at us we had a dreadful moment of fear lest their western line of approach, which placed us on the left of the main camp, made them think we were where the Heinkel works would have been if they had come straight in from the south. As we waited for what might have been our awful end the helmeted guards were already below ground in their private dug-outs from which they eyed us somewhat shamefully through the slits.

At the last moment, within what seemed less than 300 yards, the leading formation veered south, the target-pointer dropping a smoke bomb to point their objective to the rest. And now the bombs rained down, forming a pattern over the doomed factory and surrounding houses and for over an hour the deafening crumps shattered everything below and shook the whole district to its foundations.

No single bomb fell inside the camp, whose walls were be-spattered by flying bricks and masonry.

As the huge wave passed over, little white puffs in the sky pointed to crews who had had to abandon their flakstruck 'plane, and here and there a limping bomber could be seen heading north in the hopes of reaching Sweden or at least avoiding further trouble. Half a dozen aircraft whined their way down to final destruction and one, whose tail had been shot off, came spiralling down in the fatal corkscrew dive that pins the crew hopelessly to its walls. One parachute came down so close to our camp that we feared the man might land on the electrified wire, but whilst still half a mile up he swung away to fall onto the parade ground in the very centre of the S.S. camp. His fears may well be imagined as he saw the style of reception committee eagerly awaiting his descent. Nor were these fears unfounded, for in a War-Crimes Court after the war, an S.S. sergeant was condemned to die for kicking this man to death.

For forty-eight hours after the raid time bombs went off over the target area sending houses a hundred feet into the air. Whilst the spectacle of the end of this factory was heartening it was difficult to forget that, in the eyes of our captors, we spoke the same language as the "Terrorflieger" who had caused the destruction.

Christmas passed peacefully enough and, in like manner, January and February of 1945. For five months Judd's behaviour had been exemplary and it looked in every way as though the time might come when I should unscrew the steel plate below and surrounding the base of the stove and fish out his signed confession for a ceremony I longed to perform.

Just as we had rejoiced over D-Day, and waited anxiously for some advantage to result from the 20th of July attempt on Hitler's life, so we had grieved over the tragic fate of the Warsaw Rising. On August 1st when General Bor-Komorowski had signalled the start of what was to be the most heroic siege in world history, Bessonov said to me,

"The Russian Army has reached the banks of the Vistula and has already dropped leaflets over the capital and blared across the river through amplifiers, saying, 'Citizens of Warsaw, the hour has come to strike. We, your Russian allies, will help in every way to expel the hated common foe from your soil. Hand in hand we will march towards victory. Citizens of Warsaw, rise!'"

"Why, this is terrific news!" I had said. "I must go and tell Jan and Leshek."

"Whatever you do, don't do that. Believe me, Herr Hauptmann, I know what is in Stalin's mind. The Russians will not lift a finger to help the Poles. They will sit on the banks of the Vistula and watch the destruction of Warsaw."

"I can't believe it."

"Wait and see, and then perhaps you will begin to understand my endless efforts to explain the grave dangers that await your great but weary land, the credulous United States and all the other ostrich-minded countries which may only begin to see the writing on the wall when it has become indelible."

I was much shaken by these words, for they had come from the horse's mouth. Time and the ghastly truth of Bessonov's pre-vision only served to shake me more.

Now, at least, I thought, Winston Churchill has ample proof of what to expect. His heart must be heavy for the Poles and he must have ground his teeth with rage when Stalin refused to allow his bombers to land on Soviet aerodromes after the long flight to replenish the beleaguered capital from the air. Only when it was too late to help, did the constant pressure on the Kremlin bring forth agreement for such an operation to take place. The grim tragedy that was then witnessed by the starving hollow-eyed defenders of Warsaw cannot be told too often.

As these survivors looked up through the ruins of their shattered city on October 3rd they watched the life-saving parachutes descending, with tears of relief pouring down their grimy faces. As the thousands of precious containers came closer, an adverse wind blew the whole lot over the Vistula and into the Russian lines.

So the great heart of Poland was broken; so ended a criminal Soviet victory.

"The advance will now proceed," said Bessonov.

"What about the delay?" I said. "Our chaps are coming up pretty fast on the other side."

"At Yalta and the other meeting places of the Allied Leaders, The Little Father will see to it that the delay does not handicap the Soviet Union in the final spoils."

The prophet Bessonov never missed a beat.

I spent hours with the N.K.V.D. man hoping to imbibe the maximum of his vital political knowledge.

Five months had now passed since the fall of Warsaw and the sounds of battle were now raging within earshot of the camp. As I walked up and down with Bessonov at this time, with German aircraft dashing about the sky like angry hornets, he said,

"This is bad for me. If we are overrun by a Soviet Division, it is not the soldiers I fear, but men like myself who will go straight to the files and look up our stories. We shall not be allowed to leave the camp and wander about in freedom. When they read my file, they will simply string me up to the first tree. As for you, Herr Hauptmann, you will not get back either. Men like you are valuable to the N.K.V.D. Your first move will be to the twelfth floor of the Lubianka Prison in Moscow, where I have helped to put people like yourself before. After some six months of dead silence you will be taken out and transported to quite a comfortable villa in a settlement in the Steppes of Siberia. There you will be left to mature like wine. In the meantime your anxious relatives will be having questions raised in the House of Commons over the mysterious silence that will have enveloped you since you were last seen in the company of certain Russian officers.

"Representations by the British Ambassador in Moscow will be received with a shrug of the shoulders and a vague promise to look into the matter; but nothing will be done although they will know exactly where you are. A second visit by the Ambassador, some six months later, will produce the counter-proposal that if Captain Gregorieff, now residing at 968, Hagley Road, Birmingham, could be extradited, it might be possible to discover your whereabouts and to consider an exchange.

"You see, Herr Hauptmann, they like to collect people like you so as to get people like Captain Gregorieff away from countries where they are harming the Communist cause by telling the truth about it. I need hardly tell you that they will not send Captain Gregorieff to enjoy his retirement in the villa that you will have vacated, for his will be a total retirement."

"Good God, Herr General!" I said. "What a cheerful prospect."

"For you it would not be so bad. These villas are quite comfortable and maybe some time I will tell you some interesting stories about them, but for the moment I am not in the mood; the sound of my compatriots' approach gives me a curious feeling as though a rope were tightening around my neck."

The sounds of the Battle of Küstrin on the Oder—not twenty-five miles distant—were listened to with mixed feelings by the members of Sonderlager "A". The Irishmen, whose files contained matter that would certainly be of interest to the British Security Branch, from what they had told me, and which might necessitate a tiresome enquiry, were in two minds as to whether a free trip to Russia might not be a good thing. The added delay to their return would confuse the issue to such an extent that by the time they got back the authorities would be glad to cross them off their books.

With the exception of Fiodr, the Russians all knew what to expect, for Privalov and Brodnikow were in the same boat as Bessonov, having been members of the Wlassow Army whose aims it had been to free Russia of Communism, help in the extermination of Stalin and the Politburo and give up the Ukraine to Germany. Their court-martial would not take long and they did not need Bessonov's lurid descriptions of their eventual fate to know what awaited them. As for Stefanov he, too, was an avowed anti-Communist and, however patriotic his designs, he was tarred with the same fatal brush.

The Italians were not at all keen on being rescued by the Russians, for they knew that this spelt a long delay before they would ever reach home.

The Poles were quite naturally terrified of the idea, for from Russia there could be no return to the U.K. with a chance of starting a new life and breathing the air of freedom. They might, at best, be sent back to Poland, which was virtually the same thing as staying in Russia.

To Judd the din of the battle held out great promise and completely unsettled him. This I could well understand; but what defeated me was his reaction to an occurrence that coincided with this event.

On the night after Bessonov's graphic portrayal of our futures, I happened to be talking to the guard on duty in the passage. After I had given him a cigarette, he put his mouth to the square wooden hole in my door and said,

"I have some good news for you, Herr Hauptmann. Tomorrow morning the escaped British officers will return to this camp."

"So they were captured after all," I said.

"They hadn't a chance. The whole country was looking for them."

"Where have they been all this time?"

"Over the wall in the camp cell-block."

"What, in solitary?"

"Yes, but I think they are lucky to be alive."

"So do I, Herr Posten, in view of some of the local habits! Thanks for letting me know."

CHAPTER

V

Early next day the entire hut was ready to welcome back their friends. Look-outs were posted from 8 a.m. onwards to spot their arrival. Everyone was shaved and dressed as smartly as possible.

Suddenly the word went round, "They're here!" and instantly the prisoners lined up by the entrance gate to the compound. There was no scrambling for position in this strange allied "Guard of Honour". Russian Generals lined up beside privates and all were now pleased at having been at all associated with this daring escape, even if it had only meant extra restrictions.

I was allowed the honour of standing at the end of the line nearest the gate. As the four men entered the compound escorted by a Captain in the S.S. the line stiffened to attention and feeling a little foolish, but meaning every word, I said:

"We salute four brave men."

And now they passed down the line shaking hands and having theirs warmly shaken by Generals and batmen alike. It was a great moment and even the S.S. officer had nothing to say at this demonstration.

Johnny Dodge was not of the party. He had been captured and was now as safe as one could be in Berlin where he was holding conversations with members of their Foreign Office which he may himself relate one day.

Little by little, in their own sweet time, they told me their stories. It required much prodding and patience to get them to open up, for after their long spell of solitary confinement, they had lost interest in what they considered their dismal failures. But since these failures were rewarded with three M.C.'s and a D.S.O. for dauntless courage in the knowledge that capture might mean death, I give their stories briefly below.

When they reached their hut after saying good night to me on September 23rd, they were locked in as usual. The black-out was in position throughout the hut and the lights would be put out at 10 p.m. Before then they could move about between rooms in preparation for zero hour without attracting attention. It was over a year since anyone had bothered to come sniffing around with dogs after nightfall. Why take such precautions in a fool-proof meat-safe? Experienced Wehrmacht and Luft-waffe Camp Commandants could have answered that question very easily.

By the time the lights had been switched off at the main in the Guard Commander's hut all preparations had been com-pleted inside, and the three senior officers settled down to wait for the return of Dowse and James who were down the tunnel finishing the break-through at the far end.

They had decided to leave the camp around 11.30, by which time the sentries who had been on duty since 10 p.m. would be getting tired and very wet and their thoughts would be centred on the comfortable beds that awaited them in their warm hut.

Time seemed to drag endlessly for the waiting men. 'Wings' ' knee which had only been deflated two days before had swollen up again and felt like a football inside his trouser leg. He hoped to God that he would not faint inside the tunnel. He had got stuck in there before and had been horribly reminded of the experience in frequent nightmares.

The Major thought of the people in the other hut. They were probably all going to sleep. Perhaps he would never see them again. All Hell would be let loose in the camp when their absence was discovered. How good it would be to stretch his long legs in getting away from this place.

Jack Churchill concentrated his entire thought on getting quickly across the road, once he was out of the hole. He was well acquainted with the tunnel and knew little about fear. This was just another marvellous adventure in a life packed full of action. He was only thirty-seven and belonged, so to speak, to the first eleven of his country. Anyway it was his birthday so nothing could go wrong.

All this time Dowse and James were tearing away at the earth as fast and as silently as they could. Time was passing rapidly and still the sound of the earth gave no hint that they were approaching the surface. Despite his vast experience in tunnelling Dowse went through horrible moments of panic lest his calculations had been wrong.

At last the knife with which he was excavating the sandy soil came in contact with something hard. He swore softly. They had gone too far and this must be the concrete path beyond the grass verge they were aiming for. Now they would have to bring the hole out at least two feet behind the present position. He and James hacked away at the earth in turns and, after another half hour's desperate work, they pushed through into the open. It was now child's play for the two men to finish off the opening and to cover it up with their home-made lid, which would prevent its being seen from outside.

Having disposed of the earth they crawled back to the hut to report and have a wash and brush up before the start. Their reappearance was more than welcome, for their absence had lasted far longer than had been anticipated and the three waiting men had begun to imagine that all kinds of accidents must have befallen the diggers.

Now all was set and the five men lined up with their kit for the departure. James and Dowse went first, then Jack Churchill, followed by 'Wings', and last of all the Major who replaced the trap after drawing the bed back into position.

On hands and knees they slowly crawled through the tunnel, reaching the end without incident. Dowse pushed away the lid and crawled out into the sopping night. He took a quick look round to see that the coast was clear before helping James out after him. James remained in his turn to give the Colonel a hand out and also took his bags as well as those of 'Wings' and of the Major. All this made some little commotion and the wall of the compound was only some four or five feet removed from them. In addition James saw the light of a torch flashed on for an instant some quarter of a mile down the road, giving him an uneasy moment. He whispered to the Colonel and, as soon as expedient, scooted across the road to relieve the congestion at the tunnel exit. They waited, as arranged, by the wall of the new and not yet occupied camp. The Colonel now gave 'Wings' a hand up. By now their feet had dislodged quantities of sandy earth which ran down into the steeply uprising tunnel mouth and onto the Major. As he was half as large again as any of the others and the hole was getting smaller, the business of getting him out was extremely difficult. He managed to pass one hand and his head through the narrowing exit, whilst holding his bag of provisions behind and below him. The other two pulled on his free hand and as he pushed and scrabbled against the now slippery or broken wooden steps he found himself hopelessly trapped in the exit. It was a grim moment for all three as they struggled to get him loose and the two who were waiting out of sight could not imagine what had gone wrong. Eventually with grunts and

M

groans from the Major they managed to pull him free and all dashed across the road making rather more noise to their own sensitive ears than to the drowsy ones of the sentries and the dog. By the time they reached their rendezvous both parties were so jittery they each imagined the other must be Germans.

The ladder, which they had seen by standing up on the parallel bars inside the camp on the same afternoon, was happily still leaning against the wall of this new camp. All five were soon over the top and by the grace of God the wire was not yet charged with electricity. One by one they dropped down into freedom. Without much talk the three parties spread out in their pre-arranged directions and vanished into the night.

*   *   *

Having dropped down to freedom 'Wings' and Dowse made their way to the "S" Bahn Station. 'Wings' was in considerable pain from his bad knee which had not been improved by jumping off the high wall.

They were hardly back on the road after emerging from the wood before they saw two men walking slowly before them in the same direction. Since they would have to get accustomed to seeing other individuals in Germany they pressed on and overtook them. As they passed they were horrified to see that they were armed guards, presumably patrolling the outside of the Concentration Camp. They walked fast and were well ahead when one of the men called out: "Halt! Who goes there?" They paid no attention and, with their hearts in their mouths, awaited the inevitable spray of bullets in their backs. Nothing happened. Only the seconds that crawled by were lead-bound. The relief was almost painful. They plodded on through the rain. Their next fear was that they should have missed the last train. So much time had been spent completing the tunnel and in dragging out the Major.

And now in the black-out they lost their way. The next thing they knew was that they had collided with a six-foot policeman.

With great presence of mind 'Wings' instantly asked him the way to the station and this information was given in loud and affable tones. Before the man had time to say anything else they were well on the indicated road, but what kept them going was somewhat of a mystery to them for their blood had turned into water with all the shocks they had encountered in so short a space of time.

Eventually they found the station and Dowse booked two singles to their destination some twenty-one miles on the other side of Berlin. He asked when the next train was due and learned to their dismay that this was not until 5 a.m. They had, therefore, nearly five hours to wait. But in spite of this set-back he gave a cheery smile to the girl in the ticket office which earned him a very pleasant one in return.

'Wings' and he then decided it might be wiser to make themselves scarce until it was time to catch their train, so they walked away from the station and sheltered from the rain and public scrutiny beneath a nearby bridge. They were soaking wet and very cold and their only way of keeping warm was to huddle up close together to pass the long hours of waiting.

At last it was time for their train and they could enjoy the luxury of walking back to the station, even though it was still pouring with rain. On passing the ticket office they were not too far gone to raise a flashing smile from the ticket girl who was still on duty and soon they had boarded their train without having attracted any other attention to themselves.

Their journey passed without event. They did not talk to each other but pretended to doze. Their luck held, for at no time were they asked for their identity papers—of which they had none—and, after changing trains, they got out at the right station.

Knowing exactly where their safe house lay, they made off in its direction. It was four miles from the station and they stepped out smartly so as to reach it before daybreak.

As they approached the house their worst fears were realised. The place had been bombed into a complete wreck, as well as most of the other houses in the neighbourhood. They climbed through the debris and went into a back room to shelter from the rain and make fresh plans.

Theirs was a sorry plight. Dawn would break at any moment. They were very wet and 'Wings' was in no condition to start walking to Switzerland or, for that matter, to any other place.

Unknown to them they had been seen by a member of the Hitler Youth and this little fiend had wasted no time in spreading the happy news that two suspicious characters were hiding in a bombed-out house.

Before the first light frowned upon a dismal dawn the place was surrounded and 'Wings' and Dowse found themselves inside an even more gloomy Black Maria. They were taken to the local Police Court. From there they were dragged to a Berlin Lager. Then they were transferred to the Lehrte Strasse Prison. This was followed by the doubtful honour of a visit to Gestapo head-quarters in the Prinz Albrechtstrasse. After a few hours they were taken back to Sachsenhausen in one of the camp Black Marias. Each was placed in solitary confinement in the prison block of the Concentration Camp itself, and subjected to constant inter-rogations without a hint as to how long this treatment would last.

*   *   *

Jack Churchill and James set out to follow the banks of the canals and rivers according to their plan.

It was no easy matter finding their way on such a black night. Sometimes they went wrong and had to retrace their steps, but in that first night they somehow managed to cover a fair dis-tance.

At dawn they found a suitable wood where they hid and rested, but sleep was out of the question.

It rained all that day and continued throughout the night. They proceeded in this manner for four days and nights, keeping close to the railway.

On the fifth night they came upon a very small marshalling yard in a place called Dannenwald, and here was the very thing they were praying for—a goods train with notices on each truck indicating its destination. At last they found some Rostock wagons, but as they were unsuitable, Jack Churchill unpinned one of these labels and replaced it over that of a suitable truck. As there seemed little likelihood that this train's departure was imminent, he mixed up the labels on the other wagons just for fun.

Not knowing when the train was due out, they contented themselves with reconnoitring the goods yard on the first night and on the following day hid themselves in the thick wood that bordered the place.

By good fortune the engine for their train was not reversed into position until the next evening. Seizing their chance they climbed up onto the buffers of the penultimate wagon, which was the one they had chosen. The train then shunted back and forth several times, finally coming to a halt in the middle of the station.

Suddenly the clanking of wagons began again and the two fugitives realised that their train was moving forward once more. As the sounds of the clashing buffers approached them Jack Churchill suddenly slipped down onto the line, having dropped his bag of stolen vegetables and James, imagining that he must have seen someone coming along his side of the track, dropped down between the wagons beside him.

They had been prepared for a good deal of hide and seek in such a public place, but before they could make out if there really was someone there, the wagon on whose buffers they had been standing began moving forward over them. It then jerked to a stop and before they had time to throw themselves out from underneath, the train began to reverse, gathering speed by degrees. It was too late to do anything now but lie down and hope for the best. This they did, spreading themselves flat on their stomachs while the wagons clanked relentlessly over them.

By looking up a little they could see by the light thrown from the overhead lamps along the track and there seemed to be a fair clearance for several hundred yards ahead, for it was a long train. They lay in a sweat wondering just how far it would run back. The wheels continued to clank beside their ears without any signs of slackening speed.

Suddenly Churchill and James were gripped by a most horrible fear, for they could now see the red glow from the locomotive lighting up the track and moving steadily towards them. The light prevented them gauging the amount of clearance below the engine, but to their terrified eyes it did not seem sufficient to clear a plate of soup.

It would be suicidal to try to dash sideways between the wheels, although the long log wagons made this look tempting. It was equally fatal to be crushed by what was coming.

They were trapped. Cursing the sleepers they pressed their bodies into the track and closed their eyes.

A mighty hissing penetrated their heads and two long seconds later they felt the thrice-blessed rain pricking their hands and the side of their faces.

It would have been a legitimate luxury to pass out at the moment but the Colonel and Jimmy James were not exactly the fainting type. Anyway there was a sound of brakes being applied. The train now stopped as suddenly as it had started and there, in the full glare of the headlights, lay the two prostrate men.

Not wishing to be picked up after so close a shave and having no desire to repeat such a scare they quickly removed themselves from the permanent way and, as there was nothing else for it, they casually walked back to the end of the train as though it was their custom to lie on the track and then stroll back under the arc lamps as if to do it again.

After passing some seventy wagons they found themselves back once more where they had started, but due to the presence of shunters they hid themselves for a time at the side of the marshalling yard.

When the coast was clear they climbed up onto the iron plate of what was now the penultimate wagon. They had a bad moment when a shunter sneaked up below them and uncoupled the last wagon, his head being only a few inches from their feet.

For greater security they then climbed up on to the smooth logs with which this wagon was loaded and the Colonel perched himself near the end.

And now the train repeated its reversing procedure for the nth time. When the sound of the buffers came closer they automatically took a good grip on what there was to grip, but their wagon came to a standstill with such a jerk that the Colonel was left in mid-air before gravity sent him crashing down ten or twelve feet onto the track below. The fall sprained one of his ankles and broke both his water-bottles. He was lucky not to break his neck.

James scrambled down from his perch, dragged his companion clear of the line and then with a tremendous effort hauled him up again onto the iron plate. By a stroke of luck to which they were more than entitled the train stood still during this performance; nor was there to be any further shunting.

At last they got under way and both men settled themselves as comfortably as possible on the smooth tree trunks on what was now the end truck.

For a while they could relax, if only mentally. The train crawled through the dripping night at some twenty miles per hour. Presently the full pain in the Colonel's ankle made itself felt. It was almost unbearable.

After twenty minutes they pulled up in a station under the arc lights. Both men kept dead still. Then the sirens went and all the lights were turned out. The train moved on.

Half an hour later it stopped again at Neu Strelitz immediately below the signal box which was illuminated like a gin-palace. The signalman put his head out of the window and began discussing the poorness of the German war effort with a porter standing barely five yards from them. For a quarter of an hour this enlightening subversive talk continued before the train moved off.

And now one of those ludicrous physical reactions to constant nervous strain took a hand in their fate. One of them simply had to relieve himself, and although the other implored him to consider the vast distance they could still cover on this train before daylight, there was nothing for it and both men slid down the side of their wagon to disappear into the shadows.

After leaving the train the Colonel was unable to move, so James went off to find a suitable wood. Having found it a half-mile off, he returned and picked up the four bags. His companion meanwhile took off his gaiters, wrapped them round his hands as shoes, and crawled his way into its welcome shelter. Having made some cover out of broken branches, they settled down to spend the rest of the night and most of the following day there. It was bitterly cold and, as usual, they were soaking wet.

During the afternoon a soldier walked past their hide-out, almost stepping on them, and circled it in a rather suspicious manner before walking away.

This was sufficient warning for the two men. They quickly gathered up their belongings and left. Eighty yards away they found a hollow between the wood and the railway embankment; and there they covered themselves completely with leaves and branches.

Some twenty minutes later the sounds of shouting and cursing that emanated from the place they had just left proved the wisdom of their move.

Night began to fall. It was their seventh away from captivity. James crawled out of the gulley to reconnoitre the marshalling yard for another north-bound track. He was unsuccessful, but nearby he saw a very convenient haystack to which he helped his companion.

For the first time they began to feel warm and passed an excellent night. They also spent the next day in the stack, whilst all around them people were working. The rest and sense of security did them both good and the Colonel's ankle pained him less.

On the eighth night they left their warm haven and proceeded slowly along the railway line. After a while they found they were going due east. They then cut off back through a wood and after walking at a slow pace all night finally struck the Rostock line. The next day they spent in a wood and at nightfall set off along the line again in pouring rain.

After some hours they came across a small railway hut where they rested until dawn because the Colonel was rather done in. Later on they found a wood in which to pass the daylight hours.

During the day Churchill told James that he was fairly certain that he had heard some people on the outskirts of the wood talking Russian. James, who spoke the language fairly well, went over to investigate. He found that they were indeed Russians. In the morning he went round to the edge of the wood and attracted their attention. They came over and turned out to be very friendly, giving James bread and butter and filling their water bottles for them. When he explained that he had a friend and that they were both British R.A.F. officers his success was astonishing. Both were invited to call on the Russians at nightfall in their huts. The sincerity of the invitation was such as to exclude any shadow of possible betrayal.

At the appointed hour Churchill and James, having shaved, called on their new friends and were received like Ministers Plenipotentiary, and provided with a delicious hot thick soup, out of doors beside a wood fire. James's months of Russian study had borne fruit. There was no doubt that these simple men were flattered that an Englishman—of all people—should speak their language.

This was the first time for days that they had felt warm. The two Europeans thanked their Asiatic friends for their most delightful party and gave them their English addresses. With their clothes dry, thanks to the fire, and their stomachs full of good food they made off for the railway line in a mood that gave a humorous aspect to all their past troubles.

That night they made good headway.

The next night they had to pass through the town of Warem, beside a lake. They passed policemen and soldiers without being stopped. Then they went through the marshalling yard and their unconcern was such that they even passed in front of an armed sentry whose particular assignment in that place was to challenge tramps of their calibre and then take them in charge.

Towards morning, after a steady walk along the line, they came across a signal lamp. They had seen plenty of these before and successfully 'milked' them, but as they were now in possession of a miniature primus stove nothing would alter the Colonel's decision to wind down the lamp in order to 'borrow' some oil. It took them nearly half an hour to wind it down and take it to pieces. So intent were they on filling their oil bottles that they were quite unaware that a very elderly signalman, who had seen one of his lights go out, had come over to investigate and was actually watching the proceedings.

"What goes on?" they suddenly heard at their elbows.

"We're Official Controllers carrying out an inspection," said James without a qualm and in a very fair German accent.

"Oh, I see," said the real Official, apparently believing this fairy tale.

As he walked away James called after him:

"Don't catch cold. Heil Hitler!"

So confident were the two men that instead of clearing out there and then they continued to fiddle about with their bottles. In an instant two Germans arrived on the scene with long quarter-staffs like boy-scouts' poles, James fled down the bank but the Colonel was caught on the platform below the signal lamp trying to grab his two sling bags. He was treated to a first class beating although he managed to ward off the more fatal blows to the head by protecting himself with his cumbersome kit.

One of the Germans was wrestling with him on the ground whilst the other stood by and aimed blows at him with his pole. Sometimes the latter was able to give a violent wiggle at the right moment so that his opponent got hit instead of him. Meanwhile Churchill was bellowing for James to come and distract the man with the pole so that he could attend to his own adversary.

James hurried back up the bank and so as to cause a diversion grabbed the bag that one of the Germans had snatched from the Colonel. A general tug of war now took place during which the Englishmen were treated to a hail of blows.

But while James was tugging away at his opponent's prize the German's handle broke and James fell head over heels backwards down the embankment. This turn in the battle allowed the Colonel to disengage from his man and tumble down the bank after his rescuer.

Churchill was in a very bad state with black eyes and a bleeding head, but fear almost enabled him to keep up with James whose recent valour was now being followed up by a long burst of discretion somewhere in the neighbourhood of twenty miles per hour. In case the Germans had seen them they made a detour before retracing their steps, crossing the line higher up and proceeding some three miles in the other direction.

By this time dawn was breaking and they found an ideal wood with a small lake in its centre. After sleeping until the sun had risen above the trees they began to lick their wounds and finished by having a refreshing swim in the lake. It was the only sunny day of their whole escape.

That night they tried to go across country but the going was so heavy that they soon cut back to the railway line. A couple of days later, for no apparent reason, it was James's turn to slow up their progress, for he suddenly caught cramp in one of his knees.

As the light came the cramp wore off. But then the Colonel's knee developed some fresh trouble and they found themselves in open country without cover except for a thick ground mist. Suddenly towards them out of the mist came a large gang of field-workers. It turned out to be a crowd of Polish women and boys in the charge of a very large farmer who was walking with a heavy stick. The farmer came up and challenged them. James pretended that they were Frenchmen who had missed their train and were walking.

"Where are you going?" asked the farmer.

"To Farmer Schmidt's," invented James.

"Is that so!" laughed the unhumorous farmer. He then yelled out to a Polish youth to escort the two men to the nearby barracks, still invisible.

It was a simple matter for James and Churchill to give this youth the slip in the mist but once they had left him they did not stop running for three miles.

Then they hid all day in the thickest wood they could find. Towards the afternoon James saw a figure walk past their spot with a gun. He had a feeling that someone must have seen them entering the wood. He whispered his fears to the Colonel and they decided to climb into a thick tree. They got up off the ground and were just stooping to pick up their kit when a voice shouted:

"Hands up!"

Three men with guns surrounded them.

The spokesman asked their nationality.

"British," came the answer, for the game was obviously up.

They were led to the local pub to await an escort. Here they immediately began to bolt all their remaining food. The Colonel asked the publican for two bottles of white wine on payment, but as there was none, two pints of beer were produced for which payment was refused.

The S.S were soon on the scene with their fast cars. They were taken off separately to Gustrov jail—a mere twenty-five miles from the Baltic. Their gallant escape was over.

Next morning they arrived back in Sachsenhausen and were locked up in cells not far from 'Wings' and Dowse.

It seemed incredible to them that this comparatively short motor ride should have taken them thirteen days to accomplish the hard way.

*   *   *

The Major started out upon his solitary trip by following 'Wings' and Dowse for 200 yards until they had passed the wall of the new camp. Here they waved to each other and parted company; they for the station and he to the nearest point of the railway line.

His one ambition was to avoid any kind of contact with Germans, verbal or otherwise—but especially verbal, for he fully realised that despite months of serious study his linguistic assets were practically a dead loss.

There were two things, however, concerning this escape about which the Major was totally unaware. The first was that as soon as his absence was known inside the camp the betting against his surviving the first twenty-four hours found few takers owing to his height and easy description. The second was that his lucky star, although hidden by dense cloud, was twinkling away in his favour against these generous odds.

He had hardly reached the railway line before a train came in sight. Seeing the level crossing lights he slipped through the barrier and followed the track beside the moving train. When it had passed he, too, had left Oranienburg behind him and was already heading north along the Rostock line.

He breathed an immense sigh of relief, for the worst was now behind him and it would be at least seven hours before the hounds could be after him.

He tried walking on the sleepers but it was so dark that he had to feel for them and then, owing to the rain, he occasionally slipped, so he tried the cinder track and found that by lightly brushing against the signal wires he could keep his direction and maintain a good speed.

He kept this up for two hours and, thanks to the regular exercises he had performed in the camp, he felt no fatigue whatsoever.

Presently he came to a station. He tossed up in his mind whether he should by-pass it or go straight through. He wrongly chose the latter course. Under the very first arc light he was challenged by a German. Panic seized him and he saw himself being ignominiously dragged back to captivity hours before the escape was even discovered. He vainly tried to produce one suitable sentence from the hundreds he had learnt by heart for this very emergency but nothing would come. He mumbled something vague in the unmistakable accents of Throgmorton Avenue, whereupon the German instantly directed him to a French labour camp which, by a stroke of immense fortune—except for its inmates—happened to exist in that vicinity.

Murmuring a heartfelt thanks he moved on.

And now the rain stopped and he passed through some beautiful wooded country with lakes on either side.

Some two hours before dawn he saw the red tail-light of a train. Here was the ideal kind of transport made to order. He sauntered past the last truck and climbed up onto the next one. He was hardly up before the train set off. It was too good to be true.

The problem now was to get off this goods train before dawn so as to hide throughout the coming day. Fate again settled this matter, for the train stopped some thirty miles further at the correct time and his coal truck was conveniently short of the station to allow him to walk round, and past it, unseen.

He followed the steep embankment and presently sighted an ideal hide-out—marshland amidst trees. When dawn broke the Major was completely hidden from view, in the reeds.

Though he was wet through and the swamp did not exactly improve matters he was delighted at having put so many miles between himself and Sonderlager 'A' on his first night. He ate something and even managed to sleep a little. A variety of birds and a herd of cows kept him company all next day.

At nightfall he made his way back to the station in the hopes of catching another train. As he approached the place he heard voices coming from the platform, so he hid behind some shrubs. But someone must have spotted him for a powerful torch was shone in his direction and one of the voices called to him to come out. When he did not move someone came in his direction. At this the Major took to his heels. The man ran after him and was joined by others. The Major careered down the embankment and back to his hide-out in the reeds. The darkness seemed to be baffling his pursuers for their cries of "halt" seemed farther away. None the less he kept running and went due east across a field and away from the railway line for about a mile and a half. Then he turned north once more. But now the rain was pouring down and, added to this, it was blowing a heavy gale. The Major lost his sense of direction and being unable to find it by means of the stars—now blotted out by clouds—he sheltered for the rest of the night under a hedge.

At daybreak he could see the railway in the distance and in order to improve his spoilt average he walked parallel to it as warily as possible.

By noon the sun came out, so he very wisely undressed and spread out his sopping clothing on a hedge.

Seeing workers some way ahead he stayed put and spent three hours sunning himself.

At about 6 p.m. he moved on and found the main road which ran parallel to the railway. This led him to a small village. Abandoning his recent caution he barged straight through it. Again his luck held and, following the road which now crossed the line, he decided to hide and return to the small station after dark to attempt what had failed on the previous night.

He had not gone very far before a farm cart overtook him. In it were two French prisoners of war. The Major stopped them, told them who and what he was and asked if they would hide him. They courteously declined. On thinking the matter over he was not surprised, seeing that it was still twilight and he could have lobbed a ball into the village with a number five iron.

Later in the evening on his way back to the station he met another French prisoner walking towards him. They spoke together and, as it was almost dark and they were much further from the village, the Frenchman said that he would certainly help the Major to hide. He told him to go through the village and up to a barn just beyond and that when it was pitch dark he would come and see him there.

Johnny Dodge found his barn without difficulty about a quarter of a mile beyond the village. He passed it and carefully reconnoitred all the surroundings. Shortly afterwards he heard the whistling signal that had been agreed upon, and there was his Frenchman accompanied by two others. The latter two went ahead as scouts and the party moved towards the barn. They opened the door and told the Major to hide in the loft. They left him haversacks of food and bottles of milk and coffee. They told him to keep well out of sight and added that they would return either before dawn or after dark with more food.

It appeared that he was in a village called Seilershof, that the two Frenchmen had to work all day, that they could only get away from their camp for a very short while at a time, and that they would try to pass him on to other Frenchmen at Rostock by putting him into one of the potato trucks which they loaded from time to time.

This barn was to become the Major's home for a whole fortnight. Time was no object so long as he was in comparative safety, for it was obvious to everyone that the war was in its last stages and he felt safer waiting for the final victory, out of sight, than parading his six foot three inches in a country which, although obviously on its last legs, was still very much on the alert to catch him.

He dug himself a deep hole in the wheat-sheaves, leaving plenty of loose straw within reach, to pull down over his head in case of need.

It was a delightful spot in which to await the arrival of the allied armies. At night, under the moon, the deer would come out of the woods and browse near the barn. In the daytime, through slits in the beams, he could contemplate a splendid herd of Holstein cattle which pastured in a beautiful open meadow close by. Further off a flock of geese waddled around the farm buildings. People passed to and fro all day long and the changing scene was a constant delight to the Major.

His French companions had taken a liking to him and looked after his needs with unfailing regularity and kindness. He called them the Three Musketeers.

One morning, soon after the Frenchmen had gone, he heard the barn door open. He fled to his hole but knew it was too late to bring down the loose sheaves over his head as the intruder would certainly hear the rustling straw. He heard footsteps on the ladder and then saw a face looking down into his. It was a bad moment for the Major until the newcomer had convinced him that he was nothing but a Polish worker from the farm. On hearing who the Major was he became most friendly, clasping both his hands. He asked if he could bring food or anything. The latter replied with all the German at his command that he really needed nothing and he besought the Pole not to mention having seen him to anybody. The Pole promised to keep quiet, drawing a finger across his throat, and after wishing the Major good luck he retreated down the ladder.

During the afternoon the door opened again, and again the same face peered down at the anxious Major. The same halting conversation took place before the Pole finally departed.

Before dawn on the next day the three Musketeers burst in in a state of great vexation and excitement. They accused the Major of having allowed himself to be seen, adding that the Pole had told his wife and that now it was common knowledge all over the district that a British officer was hiding in the barn.

The Major was very unhappy at having inadvertently shown himself, thus making things awkward for his good friends.

The leader said: "We can't possibly keep you here any longer now. We'll come and take you away tomorrow night to some other spot."

True to their word the three men came for him at the pre-arranged time. They went off together across country to a small village about five kilometres away.

Following his inactivity in the barn the Major experienced great fatigue covering the ploughed fields. By the time they had reached the village he was completely exhausted and in this state he found no objection to being bundled into the local *estaminet* whose blaring radio had been their guide for the last mile or so.

Inside he flopped down on a bench amid some fifteen French workers. An old German with grey hair was behind the bar. Someone slapped the Major on the back and, indicating the German, said: "Don't worry about him. He's stone deaf. Besides, the only policeman in the place is a Luxemburger and he never bothers us."

N

Apart from the dazzling effect of the first bright lights he had seen for quite a time, his fatigue, the noise and the effort of following the swift French talk, the Major felt comparatively safe and he gladly accepted the beers that were passed to him by these friendly allies in misfortune.

One of his particular friends said to him:

"Yes, since the Pole told his wife about you, the local policeman has known all about you. He is much amused at your presence in his district. So long as you don't throw yourself into his arms he'll leave you alone.

As beer followed beer and names and addresses were exchanged and memorised, a sudden hush came over the assembly and in that silent gift of simple people there penetrated the confident voice of the B.B.C. announcer bringing to one man in exile the joy these Frenchmen knew it would.

The Major was deeply moved at the gesture and covering up his confusion to the best of his ability he delighted his hosts with a translation of the latest allied successes that would have had any boy of fourteen expelled from his private school.

On this happy note the party broke up. The Major was introduced to the leading Frenchman of the village and after a warm leavetaking with his Three Musketeers he was led off to his new abode.

This was another loft at the end of a cowshed, only just outside the village. Before leaving him for the night his new guardian said:

"Now don't let yourself be seen by anyone here except the Russian P.O.W. who comes in to milk the cows and who will give you a pail of milk each morning. Either I or a friend of mine will bring you food every day."

There was real sweet-smelling hay in this barn and the Major considered himself to be definitely in clover.

At dawn he made the acquaintance of the Russian who brought him an ample pail of fresh warm milk. Then he was brought some fresh hot water in which he washed and shaved.

This barn seemed to the Major even more agreeable than his last one and its pastoral scene even more varied.

He was quite prepared to put up with a long stay here, his only worry being the amount of trouble to which he was putting his friends, the risks they were taking on his account and the food they so generously provided from their meagre rations. However much he looked forward to compensating them handsomely if he ever got home, he realised that he could never really square such an account.

But he was not to stay here very long, for again someone unreliable caught him in the hay and on the strong recommendations of the French, who knew exactly how far they could go, he was hustled off in the night and handed back to his three original friends.

This time the Major thought the French overcautious, but on the way back to Seilershof his friends persuaded him that the local men's judgment was not at fault as they knew all the conditions intimately.

He was to spend the rest of that night in a tiny outhouse not fifty yards from the Frenchmen's camp. Sleep was impossible for there was a constant scuffling sound going on all night. A large-sized rodent stumbled over his face.

In the morning he saw that he was in a rabbit hutch and no doubt his presence on the floor was as great a surprise to these animals as theirs was to him.

That night one of his friends came and took him away. They walked behind the houses lining the main street of the hamlet. Once beyond these they got back onto the main road. A short distance then brought them to an isolated building beside which was a five-foot wall. Up this they climbed and the Major found himself on some straw. The Frenchman told him to lie down and then proceeded to pile up the straw between him and the edge of the wall so that he could not be seen from the road. The Frenchman promised to bring him food on the next day and after the usual urgent recommendations to keep out of sight he jumped down into the road and made off back to his camp.

On lying down the Major found himself slipping through

the straw in a most disconcerting manner. He felt around with his hands and discovered he was lying on horizontal poles with large gaps between each. By lying across them he managed to stay up.

From close below there rose a prodigious noise that reminded him of the slaughterhouses he had seen in Chicago. He spent a sleepless and rather uncomfortable night.

In the early morning he heard a door open beneath him and there came the sounds of a man's and a boy's voices. They were Poles. As daylight came he realised that he was in the rafters above a giant pigsty containing some 100 pigs.

The Major was now able to arrange the straw to his satisfaction. He breakfasted and began to feel better.

He spent a week on this odd and rather smelly perch. Every other day his friend brought him hot food.

The Major's life became a regular routine. He took great care to keep out of sight for he neither wished to be caught nor to jeopardise his excellent friends. To his questions as to how they managed to find him so much food there came the invariable reply that it was no trouble at all.

On the seventh morning the Major was peacefully studying German from a little book when he heard footsteps approaching the pigsty. The footsteps stopped outside the door and instead of a Polish voice he heard the unmistakable German words: *"Kommen Sie mit!"* Peering through the straw he saw the farmer with a Luger in his hand which was unquestionably pointing at his head.

The game was up and the Major wondered who had given him away. He remembered his fear of having been seen by the Poles when he had been answering a call of nature five minutes later than his usual time.

The farmer, though courteous enough, was in a hurry. He would not even let the Major put his shoes on, but walked him barefoot up the main street into the boiler-room of an alcohol factory. Here he was allowed to wash his feet and someone fetched his shoes.

Shortly afterwards the Luxemburg policeman arrived on his bicycle and led him away.

In a secluded spot in the woods he said to the Major:

"I've known all about you for the past three weeks. Some idiot must have given you away. It's a pity." Then drawing out a copy of the *Police Gazette* he showed the Major pictures of himself, James and Churchill. He then added:

"I could have handcuffed you, but I didn't, so please don't run away or you will get me into a peck of trouble. Is there anything I can do for you while you are waiting in the local cell for the arrival of the Sachsenhausen Guards?"

"Yes," said the Major. "When you get back to Luxemburg let them know in London that you saw me and take this list of names of people who are now in Sonderlager 'A', because as far as their relatives are concerned they have been reported missing."

The policeman took the list of names which the Major had already scattered amongst his French friends, verbally, and after locking him up apologetically he brought him a first-rate meal.

It was the Adjutant of Sachsenhausen Concentration Camp who called for the Major.

The return drive—in handcuffs—took about one and a half hours. It was not done in a Black Maria so the Major could fully enjoy the beauty of the countryside on this sunny afternoon of October 23rd, 1944.

He spent a dismal first night in the camp prison but on the following afternoon when he was taken out into the courtyard it seemed almost like old times, for there, waiting for him, was the rest of the gang: 'Wings', Churchill, Dowse and James and in their smiles of relief and welcome there was also a look of no mean admiration for the last man to be caught.

CHAPTER

VI

It might have been supposed that the return of the five escapee officers—clearly the signal that we were about to be evacuated—would have inspired Judd to keep up his good behaviour, if only to confirm the tales that all would gladly have told if given half a chance. But Judd never gave anyone the opportunity of bringing up the subject. Nor was there any reason for my compatriots to suppose this miracle had ever taken place, for, from the moment they returned, Dr. Jekyll vanished for good to be replaced by the infamous Mr. Hyde.

Judd's sudden and unexpected relapse into a being of evil was a double blow for me. Apart from the five months of complete harmony, I not only saw my efforts dwindle to nothing, but there seemed little point in telling 'Wings' what had happened, for I should simply be laughed out of court.

It looked as though pride in his foul reputation had won the battle in which his life was at stake. Perhaps I should have foreseen that in the struggle between good and evil, Judd's obsession for notoriety at any price was so predominant as to tilt his schizophrenic scales towards evil so that the consideration of his life in the balance was reduced to the weight of a feather.

I could not help confiding some of my disappointment to 'Wings' and, choosing what I hoped was a good moment, I told him about the signed confession. I seem to remember his claiming that such a document would not carry much weight and that, in any case, the evidence against the traitor from other sources would prove conclusive enough.

What with the ever-approaching rumble of gun-fire and all that this signified in the race to avoid being overrun by the Russians—a race which we were positive meant as much to our captors as to ourselves—the problem of the traitor now became of secondary importance.

After our long captivity we were now entering upon the final act of the drama and until the curtain rang down for the last time our lives would hang in the balance. With all that this meant in terms of possible survival it was hardly surprising that I should dismiss Judd and his confession from my mind until the die was cast.

The dormant butterflies of hope roused themselves anew. At the rate things were going, a lucky toss of the coin and I should be out of this madhouse in no time and back in the world of dreams looking for Odette; or would it be the other way around? Or would neither of us . . .? but no, surely at this eleventh hour the cup of bitterness had been drunk to the full.

In a state of mounting tension the days dragged by and the battle came so close that even Bessonov began to fear it would be too late.

It was only in the second week of April that the move came. Warned of our departure the night before, the whole camp was packed and ready for the following day.

Led off before first light we were driven to the station under the supervision of George's guard. As we waited outside the station-yard for the next move we were ringed round, each guard turning on the electric lantern with which he was provided and holding his sub-machinegun at the ready.

At length we entrained and our long journey began. It lasted all day and all that night as well as the whole of the following day. Our party was under the command of a Gestapo officer whose duty consisted in handing us over to the Commandant of Flossenburg Concentration Camp—a place of which we had never heard.

He and George behaved with punctilious correctness throughout and 'Wings' made sure that the former told our new Commandant the sort of treatment to which we were accustomed.

If my arrival at the gates of Sachsenhausen had given me a shock, the first sight of Flossenburg in a bowl at the top of a hill, with its high electrified stockade, was something that none of us would ever forget. The local guards began screaming their hymn of hate as soon as the gates closed behind us.

We were led to the camp hospital, the best ward of which had been prepared for us in advance, and here, according to the Commandant, we were to stay until further notice. Escape, he warned us, was out of the question, since mines lay hidden all around the boundary walls.

We stayed five days in the hospital, never leaving the ward, but through the windows we could see what manner of camp this was. Smoke rose all day from the crematorium and the men we saw moving about were nothing but skin and bones. From time to time a stretcher party would pass with the blanket-covered remains of the latest man to die of overwork and starvation. Our toilets were shared by those who were dying in the next ward. Men weighing no more than five stone would come in wearing short-length shirts hardly covering their nakedness and would look at us over the next stall with the eyes of those who have not long to live. Even if the Anglo-American advance were to arrive tomorrow or in five minutes, it would be too late.

How many camps of this sort existed in Germany? How many hundreds of thousands of human beings—men and women— would see the gates opened by healthy soldiers in khaki, only to look at them with uncomprehending eyes before death closed them for good?

One day a new intake arrived. Passing through a hut they emerged naked from the showers to be hustled towards other huts where deloused clothing awaited them. Over the intervening hundred-yard space which they had to cover, we had an un-interrupted view of some 500 walking-dead, still good for a few hours forced labour on starvation rations. Some fell through sheer exhaustion as they descended the few steps to the main compound, only to be kicked back into line. Some who stuck together and had maybe known each other in better days when there had been flesh on those bones and a smile on a happy face, now drawn into a premature death-mask by degradation and unspeakable pain, put their arms under the more feeble shoulders of their flagging comrades and shuffled out of sight.

Here there was no wall as there had been at Sachsenhausen to prevent us seeing what our imaginations had pictured. But during our weekly visits to the showers we had never seen walking skeletons on this scale. Truly Sachsenhausen was a rest camp for its inmates compared to Flossenburg. Looking through the large windows we were more conscious than ever that there, but for the grace of God, went we.

On the fifth day we were transferred to the prison-block and here, in compensation for the comparative freedom of the hospital, we were allowed to walk freely up and down the corridor and were only locked into our cells at night.

Every day we were also allowed a short stretch in the yard and here we saw the sheds about whose foul purpose we were to hear so soon.

We took advantage of our free run of the corridor to knock on every cell door and, after discovering the nationality of its tenant, we said in his language:

"Keep your chin up! The Allies will be here in a matter of days."

The voices within replied:

"It had better be soon. Only yesterday they took out four men and a woman and hanged them in the shed outside. I saw them pass through the slits in my door. All were naked, all young and the girl was beautiful and walked like a queen,"

or,

"Am I glad to hear you? This means that things are going badly for these swine. Hurry up, the Allies! Only three days ago the Adjutant opened the food hatch of the next cell and shot my neighbour. I saw them take his body away and I can still hear the echo of those shots and the screams of my poor companion,"

or again,

"My name is Josef Müller. I am the Chief Justice of Bavaria.

Yesterday they took me to the hanging shed and I refused to be executed without a court-martial. Perhaps now, with your arrival, the danger is past. Maybe we shall soon meet and I shall be able to tell you this nightmare story."

Yes, it had better be soon. Orders were coming through daily from Gestapo H.Q. for the liquidation of one or another. Hitler was also taking a hand in the matter. Ensconced in his Berlin bunker, he was witnessing the relentless destruction of his capital. "Baptism of Fire", which had been his proud propaganda film to show any adversary what to expect from the Luftwaffe if they resisted his ambition for world power, was catching up with him. The flames that he had spread around the world were now licking their way closer and closer to his bunker and his ears could pick up a faint grumble of crashing buildings that shook the very foundations of his underground lair.

Would he leave all this for the Austrian redoubt, or would he remain in his hole to the bitter end whilst crossing out, one by one, the names of his hostages that were listed on the wall?

In view of the imminent fall of Germany, would the S.S. carry out their orders and execute us in turn as our names appeared for liquidation?

This was the situation of which we were all aware during these last anxious moments. Admiral Canaris—Head of the Abwehr—had been done to death in this very prison only a few days back. What was to prevent us from falling to the same axe?

But on the fifth day we prepared for another journey. Just as we had flown before the Russians, so now we were to retreat before the advancing Anglo-Americans so as to get nearer to the centre of the ever-diminishing circle.

A twin-benched eight-seater Black Maria with one small single cell compartment and a lorry represented the transport for the survivors of the cell-block. This convoy was under the command of an evil S.S. Captain who handpicked us for the joys of being crammed into the minute van.

For daring to raise his voice in protest at the conditions of over-crowding in the Black-Maria, Dowse and all those who backed him up by word or look were squeezed into its restricted space. Thus I found myself among the twenty-one prisoners in a van intended for the transport of nine persons over short distances.

The floor was strewn with sacks containing triangular wooden chips which were to serve as fuel for the charcoal-burning engine. To sit on these for ten minutes was an agony. To stand meant crouching so as not to bump the roof.

Amongst those who shared the 36-hour journey with me in this sardine-box without windows were Dowse, Cushing, Walsh, Lieutenant Fabian von Schlabrendorff, Prince Philip of Hesse, the sixty year old Baron Wilhelm von Flügge, Josef Müller, Wing-Commander Dragic of Yugoslavia, Carl Edquist—a Swede, and ten others.

We had no notion where we were going any more than our friends in the lorry who were no better off than ourselves. If we were stifled by overcrowding they, too, had twice as many people on board as the vehicle was meant to carry and, as against the heat from which we suffered, they were to be frozen stiff and covered in dust so as to become unrecognisable.

At one point on the first night the Prince of Hesse, whose wife was to be killed a few days later in Buchenwald Concentration Camp as the result of an allied raid, fainted and Dowse, who was standing in the front of the narrow corridor, was able to revive him with water which he obtained from some villagers beside whose house he had been disdainfully flung onto the street.

During most of this journey I sat on a sack of wood resting my back against Baron von Flügge's knees. If anyone so much as put a finger on one of my knees I could feel the weight going right through my heel like a stiletto, but the elderly Baron made no complaint throughout the long journey and spent the time entertaining us with all manner of topics from his vast knowledge of the world, its languages, arts and letters.

After occasional stops for meals and refuelling, when we could stretch our cramped limbs, the convoy pulled up outside the gates of Dachau Concentration Camp. As we waited to pass through the barrier, Cushing, Dragic and I began to sing softly the songs that people sing all over Europe. Dragic had a lovely voice and Cushing, who had soldiered over half the world, knew all the tunes and could hold them to our harmonising.

When we finally disembarked inside the camp, Josef Müller slipped up beside me in the dark and said:

"I shall not be coming along with the rest of you, for they are taking me to a special cell. I just wanted to tell you that if this is the end for me, as I fear, I shall think to the last of the lovely singing that you and your friends performed as we entered this infamous camp." He searched for my hand and said, "Goodbye, my friend."

I forget what I told Josef Müller as we shook hands in the dark. Each one of us was guided by his own intuition and even here in this camp of 20 or 30,000 souls, to die meant dying in solitude. As I saw his grey tragic face move out of sight, the realisation that each one of us might still be segregated in turn, like Müller, came back to me in full.

We were now led to a large and well-appointed hut already half full of other political prisoners. Here, clearly, were the real Prominenten and here, for the first time, I was to shake hands with the anti-Nazi German Ambassador to Madrid and his wife, Dr. and Frau Erich Heberlein; Richard Smitz—Mayor of Vienna; Dr. Kurt von Schuschning—late Chancellor of Austria—and his charming wife, Vera, who had voluntarily joined her husband to be interned for years in one of the four villas in the next compound to ours at Sachsenhausen, where their daughter, Maria-Dolores, had been born.

Here I met Martin Niemöller, the famous Pastor and ex-U-boat Commander. My first impression on shaking hands with him was that I was in the presence of a forty-year-old ski-ing instructor. The clear intelligent brown eyes looking out of his sun-tanned face—he had been allowed out of his cell—told me that here was a man of great personality and charm.

Bishop Neuhaüsler of Munich and Gabriel Piguet, Bishop of

Clermont-Ferrand, were other outstanding people in this distinguished assembly.

Here and later on came the opportunity of getting better
acquainted with the five Greek Generals who had inhabited a
hut in a compound beside ours at Sachsenhausen, on the opposite
side to that of the Schuschnings. After saluting them as they had
occasionally passed through our compound we had found ourselves
in the yard at Flossenburg with them on occasions and now we
had joined up for good. Besides the outstanding Alexander
Papagos, Commander-in-Chief of the Greek Army, there were
four Lieutenants-General: Pitsikas, Bakopoulos, Dedes and
Kosmas.

But amidst all this galaxy of historical figures I was drawn most
by the outstanding personality of Colonel Ferraro of the Italian
Partisans. A tall, powerfully-built man with a ruddy complexion
and curly brown hair, he smoked his pipe placidly amidst the
hubbub and looked for all the world like a champion golfer
waiting patiently in a crowded club-house for his turn to tee off.

Brought up on the tough battle-grounds of the French Foreign
Legion he had risen from the rank of 2nd-Lieutenant to full
Lieutenant and then to Captain, being awarded the Croix de
Guerre and two Palms for three outstanding actions that had
resulted in his promotions. Surrounded in the mountains by
Germans in his fight against Fascism, Ferraro was in the same
boat as Bessonov or any of the others who had dared to oppose
their totalitarian régimes. But if beside Ferraro, Bessonov seemed
somewhat dwarfed in stature, then Ferraro's Chief, General
Garibaldi, was an even slighter figure.

Grandson of the famous Liberator of Italy, this sixty-year-old
General had been arrested in Bordeaux for Resistance activities.
His rank had not saved him in Dachau from being assigned the
degrading task of cleaning out the camp latrines, which duty
necessitated his rising at four o'clock every morning, nor from
receiving a brutal kick in the most intimate portion of his anatomy.
He was further subjected to ill-treatment when his arm was
broken with the butt of a German rifle for being slow in climbing

into a lorry. None of these things had helped to rejuvenate the wise and kindly man I was to get to know and appreciate more and more.

Bartoli and Amici naturally looked on their high-ranking compatriot as a long lost father. They asked me with great tact if I minded if they now transferred their services to him and Colonel Ferraro. But before doing this Bartoli introduced me to General Garibaldi in such glowing terms that the latter was left in no doubt that he was looking on someone who was a friend of Italy.

It was thanks to Ferraro's influence that Garibaldi had been transferred from the main camp to the far better conditions that obtained inside the prison block.

No sooner had we arrived in this hut in Dachau than 'Wings' and Dowse gathered all the spare bread they could lay their hands on with a view to hiding in the triangular space above the ceiling and below the rafters. They discovered the entrance in the showers and determined to await there the arrival of the allied troops.

On the very morning after our arrival we were warned to get ready for the next move, so 'Wings' and Dowse prepared themselves for the siege. When Ferraro discovered their plan and heard—not through me—that they were already in hiding, he implored me to get them out, saying:

"The dogs'll sniff them out straight away and they'll be goners. Tell them that we're going to Italy. I promise they'll be all right there. We shall manage something once we're over the border."

I was so fearful for the lives of Dowse and 'Wings' in what I considered a most risky enterprise that I took it on myself to climb up through the showers and pass on Ferraro's message. They were not pleased at this interference with their plan and much against their wills, allowed themselves to be dissuaded by the gravity of my entreaties.

We were now marched through the camp in front of several thousands of its massed inmates. The British contingent gave these men the thumbs up sign all the way. At one point I heard someone call out my war-name from the centre of the throng. I searched eagerly amongst the sea of scarecrow faces but all the shorn heads looked exactly the same. Hearing one of their number calling out had started a general murmur from which it was now impossible to trace the original call, and as the man who knew me tried to attract my attention by returning the thumbs up sign, a hundred neighbouring thumbs copied the gesture.

If this was annoying to me I could imagine the frustration of my friend—either a Frenchman or a British officer—for one always wanted to be recognised so that word would get back by one or the other that he had been seen.*

We now joined forces with several more Prominenten who had been kept inside the Dachau prison block and together we were driven in two coaches to the Concentration Camp of Innsbruck.

Our journey took us through Munich, that lovely town of pre-war days: Dachau was a mere stone's throw from it.

Passing through the streets we had our first view of the destruction wrought by pattern bombing. No single house remained standing, only an odd wall here and there; the rest was rubble. The trams were still running with cardboard squares replacing their broken windows. People stood at various points they recognised as tram stops, but from inside the coach one marvelled that anyone was still alive in Munich. One wondered where they could possibly live and what point there could be in taking a tram to go nowhere.

Now that the Allies were so close at hand our aircraft were never out of sight. Sometimes the coaches stopped whilst the guards took cover, but our luck held. When night fell fires could be seen all around. A few more days of this and every house on enemy territory would be destroyed. The Germans could not possibly hold out much longer.

We reached our new camp at about ten o'clock; the date being roughly April 21st. Though it was dark we noticed that this could only be a small camp. It was encircled by snow-capped mountains visible in the starry sky.

* See Appendix.

We celebrated our arrival with a sing-song in which most of the members of our large room joined. Presently this gaiety was interrupted by loud bangings on the wall from the guards in the next room.

"Shut your traps!" yelled a guttural voice. "How do you expect people to sleep with that filthy row?"

Jack Churchill walked up to the wall and banged back in his turn, yelling out in perfect English,

"You shut yours! It's about time you heard some decent singing now that your marching songs have led you to defeat."

We sang on.

The next morning broke fine and the blue sky remained filled with R.A.F. bombers all day. We now had a clear view of the surrounding mountain scenery. It was quite incongruous to find oneself in a camp in so glorious a setting.

Another convoy of political prisoners arrived to complete the 132 Prominenten of twenty-two nationalities which were now to remain together until the end.

Amongst the new arrivals were Léon Blum and Madame Blum; the Hungarian Prime Minister, von Kallay and the entire Hungarian Cabinet; General Alexander von Falkenhausen, until recently C.-in-C. German Forces in Belgium; General Thomas, Colonel-General Franz Halder, Prince Frederick Leopold of Prussia and all the closest relatives of Goerdeler, the Mayor of Leipsig—principal civilian figure of the German Resistance Movement, who went into hiding after the Movement's failure to assassinate Hitler on July 20th 1944, only to be betrayed later by a woman who could not resist the million marks reward for information leading to his capture. Added to these were a large number of men and women related to Colonel von Stauffenburg, the man who had left the time-bomb in a brief-case under the table at Hitler's Rastenburg H.Q.; all had been roped in as hostages.

Other noteworthy prisoners included Fritz Thyssen of Krupps, Dr. Punder, a Secretary of State, and Dr. Schacht, President of the Reichsbank. The military element was enhanced by the presence of the tough, masterful Colonel von Bonin, G.S.O.1 of an Eastern Front Division, of whom more will be heard later.

Amongst this gathering I was relieved to find Josef Müller back amongst us and delighted to rediscover Hans Lunding of Albrechtstrasse memories. With him were five members of the Danish Resistance Section of the War Office.

Here, as in Sonderlager 'A', rank was of no account and all could converse with one another, for all were in the same boat. In this way I grew acquainted with most of my companions in distress. Whilst it is difficult to single out any one particular individual amongst such a gathering of important people, I think most would agree with me that the elderly Léon Blum was an outstanding example of an alert mind, an unquenchable spirit and a uniform charm of manner that would have made all French hearts glow with pride, whatever their politics. I well remember a half-hour's conversation with him which was interrupted by his wife who quite rightly insisted he should sit down and stop talking politics.

The British Colony had now increased by three new members: Hugh Falconer whom I knew from Gibraltar days and who, after being one of the experts of the "Rock's" hidden radio installations, and captured on a secret mission to North Africa, was beginning to put on weight and colour after the bad time he had experienced prior to our first meeting in Dachau; then there were Captain Best and Colonel Stevens, both kidnapped before the outbreak of hostilities at Venlo in Holland.

I first saw Richard Stevens through the window of a room where he was mysteriously kept in splendid isolation. As I caught sight of him standing there in a sports jacket and grey flannel trousers I immediately recognised the Indian Army officer and gave him a huge wink. His puckish face broke into a cheerful smile as he returned it and both of us knew that we should be friends. Fortunately he was soon released from his original restrictions and we spent much time together thereafter. From him I heard the story of how he and Best had been led into a trap by the Gestapo and of their long imprisonment in the cells

o

of Sachsenhausen and Dachau. Stevens' great friend was Count Leshek Zamoyski, a Pole who had survived a long stretch in the horror-camp of Auschwitz.

One of the women prisoners, Isa Wermehren, came from a camp whose name—Ravensbrück—was new to me. Learning that there were two Churchills in the group she searched me out first and asked if it was my wife who was in that camp. I asked her for a description and then knew it was Odette. Isa Wermehren told me that she was in excellent health and spirits, that although she was called Frau Schurer on the Commandant's orders, certain people knew her real identity. She then informed me that Baron von Flügge had been in closer contact with Odette than herself, so I hurriedly went in search of my room-mate. When I had found him I broke the strange news that he had actually known my wife under another name. Smiling with delight at this coincidence I pulled out the snap that I kept in my wallet. Von Flügge took it from me, looked at it and, handing it back, said,

"I'm sorry. This is not the woman I knew."

Then, seeing the look of shocked surprise on my face, he said,

"Let me have another look. . . . Yes, yes. . . . It might be she. . . . People can change so much in prison. . . . Forgive me, my dear Churchill." He got up, handed back the photograph and walked heavily away.

I remained alone in the room with my dreadful fears. Soon, soon I should know what they had done to her. All the agony of uncertainty came welling back into my mind. There was one consoling factor in the thought that if we both survived, I at least would be in condition to look after her and try to make her forget the horrors she must have known so as to have altered beyond recognition.

But now the thing to do was to avoid thinking and working myself into a state of despair which could in no way help the situation. There were plenty of prisoners around me whose plight, if not precisely the same, was at least as grim.

Generally speaking, people did not divulge the whole story

behind their arrest, for no one could be certain that it might not reach the wrong ears. Little by little, however, everyone's reason for being here became known. As far as the Germans were concerned, those who had not been arrested as a result of the 20th of July affair, found themselves here because their behaviour and conversation had shown them to be anti-Nazis.

General Falkenhausen had been arrested, it was said, for refusing to carry out Hitler's instructions to execute all Belgian saboteurs without trial.

Colonel von Bonin's unit had had to retreat from untenable ground on the Eastern Front which Hitler insisted should be held. As someone had to be punished for disobeying the great "Corporal's" orders, it was von Bonin who took the rap. This officer was a handsome upstanding German whose bearing in the presence of the Gestapo guards never wavered. He addressed them constantly like menials and was not in the least cowed by any of their threats.

We spent some ten days at Innsbruck and during that time we were locked into our huts so that a hanging could take place undisturbed and unwitnessed. The poor victim was not one of our number.

CHAPTER

VII

At the end of April we embussed once more and, followed by a coach-load of guards and provisions, we set out for the Brenner Pass.

The entire route up to the pass was lined with Italians returning home on foot. There was no need to be sorry for them; they were going in the right direction.

Near the top our coaches were stopped for another air-raid and during the halt the usual soft singing broke out. This time it was silenced by von Schuschnigg. Turning round he glowered at us and said,

"How can you sing in this grave hour?"

It was a difficult question to answer, but for the sake of those who felt like him we desisted. Perhaps we were singing so as to temper the gravity of the hour. Perhaps we were thinking of the thirty odd Poles at Innsbruck and the way all of us had gathered round their separate enclosure one evening as they sang the Polish Partisan song as a farewell to their companion, hanged that very afternoon.

Thanks to the silence that now reigned we were able to over-hear the whispered conversation between a scar-faced S.S. guard and the driver. The former said,

"If Hitler should be killed in the bombing of Berlin I'll mow down these bastards like nine-pins."

Everyone was conscious that whether these words had been expressed or not, this was the thought we had all read in the eyes of the arrogant guards who were leading us into the last lap.

By the time we began the run down into Italy night was falling. The oncoming traffic of German lorries was quite heavy and here and there abandoned trucks lay by the roadside. From von Bonin we learned that only the German Fourteenth Army lay between us and the advancing Allies.

During the long slow run some of us dozed off and I, for one, awoke to find our convoy of three coaches halted in a small side road within a few yards of a railway crossing.

It was from this point onwards that we began to notice a slackening of discipline in our guards. Like them we were con-scious that with the Brenner between us and the last Concentration Camp of the Greater German Reich we were a long way from the land of militarism and its highly organised machinery for the enslavement of human beings.

Without asking for permission prisoners left their coaches, sauntered around to attend to their needs and knew that they could walk away freely into the night. Whilst it was tempting to do so, such individual action might easily have jeopardised the chances of the women and the elderly members of our party who were not in condition to spend several nights in the mountains whilst awaiting the allied advance. The party therefore limited itself to visiting friends in the other coaches.

And now several events occurred, sometimes simultaneously and sometimes in swift succession, so that it was impossible to be a first-hand witness of them all.

The first event that came to my notice was the discovery that the level-crossing's keeper was an N.C.O. of Partisans. Before daylight, in the morning after our arrival in darkness, this man entertained Garibaldi, Ferraro, Bartoli, Amici and myself to a large breakfast with such items of food as we had not tasted for many a day. From him we learned that the nearby village was Villabassa in the Puster Valley.

After breakfast Bartoli was sent to convey Garibaldi's compliments to 'Wings' and another officer and invite them into his master's presence. He returned with them shortly afterwards and they entered the level-crossing's shack.

Garibaldi received them with his usual courtesy and asked me to act as interpreter for what he had to say.

"Gentlemen," he began, "I have asked you to come here so as to give you the picture of the situation as we see it and also because Colonel Ferraro promised we should find means of escape once we reached Italy."

I rattled this off in English and Garibaldi then proceeded,

"Fifty yards away in the wood over the level-crossing lies freedom. The wood also hides some units of our Partisans. According to our host, several cars are at our disposal to go and join these and other units, but we should certainly not require cars in order to reach the wood. The position, therefore, is as follows: If we join the Partisans, who have invited me to be their leader, we could then surround Villabassa and rescue all the prisoners. On the other hand our temporary absence might jeopardise the lives of the people left behind and in that event I can arrange for the Partisans to surround us without our being with them."

I translated these words and Garibaldi now came to the crux of the matter:

"I am now going to ask you both what you think we should do. Wing-Commander Day, may I have your views, please?"

'Wings' did not hesitate long before replying,

"On the whole I think the second plan is less risky for the majority."

I translated. Garibaldi turned to the other officer and said,

"And now your opinion, please?"

"I think we should escape while the going's good."

"Thank you," said Garibaldi. "And now your views, please, Ferraro?"

"I agree with Wing-Commander Day."

General Garibaldi took in the gathering with an all-round sweep of his eyes and said,

"Gentlemen, the majority votes for the second course of action which I shall now set in motion. I thank you all."

I left the shack with the others and could not help thinking how greatly tempted Garibaldi and Ferraro must have been to take the easy course and make sure of their own lives. I wondered what I should have done on finding myself fifty yards away from British Partisans who offered me their leadership after spending two years in a Concentration Camp.

The next time I saw Garibaldi in the course of that morning he was in the uniform of an Italian General with all his decorations up. Things were moving quickly.

Early the same morning momentous happenings were reported from the other coach. Rumour had it that, as a result of drinking the greater part of a bottle of alcohol, one of their guards had fallen into a drunken stupor.

Some of the members of the coach apparently found another bottle which they gave him when he woke up. As he got well under way with the second bottle, someone managed to extract his wallet whilst another prisoner was loosening his collar. In the wallet they found orders, above an illegible signature of someone in Himmler's office, for the execution of twenty-eight members of our party including the names of all the British officers as well as the rest of the military prisoners.

When von Bonin heard about this he went straight off to the Villabassa post office and managed to put through a call to Kesselring's Fourteenth Army Headquarters in Italy. By chance he found himself connected with a Staff Officer whom he knew. He rapidly explained our position and asked for a company of the Wehrmacht to come and rescue us from the hands of our murderous S.S. guards. The company was promised for six o'clock on the following evening. In the meantime Garibaldi was informed of this latest move and agreed to countermand his previous orders to the Partisans, preferring the rescue to be handled by experienced troops.

There now remained two days and one night in which we must all live in suspense. If the S.S. were to act they would have to act now.

We lunched that day in shifts at the local hotels, the arrangements being made by the South Tyrolese Resistance Movement. This was our first experience of a communal meal with neither guards nor electrified wire in the vicinity. With a little research one could no doubt discover who paid for these 132 lunches and all the meals that were to follow, but whoever it was, we were all made to feel very welcome by the hospitable and friendly hotel folk of Villabassa. This was the Austrian Tyrol with a strong bias towards Italy and the only German element here was the society of Colonel-General Halder and his wife who sat opposite me at a long trestle table, whilst Lieutenant Fabian von Schlabrendorff sat on my right and my friend Baron von Flügge on my left. During this lunch Schlabrendorff told me his story.

Quietly and with modesty he told me of his long family connections with England, of his invitation with his wife to Buckingham Palace before the war, of a picture that he had received from the Royal Family and had returned to them just before the outbreak of hostilities in his fear that such a valuable original might be destroyed in the coming war. He spoke of his constant hatred for the Nazi régime, his pre-war attachment to the Kreisau

Circle, its struggle against Hitler before and after the outbreak of war, its idealistic leader, Count von Moltke, and his tragic end by hanging.

From the very outset of the war he had been the principal liaison officer between the Army and the civilian elements of the German Resistance and his main negotiations had been between General von Tresckow, his Chief on the Eastern Front and also ring-leader of the Generals' rebellion against Hitler and inspirer of his colleagues and Field-Marshals to unite against the despot, and Geordeler, the violent anti-Hitlerian Mayor of Leipzig, whose lack of security and secrecy in these subversive plots had been a constant source of anxiety to all concerned.

Schlabrendorff told me how one after another the attempts on Hitler's life had failed, how we, in England, might never know how many of these attempts there had been and he asked if it would bore me to hear of his own private effort.

I needed no coercion.

"The great problem that always faced us," said Schlabrendorff, "was the fact that it was almost impossible to get Hitler alone. There had been volunteers to enter Berchtesgarten and shoot him in cold blood, like Rasputin, but the snag was that no one was allowed in armed. Nevertheless one such attempt was made and the volunteer got cold feet at the last moment. Another man volunteered to shoot him whilst wearing a new bullet-proof uniform which Hitler was to inspect; but the inspection was always postponed at the last moment, until the volunteer became a nervous wreck. Either Hitler had a charmed life or his star-gazers warned him of danger with uncanny accuracy.

"We therefore decided that we must do away with him, even at the cost of other lives—sometimes those of our own friends. It was on one such occasion that it fell to my lot as a Staff Officer who always attended his periodical discussions with the East Front Command to place a bomb in the aircraft that was to fly him back after the meeting.

"We had discovered that the most potent and efficient explosive was the plastic which was dropped to the French Resistance.

After many trials with this stuff I devised a home-made bomb that passed repeated tests. It was a hollowed-out brandy flask and the only brandy in it was coloured water visible through the glass slot; the rest was crammed with plastic which was to be set off by a half-hour time pencil.

"Choosing my moment carefully I broke the time-pencil and gave the flask to one of Hitler's Aides-de-Camp—a Colonel— just as he was boarding the 'plane. I asked him to present this gift to General X in Berlin with von Tresckow's compliments.

"The 'plane took off, circled the aerodrome, and I watched it from one of the office windows until it was out of sight. According to my watch the explosion would take place in exactly ten minutes. I lit a cigarette and waited, my eyes on the telephone. The aircraft's movements were known to every unit, every flak battery, and every Luftwaffe squadron along the run. These things were never left to chance. In Berlin our friends were anxiously awaiting my telephone call to confirm the crash and then things would start to happen.

"Four minutes to go. I need hardly describe my feelings. I was the hand that was going to alter the destiny of millions; my heart was jumping with emotion. It was 1943. For three years we had been trying to do this and now, in less than two minutes, this madman would be blown to bits and peace would return to the world.

"I lit another cigarette. Time was now up. At any second the telephone bell would sound like a scream in my ears. Yet I must give the time pencil five minutes grace; they were not accurate to a second. Also the ground forces would require a few moments to gather their wits before sending out such shattering news.

"I waited and waited and chain-smoked until my cigarettes were all gone. Slowly it dawned on me that my mission, like the others, had failed. Something had gone wrong. The demon with the charmed life would now go on spreading fire and misery until we eventually got him.

"When his aircraft was due back in Berlin I rang through as though to make sure of its safe arrival. True enough, it had grounded five minutes earlier. The passengers had all left the aerodrome in a fleet of cars.

"Now at all costs I must stop the brandy flask from reaching the General. Two or three hectic telephone calls and I was through to the Colonel. When I gleaned the fortunate news that he had not yet delivered the gift I told him some cock-and-bull story that the orderlies had mistaken von Tresckow's instructions and put in the wrong brandy. He promised to keep the flask until I brought him the real stuff. I then caught the next 'plane to Berlin and swapped flasks.

"Now I could hardly wait to see what had gone wrong with the igniting mechanism. On the return flight it occurred to me what a prime jest it would be if the thing blew up now.

"Back on the Eastern Front I took the thing to bits and noticed that the acid had unaccountably stopped burning the wire that releases the striker pin only a quarter of an inch from the end. To this day I cannot understand how this could have happened.

"When Colonel von Stauffenburg's bomb also failed to destroy Hitler on July 20th because, owing to the heat, he had chosen to hold the Rastenburg meeting in a wooden hut instead of the usual underground concrete shelter, my Chief, von Tresckow, warned us what this failure would cost in terms of mass executions. After a moving farewell to me and his other companions in the Movement, he went off alone into no-man's-land and blew himself up with a hand-grenade.*

"I was arrested shortly afterwards, as my name had cropped up in other people's trials. Though I denied complicity in the plot the Gestapo tortured me into unconsciousness on two successive occasions.

"We are not out of the wood yet, Churchill, and I feel that tonight may be a danger spot."

I thanked von Schlabrendorff for confiding his story to me. At such a time as this, it was risky to share such a tale. Ever since we had travelled together in the Black Maria from Flossenburg I had taken a liking to him. His friendship for a man of von

* "Offiziere gegen Hitler" by Fabian von Schlabrendorff.

Flügge's stamp had only served to consolidate my opinion of his character.

The experience of living close to men like these two, Josef Müller, and many others prevents one joining the ranks of those who claim that "the only good German is a dead German". I often think that most of those who make this remark have no idea that 5,000 German Resisters, including twelve Generals and two Field-Marshals, either committed suicide or were executed for their part in the July 20th plot.

During that same afternoon a committee was formed with Papagos as Chairman, the confidential man of the South Tyrolese Resistance Movement, Captain Payne Best, Colonel Stevens, von Bonin, and several representatives of our gathering as its members.

In principle it was decided that since the guards were unaware of their imminent replacement and had no specific orders as to where we should be kept, the majority of us would spend the first night in the Town Hall on straw bedding and that rooms would be found for the women.

At the same time preparations were made by the local man for our accommodation in the Pragser Wildsee Hotel up in the nearby mountains, and our transport to this place had to coincide with the all-important arrival of the Wehrmacht unit.

After dark Jack Churchill decided that he had had enough of this place. Perhaps he, too, felt that the night in the Town Hall foreboded nothing good. At any rate, after conferring with some of his colleagues at a meeting I did not attend, he started to walk home.

This independent action may, strangely enough, have resulted in saving the lives of the rest of the British contingent. As we stood around talking on the ground floor prior to going up to our straw beds, the S.S. Lieutenant in charge of the guards came up to me and said,

"Where is your cousin?"

"I haven't a clue." I replied, "Perhaps he's already upstairs and fast asleep."

"Well," said the S.S. man, "we have a special room for you British officers."

'Wings', who was now beside me, said,

"Tell him we don't want any special rooms. We'll doss down with Colonel Churchill and all the others."

I translated this and the matter was dropped. As the S.S. man moved away, the bearded Prime Minister of Hungary came up to me and whispered,

"In God's name don't go to any special room tonight. They're gunning for you. I feel it in my bones."

"Thanks, but don't worry," I said. "We feel it too."

We went upstairs and the eerie night began. At each end of the long row of sleepers sat a cross-legged guard with his Schmeisser across his knees. There was little sleep that night and much relief when dawn broke through next day.

It was fitting that the last crucial hours should fall on a Sunday and that Bishop Neuhaüsler should share the service with the Bishop of Clermont-Ferrand. The Villabassa church was filled with hostages thanking God for his protection on the previous night and fervently invoking his aid throughout this equally fateful day. And the good Lord might have been listening to the Committee's plan to save the whole group.

During the afternoon, and well before the Wehrmacht company was due, von Bonin bluffed the S.S. Commander into believing that their arrival was imminent and that the only way he could save his small group of guards was to take the provisions' bus and make themselves scarce.

In the Sunday hush of Villabassa, before the streets were thronged with the first elements of the retreating German army, the S.S. Commander had to make his choice. On the one hand he was being tempted to mow down the prisoners out of vengeance for the defeat of Germany. What was to stop him repeating the grim atrocity of another S.S. unit which had burned and machine-gunned the innocent inhabitants of Oradour-sur-Glane in the village church ? On the other hand the order to execute so many hostages, part of which he would have carried out on the previous night if he had only managed to herd the British officers into a separate room, was still in his pocket. That slip-up was now to his advantage. With these hostages alive this piece of paper would have a certain protective value if shown to the allies.

Once made, his choice soon flashed round amongst the scattered prisoners, and all came out to look with silent awe at the spot where, until so recently, had stood the bus with its pile of loaves visible through the back window.

The guards had vanished and we were free.

That evening, true to their word, the Wehrmacht force arrived.

Some were now driven and others walked up to the Pragsa-See Hotel. Situated about 5,000 feet up, this lovely place had the added attraction of a lake outside the front door and visible from half the bedrooms. Snow lay everywhere at this altitude and, in this glorious setting and under the protection rather than in the charge of the Wehrmacht unit, we felt that our freedom had almost begun.

The next to leave the party was 'Wings,' who left officially with the Austrian confidence man. They drove in the direction of the advanced units of the American Army so as to inform them of our whereabouts. With their departure we settled down to await the arrival of an American company to take over from the Wehrmacht.

Seeing which way the wind was blowing, Bessonov very wisely deserted the party. He may or may not have invited some of his compatriots to join him. For Fiodr there was no point in escaping. Privalov and Brodnikow had lost their nerve and desire to live. It was as though they were mesmerised by the awful fate that awaited them in the Soviet Union. As for Stefanov, I had promised to take him home with me to England. I looked forward to bestowing on him the affection of a brother.

Just as Sonderlager 'A' had helped to rehabilitate me after solitary confinement, so the pleasant days at Pragsa-See were like a convalescent stage after the camps. I was indeed fortunate. At thirty-five, if all still went well, I should return to freedom unscarred and unchanged in outward appearance. If I sometimes felt one hundred years old inside, those years gathered in solitary confinement had been richly compensated by the society of men of many nations who had been prepared to lose all in their fight for freedom and their example would help me to face whatever lay in store at home.

Von Bonin had the hotel widely ringed around with the soldiers over whom he had assumed command. They were mostly out of sight in the woods behind and at the sides of the hotel, so that one was hardly conscious of their presence. At a time like this there would be plenty of deserters from the German Army which contained quite a large percentage of foreign troops. These men fought in German uniforms with shoulder-flashes indicating their nationality. Almost every nation was thus represented and bore the insignia of Russischer, Polnischer, Französischer Freikorps, etc. Whereas by far the largest proportion were Russians—as already shown elsewhere—other nationals had accepted conscription into the German Army either for political reasons or because they preferred doing so rather than half starving to death over the years in P.O.W. camps. The Germans had spent a great deal of time, thought and money on propaganda for this recruiting, but just as these units were the first to surrender, so they would now be the first to go to any lengths in order to obtain a civilian suit and discard the evidence of their treasonable behaviour. It was therefore no great hardship to agree to von Bonin's suggestion that it would be wiser to remain inside the circle formed by his protective guards.

Hugh Falconer, however, still felt he had a few accounts to settle for the treatment he had received. Completely recovered from his long imprisonment he knew that his place was down in the valley where things were happening. Commandeering a two-seater car he had noticed in the hotel garage, he soon had it in working order and I joined him in the hair-raising descent over the snow-bound road to Villabassa where my presence was requested by Garibaldi to act as his interpreter.

Garibaldi and Ferraro had remained in Villabassa as the popular commanders of the Partisans. We found the square in front of the Town Hall full of these men with their funny coloured caps and wearing two Schmeissers each slung around their shoulders. Here they had remained after the rest of us had gone up to the Pragsa Hotel and disarmed all German troops retreating along this valley. Most of the time their non-stop activity had been carried out with no more flutter than is shown by an orderly cinema queue as it advances towards the ticket office.

However, one unit had not shown quite the same amenability in throwing their arms onto the growing pile and we were enlightened by Badoglio as to what had then occurred.

As soon as the Germans had opened fire on the Partisans Ferraro had given orders to retaliate and, taking part in the action himself, he had mowed down the majority of those who paid for this short show of resistance. Afterwards he had held a summary court-martial at which he condemned twelve German officers to death in the style which he had learnt from them. As the twelfth passed through the office, Garibaldi had entered and, on learning what was going on, he remonstrated with Ferraro and got him to countermand the orders. The twelfth man, imagining that he was the only one to benefit from this reprieve, said,

"If my colleagues are to be shot I prefer to be shot with them."

Garibaldi looked at the man and said,

"I commend your loyal attitude, but none of you will be executed. We shall not repay you in the coin of some of your S.S."

Falconer and I found a room in the Town Hall already crammed to the ceiling with German arms, and from another room we selected a couple of shining Lugers with holsters.

Leaving Falconer with his Foreign Legion colleague, Ferraro, I accompanied General Garibaldi towards the most advanced American unit which was in the next village some ten miles distant. The road was dotted with groups of Italian Partisans who went wild with excitement as soon as they spotted Garibaldi.

The American Captain with whom we conferred seemed to have little conception of the local situation and was far too tired to want to hear about it. In the absence of his superiors he conceded a minimum of Garibaldi's requests and excused himself on the grounds that his few men were miles in advance of the main body; they were exhausted by their rapid advance and he was worn out by the endless chatter of Partisans which he had suffered all along the route. The position was understandable, for just as in 1940 small German motor-cycle detachments had captured French villages well ahead of their main force, so this unit had done the same. Garibaldi's principal argument that the whole district was under his control made little headway with this man. I was glad I did not have to negotiate with him for the rescue of our party, but maybe he would have better understood the urgency of such a plea.

CHAPTER

VIII

BACK at the Hotel we now heard the news over the wireless that Hitler had committed suicide. The soldiers shrugged their shoulders and the prisoners thanked their lucky stars that this news had not come whilst they were still in the hands of the S.S. Truly one stroke of luck had followed the next in these last hectic days, each one of which had been charged with uncertainty as to our fate.

Now the collapse of Germany was inevitable, and the anxiously awaited American saviours were no longer awaited with anxiety.

Their arrival on our fifth morning at the hotel coincided with breakfast. Through the dining-room window I saw their Jeeps and light tanks race up the drive with Italian Partisans clinging to every available hand-hold. It was the Partisans who rushed to the German guards and disarmed them, the latter accepting this long-awaited end to their war.

Although this arrival was an anti-climax that did not even get the prisoners up from their breakfast table, I felt that a gesture was indicated, for these men must certainly have put themselves to immense trouble in getting here. I joined a small band of grateful souls and we shook hands with a bunch of very exhausted but beaming young Americans, led by Captain Attwood.

Nothing was too much trouble for this Company. As a result of 'Wings', and the Austrian's report of our position, these men had been detailed by wireless to come to our rescue. Awakened at 2.15 a.m. after only twenty minutes' sleep they had accomplished a seven hour cross-country journey to execute their mission of mercy. Now they shared all their possessions with us, made us gifts of blankets, cigarettes and food. Within twenty-four hours we were treated to a first-class cinema show and I was fitted out from head to foot as a G.I.

Having already given my name and those of all the British officers and Danish Resistance men to an S.A.S. wireless officer I had encountered near Villabassa who promised to transmit these immediately, we were now able to double this confirmation of our survival through our American hosts. Besides this we were filmed and newspaper reporters were not long in reaching us. An American General promised us transport to Verona as soon as this could be arranged and this was no hollow promise. Within two days the convoy drew up outside the hotel and we were whisked off in style.

The convoy consisted of two or three Jeeps in the lead, followed by a light tank, after which came the requisite number of 5-seater army personnel vehicles with one spare vehicle for every five of these, in case of breakdowns. There was an ambulance, further light tanks at the rear and a rear-guard of more Jeeps.

Keeping up a good average we drove west into Lombardy and towards Verona; after a stop for lunch the drive continued for some ten hours. Everywhere we met with destroyed bridges and the sides of the roads were littered with abandoned German vehicles.

If the ship of Fresnes had seemed to drag interminably at its anchor, the allegro movement in this convoy's symphony of tyres was like sweet music to our ears. One after another the kilometres ticked themselves off, almost too fast, as we swept through this lovely country bathed in the May sunshine.

The happy conversation and unbridled laughter of my companions was contagious: this was no time for doubt, fears, or

P

pessimism over what might or might not await one at home. The only man who was tired in our car was the driver, for he had had to rise early at the spot where the convoy had formed and had already done many miles before our morning departure. Between us Colonel Stevens and I kept him awake by talking to him, shaking him and turning the wheel ourselves when he fell fast asleep and our heavy car failed to follow the others round the bends.

We reached Verona at 1 a.m. on May 9th and a chicken supper awaited the party in a hotel. Thereafter some of us were driven to an American mobile hospital where we were given comfortable camp beds under a giant tent. We were received here at 3 a.m. with the utmost courtesy.

Next day we were given an enormous breakfast and sent away with gifts of toothbrushes and cigarettes, etc. Our transport drove us to the aerodrome where we beheld something like fifty shining transport 'planes capable of holding at least thirty passengers each with comfort. There was no squeezing or stinginess about the number of aircraft set aside for the political prisoners; at least six of them were used for the purpose of flying us to Naples— the Allied prisoners' clearing house.

On the way the Captain took those of us who so desired into his cabin where we met the rest of the crew and benefited from the unique view of their forward compartment. Falconer and I happened to be there as we passed a few miles from Monte Cassino. At our merest hint of interest the Captain swung the aircraft over and circled the shattered ruins of this place about which we had heard so much.

A battery of news-reel cameras and press photographers awaited our arrival in Naples, but here my objective was to make rapid arrangements for Stefanov to be able to come with me to the British quarters before he was whisked off by the Russians.

I was introduced to the British and American Generals who were there to meet us and managed to make my plea to them simultaneously. I told them that I was prepared to sign a statement to the effect that Stefanov would be no charge on the British exchequer as he would be living with me as a member of my family.

Both Generals said,

"Oh, we can't do that. He'll have to go to Rome and report to the Russian Consul like all the others."

I looked from one to the other and said,

"He doesn't want to return to Russia. You know what'll happen to him if he ever reports to the Consul in Rome."

"Nothing'll happen to him," said the British General. "It's a routine affair."

My argument that the Poles were given a chance of returning to Britain cut no ice. I could see I was wasting my time. These brass hats had simply no notion of what returning through normal channels meant to a Russian officer. Perhaps they never understood why several Russian prisoners in Sweden committed suicide rather than return to the Soviet Union. I could see I was back in the land of "make-believe" where even Generals had their heads in the sand.

I stormed off to the Russian group, and taking Stefanov aside, I said,

"It hasn't worked. I did everything I could, but they're too dumb to understand. On your way to Rome you escape. It'll be easy. Write to me and use my name as a reference whenever you think I can be of help. I shall be waiting for you at home."

Stefanov held my hand in his farewell grip and looked into my eyes. He spoke with firmness, confidence and affection,

"Thank you for trying, Peter. I shall escape, I shall write and I shall find you.

"*Aufwiedersehen, liebe Freund.*"

* * *

I hated my days in Naples. Perhaps things were coloured by the infuriating separation from Stefanov. It was not a matter I grieved over, for my friend was as smart as a monkey. He would get away all right; but it was the waste of time and the knock on discovering that Bessonov was right again. We should not understand the writing on the wall until it had become indelible. We should have to learn the hard way. I fumed at the folly of my compatriots and cursed their one-track interest in the cricket scores that blinded them to the vital issues, the real scores of our day and age.

My friendship for Stefanov was the solid type that happens, if one is lucky, half a dozen times perhaps in the course of a life. We could pick up, if necessary, after years just where we had left off. Humorous, gay, charming and modest he had laughed, ragged and spoken seriously with me, and my echo to his mood and his to mine had been effortless. We did not need to bind each other with contracts nor was our understanding marred by jealousy on either side.

Perhaps it was the high standard of American organisation, hospitality and consideration that made the British officers' quarters odious by comparison. A dingy building, sloppily run by undisciplined and disinterested Italians and overcrowded sleeping quarters without any cupboards for one's things where, in order to switch on the light, one had to cross two naked wires, was a sample of its general style.

After sending a shoal of telegrams to England I spent most of my time with Lt.-Col. Hedin of Scotland Yard whose enthusiasm in his job of finding out all he could about the behaviour of German Camp personnel I found most refreshing. I gladly stayed up till all hours writing reports whose information was cabled to his respective colleagues in the various zones. Here was a young man who deserved his rank.

On May 11th Falconer and I were called into the presence of the General in charge at Caserta. He was fully in the picture as to our talks with Hedin and thanked us for our co-operation. He informed us that an Air-Marshal was returning to Northolt on the 12th and said that he had invited us to be his guests. We jumped at this kind gesture.

Next day we were up early and spruced ourselves up as well as possible and I was not ashamed of my G.I. get-up.

A staff car fetched us in style and I, for one, was delighted to shake the dust of Naples off my feet.

As we stood on the tarmac waiting to salute the Air-Marshal we saw a German officer being led, hand-cuffed, into another 'plane. It was a sight that did us no harm at all.

At last we were off and the aircraft headed north. May the 12th 1945—a date I should never forget—a fateful day that I now dreaded, for at the end of the flight I might hear anything. No news had come through from London despite all the telegrams and all the addresses I had left. Perhaps they dared not communicate the news they had to give. The sun shone brightly out of a perfect Mediterranean sky. For twenty-five months I had been waiting for this day and now perhaps it had come too late.

Beside me Hugh Falconer was chattering away gaily, telling me about his wife, his mother, his Austin 7. How could he be so confident that all this was waiting for him? And yet he was; everything was cut and dried, his plans all laid.

We passed high over Cannes and then crossed the Alpes Maritimes. Looking down I thought of the months I had served in the French Resistance just here, but more particularly I was reminded of the painful journey Odette and I had shared when the Italian lorry had driven us along these very roads, taking us from one prison to the next; to pass over it in freedom without her meant nothing.

We lunched and the Air-Marshal was full of kind attentions towards us. He asked no painful questions. At last France was behind us and the coast of England lay ahead, green and welcoming in the afternoon sun.

Soon we were over Heathrow where all the neat houses made regular patterns from above. There was the Berkeley Arms in its little white village and there the big hangars of Northolt. Down we came, circling round into the wind for a perfect landing.

After thanking our host for his great kindness we walked towards the offices where Hugh began telephoning our respective Sections of the War Office.

A long and painful wait now began, for no one seemed to be in, and with each minute the dreaded anxieties increased. Why was a car not standing by to pick us up? Our departure had been wirelessed through. Why should we have to undergo this added torment? No doubt there were plenty of good reasons. Had all these months of patience been of no avail? Had I already forgotten the hard-earned lesson of Fresnes? At this thought I calmed down and waited with more composure.

*   *   *

The telephone bell rang in Oxford Square, the new offices of the French Section of S.O.E. Although it was Saturday afternoon, a hand picked it up and said,

"Yes?"

"You won't know me, Miss Atkins," said the caller. "I'm the S.O.E. telephone supervisor and I know people by their voices. I am going to ask you a great favour. A man called Hugh Falconer, whose voice I have known on and off for four years, is on the line from Northolt. He belongs to the Spanish Section but there's no one there who seems to know him well enough to clear him through Security. I can't bear the thought of someone returning from the Concentration Camps and being left hanging about in this way. Knowing your interest in these men I'm asking you, off the record, if you can do something?"

"You came to the right place. Put him on."

"Thank you, Miss Atkins. I'll put him through."

"Hallo, there," called Vera Atkins.

"Vera!" came my delighted reply, for Hugh had handed me the receiver on learning that he was through to the French Section.

"Peter!" she gasped. "I didn't expect to hear your voice. Are you speaking from Northolt?"

"Yes. Can you come and fetch me and a friend of mine?"

"The time to whistle up a car and I'll be with you. Good-bye."

At last the car arrived and we were welcomed shyly and happily by my old friend Vera Atkins. I had known her since the summer of 1941 when she had been a junior member of the office staff. Now she held the rank of Major, but she was still the same.

We sat on either side of her on the back seat and I waited for her to speak. During the first portion of the drive Hugh chatted away merrily whilst I could have wished to hear my news in privacy. But that was not to be and I must face it this way.

She must have sensed my fears and had no doubt prepared herself on the way out for what she had to say.

Turning towards me she began quietly,

"Well, Peter, it's good to see you back."

"How is it at home?" I helped her.

"I'm afraid your mother . . ."

"I know," I broke in. "Just tell me who's still here."

"Your father and . . ."

"Odette?" I whispered.

"She's waiting for you in the office."

A film covered my eyes and my heart wept inside me. I heard no more of what she said and sat in a numb daze until the car pulled up outside the office. I walked up the stairs behind the others and waited in a dream. Vera Atkins was saying something to me and I followed her to a door. She pushed it open and stood aside to let me pass.

Seated at a table was a Major and opposite him, with her left side towards me, sat Odette, in uniform, her hair resting on her shoulders. She looked up. A smile came over her face and her mouth half-opened.

"Pierre!" she cried, rising from her chair and coming towards me as I advanced with outstretched arms.

So we remained in silence whilst the door closed quietly behind us and we were alone.

CHAPTER

IX

LITTLE by little Odette told me her dreadful story. Since it has been accurately and sensitively told by Jerrard Tickell in his book *Odette* from which Herbert Wilcox made the film whose title role was so admirably performed by Anna Neagle, a brief summary will suffice here.

When Odette entered captivity in mid-April 1943, her fifth vertebra had been shattered two days before from a thirty-foot fall as we came down the steep snow-bound slopes of the Semnoz mountain beside Lake Annecy in pitch darkness. X-rays taken in May 1945 showed this vertebra to have shrunk away to nothing. Her period on starvation rations in Fresnes had lasted for six consecutive months as against my two and a half months, resulting in stomach pains that may be left to the imagination. A gland, the size of a grape-fruit, developed on her neck in February 1944 with a simultaneous attack of pleurisy. The Gestapo refused the prison Captain's recommendation that she be admitted to hospital and she had this swollen gland for fourteen months. The pleurisy healed itself in Germany.

In Ravensbrück Concentration Camp which she reached after a sweltering summer journey with stops at Karlsruhe, Frankfurt and Halle prisons on the way, she was kept in an underground cell for two months and ten days on end in total darkness. In August—as a token of private vengeance for the D-day landings in the south of France—the heating was turned on in her cell day and night for a week during which time she was entirely deprived of food. At the end of this treatment she was picked up unconscious from the floor and taken to the infirmary to be revived for her execution—she had been condemned to death in Paris. At this time her hair was falling out, her teeth were loose and she was covered all over with scabies. Added to this the tenderness in her toes was a constant reminder of the day in Paris during one of her fourteen interrogations, when they had pulled out all her toe-nails in an attempt to make her divulge the whereabouts of two most important officers.

She had never spoken then, nor did she now ask for any allevia-tion of her lot when the Camp Commandant called once a month to enquire if she had any requests.

As a result of his occasional peeps through the spy-hole, when he simultaneously flooded her cell with light from the outside switch, the Commandant, Sturmbannführer Fritz Suhren, was able to see the type of woman he had orders to ill-treat in this shameful manner. Walking up and down in what had been total darkness, before he switched on the light, he might behold her with her face shining from the pat of margarine she had preferred to use as face-cream rather than food, or with her hair curled in pieces of a torn-up stocking. She studiously avoided the blue eye in the spy-hole and when, on one occasion, this man, who had been instrumental in the extermination of 100,000 women in Ravensbrück, could no longer refrain his admiration and opened the door, coming towards her with his hand stretched out, her disdainful avoidance of his hand taught him the lesson that the imprisonment of the body did not always include the enslavement of the spirit.

When, in its turn, Ravensbrück was evacuated, Suhren, partly intrigued by his frail prisoner and probably hoping that if he saved a person whose name was Churchill he might also save himself, drove her personally up to the spear-head of the American Forces.

In this way Odette, by her own bearing, saved herself.

She handed over her own captor to his future captors, was pre-sented with his revolver and chose to spend the first night of her liberty in his car, contemplating the stars above. For her, too, it had lasted too long, far too long. She sat there numb, appalled by the cruelty and folly of mankind.

Next day she took his brief-case and two photograph albums and began the same period of waiting and uncertainty as to what she would find at home, as I had. She was offered 2,000 dollars for Suhren's photographs, but kept them for the War Office. These snaps of Suhren—precious treasures which he had kept to the last—and his companions being trained to run Concentration Camps served in the identification and arrest of many a German who had gone into hiding and altered his name and appearance. Amongst these was Suhren himself. He escaped from the Americans, and was recaptured only to escape again quite easily, since he was put in the charge of German guards who helped him get away on the eve of his trial. After two years of liberty he was picked up by British Security officers in a factory. Handed over to the French—fortunately—his doom was sealed, for they have no foolish sentiment about these murderers. The news of his execution was a personal satisfaction to me.

Odette's condition on her return was such that the Ministry of Pensions awarded her a life pension of 100 per cent. The Army Medical services opened their hospitable doors and offered her everything. But her peace of mind was my principal consideration. If we could help to bring that about, her physical ailments would stand the best chance of following suit. Away from her three daughters from whom she had been separated so long and deprived of my constant presence, she would languish and perhaps fade away. I therefore made enquiries and was introduced to a brilliant young doctor who has since literally saved her life on more than three occasions. My feelings for this man need no comment.

On the day after our arrival, Oliver, my younger brother, returned from his long service with the Italian Section. Six years my junior he had covered himself with glory, being a Major with the D.S.O. and M.C. as well as the Italian Liberation Medal. Together we planned our first visit home to coincide with Odette's spending her time with her three girls.

We found our eighty-year-old father in a grief-stricken state. Having lost his eldest son, Group-Captain Walter Churchill, D.S.O., D.F.C., in August 1942, followed by the death of his life's companion in September 1943—as I had feared—he had spent nearly two years in solitude trying to comfort himself with the regular monthly white lies from the War Office—issued on our instructions and saying that both of us were alive and well. His mind had gone so far that he was unable to grasp the fact that two of his sons had survived.

During his last two years of feeble life I spent my time flying between London and Malvern trying to be in two places at once to bring comfort to two beloved beings who really required my undivided attention. Added to this I was mistakenly ordered to take up an intelligence post at the War Office from which it required three weeks of tactful negotiation before I was released.

Complications made it impossible for me to have my two invalids in the same house. (This might have been done if Odette's aunt had not been killed when her London house received a direct hit in February 1944.) As a result of all this I was not at hand when my father died.

My grief at this blow and all the difficulties that beset us were as nothing compared to what other survivors of the camps had to face, for Odette and I were together. Some of our friends have still not recovered from their ghastly experiences.

In August 1946 the news of Odette's George Cross brought an invasion of Press reporters and News-reel cameras that lasted an entire day. Despite the courtesy of all these men and women to whom we are both grateful for their understanding and patience, our peace was at an end.

When Odette went to Buckingham Palace on November 17th 1946 it was arranged that my investiture should coincide with hers. On the morning of the great day I drove Odette to her doctor for a couple of injections to face the ordeal of honour.

Not realising that one is entitled to drive one's car into the Palace court-yard, we parked ours in a nearby street and walked towards the first of the main gates. As we passed each battle-dressed guard I was sure they knew who the girl in F.A.N.Y. uniform was beside me. In turn they presented arms in such a manner that it was difficult for me to see my way through the main gates after answering their salute for her. This was one of the prouder moments of a profoundly moving day.

Joining other men and their relatives on the way in, we were then led to two different rooms, one for ordinary mortals and the other for K.C.M.G.'s and similar high honours.

Odette was the only woman in this latter reception hall dotted with glass cases full of lovely china-ware; in fact she was the only woman to be decorated that day. She found herself a seat in the farthest corner and sat shyly waiting for events. She was not long alone before a charming white-haired General came over beside her and tried to put her at ease.

Presently the Lord Chamberlain was stooping before her. He said, "Madame, His Majesty has requested that you lead the Investiture."

"Oh!" she gasped, "I couldn't possibly do that."

"Oh yes, you can," he said, with a twinkle, and in tones of gentle but firm persuasion.

Odette inclined her head before this gracious command.

The Lord Chamberlain smiled and said,

"I believe two of your daughters are attending the Investiture."

"Yes," said Odette, fearing that they may have been misbehaving.

"If you will kindly point them out to me I will arrange that they are moved up close to the dais."

Odette complied and the girls were moved forthwith.

So it was that when the King entered the room of Investiture where the curtained-off musicians had interrupted their playing to the 500 guests and relatives of the 250 who were there to be decorated, Odette stood directly facing him as the band struck up the National Anthem. On her left some thirty senior officers stood in line along the red carpet that led to the dais, whilst behind her 500 pairs of eyes were watching the scene. In front the King's eyes never wavered from hers.

As the last chord died away the guests sat down and Odette's citation was read out:

"Mrs. Sansom was infiltrated into enemy-occupied France and worked with great courage and distinction until April,

1943, when she was arrested with her Commanding Officer. Between Marseille and Paris on the way to the prison at Fresnes, she succeeded in speaking to her Commanding Officer and for mutual protection they agreed to maintain that they were married. She adhered to this story and even succeeded in convincing her captors in spite of considerable contrary evidence and through at least fourteen interrogations. She also drew Gestapo attention from her Commanding Officer on to herself saying that he had only come to France on her insistence. She took full responsibility and agreed that it should be herself and not her Commanding Officer who should be shot. By this action she caused the Gestapo to cease paying attention to her Commanding Officer after only two interrogations. In addition the Gestapo were most determined to discover the whereabouts of a wireless operator and of another British officer whose lives were of the greatest value to the Resistance Organisation. Mrs. Sansom was the only person who knew of their whereabouts. The Gestapo tortured her most brutally to try to make her give away this information. They seared her back with a red-hot iron and, when that failed, they pulled out all her toe-nails. Mrs. Sansom, however, continually refused to speak and by her bravery and determination, she not only saved the lives of the two officers but also enabled them to carry on their most valuable work.

"During the period of over two years in which she was in enemy hands, she displayed courage, endurance and self-sacrifice of the highest possible order."

Throughout the reading the King still looked straight at her and now that it was over the George Cross was handed to him. Odette curtsied and walked forward. The medal was pinned on, and the King took her hand in his, keeping it there.

"I asked that you should lead the procession, Madame, as no woman has done so before during my reign."

He paid her the gracious and moving compliments that came from his heart and it was as though he did not wish the moment to pass, for he still held her hand. Of the two perhaps His late Majesty was the shyer.

Odette curtsied once more and moved away.

My turn came some 200 places later. The King knew all about my connection with Odette and I was left speechless by the sensitiveness of his remarks to me.

Le Rouret.
Alpes Maritimes,
    and
Le Vieux Moulin,
Magagnox, A.M.
France.
April—June 1954.

APPENDIX

APPENDIX

THE person I should like to name first in this appendix is my friend Roger Renaudie (p. 104) whose courage and humour did not abandon him during his long captivity. After more than eleven months of solitary confinement in Fresnes he was condemned to death and sent to Germany for execution.

On his way to the Reich in a cattle truck jammed with naked prisoners—naked so that they would not get away—he made a brilliant escape. Later he was recaptured, but finally survived.

An architect by profession he is likewise a first-class builder, decorator, farmer, potter, wood-carver, raconteur, dress-designer and cook.

To me Roger Renaudie typifies the fine Frenchman. Enthusiastic, warm-hearted, generous, quick-tempered, impetuous, hard-working, courageous, patriotic and cynical, he lives life to the full without counting the cost.

During the war we were members of the same group in Cannes.

His principal task at the time was organising the reception of the feluccas that plied between Gibraltar and the south of France. He never thought out his operations in advance but successfully improvised means for dealing with any situation that might arise. If we did not always see eye to eye on "underground" methods, we have become close friends since the war.

This book was written in his villa near Grasse. His wife, Germaine—an equally patriotic member of the same French group— joined us there after the first month and the party was complete when Odette came out a fortnight later.

* * *

Roger Bardet was the French double agent who betrayed us in the Resistance and not Marsac. The latter's falling into Henri's clever trap and giving our address was simply done in order to try and arrange for the bomber, as explained on page 40. What Marsac did was stupid, but not treachery. His folly would have been inexcusable if he had passed through our Training Schools which warned us of such traps. As it is he is forgiven. Marsac has perhaps naturally not made any attempt to contact us since.

Roger Bardet and Louis le Belge were both condemned to death as traitors after the war. After several years of imprisonment they were both unaccountably released. Post-war commitments have prevented me from seriously pursuing my curiosity in regard to this mystery.

* * *

The meeting at the Café du Rond Point des Champs Elysées was attended by Odette and myself, as it happened to coincide with a flying visit to Paris on official business. Nobody else turned up (page 101).

Marzelle wrote to me after the war informing me that his two daughters were released from Fresnes, that he had been sent to Buchenwald and his wife to Ravensbrück Concentration Camps. His wife had returned weighing only 25 kilogs. His last letter announced her death—one year later.

I still look forward to visiting him one day.

Jo Venot and his family at the Fox Bar are now old friends whom we never fail to see on every passage through Paris (p. 102).

Simone Hérail (p. 106) and her family of Languedoc wine growers are also long established friends.

I have never forgotten and will never forget the Fols. I see them as often as possible.

The wardress who brought me gifts from Odette married the Fresnes prison Captain. Before her marriage she offered her services as governess to our children.

Henri was captured after the war. He spent several years in prison both in France and England. In Paris he spent some of his time in the underground cells of the finger-print department where Odette and I had had our longest meeting. There he met Roget Bardet who had worked hand in glove with him and the latter told him that he had tried to assassinate him on one occasion in Auxerre as he knew too much against him. Henri now lives in Tettnang, Germany.

Riquet survived. (page 40.)

Marcel Fox was executed. (page 61.)

The Italian Generals of Sonderlager 'A' were sent to an Italian fort, as I had imagined they might. From it they made successful escapes and Admiral de Angelis crossed into Switzerland where he reported my presence to the British Military Attaché in Berne. This information was passed on to the War Office.

Admiral Carlo de Angelis has remained in constant touch with me since the war and last summer Odette and I visited him and his family at Falconara Alta, Ancona. His present post is on the Naval side of N.A.T.O. in Rome.

Colonel, now General, Teucci, became Chief of the Italian Fighter Pilot School in Florence and is now at the Italian Air Ministry. We correspond regularly and I look forward to seeing him again one day.

Colonel-General Marras has been Chief of the Italian Armed Forces for many years and is now due for retirement.

* * *

The Irish boys have taken up various civilian occupations except for Sergeant Cushing who is in Korea.

The two Poles live in England.

Bartoli and Amici are back in their beloved Italy. They have not lost touch.

'Wings', now Group-Captain H. M. A. Day, O.B.E., D.S.O., etc., retired, is now living happily ever after, shunning publicity and surrounded by friends—amongst whom I believe I may now count myself. If ever a man had earned a stake in his country it is he.

All the other British officers are alive and well. Johnny Dodge returned to the U.K. after a series of amazing experiences—but that is his story.

Stefanov escaped all right. In the yard at Caserta he implored Privalov and Brodnikow not to go to Rome in the big Humber placed at their disposal but to come with him in his Jeep from which he promised he would get them both away. But they were tired of playing hide and seek; tired of life and preferred to accept their destiny through normal channels.

Stefanov, who had learned a good deal of English from me, soon had the American army driver of his Jeep fascinated with his stories of the lesser-known behind-the-scenes struggle of the European War.

After two or three hours of driving he suggested that he could do with a drink. They stopped and put away a litre of Chianti, Stefanov putting his away into a flower-pot. He then asked to be excused.

Several days later Stefanov was picked up and placed in a Polish Camp. From here he managed to get himself transferred to a British Camp where, as an interpreter, he made himself indispensable to the Commandant. Here he used my name and I received a letter from the British Commandant which I answered by return of post.

Stefanov was now allowed out of the camp and the first thing he did was to get himself Italian Papers. After some time he also procured a set of French papers and, within three years of our separation, Stefanov was telling me all about it in my London home.

His adventures since the war alone would require a book to themselves, but in short he had gone back to the Dolomites and trailed Bessonov to his lair. He found him milking cows on a farm several thousand feet above sea level. Bessonov told him he was still waiting for the British to contact him.

A year later Stefanov went back to the farm and found his bird had flown. This time he unearthed him on another farm on the shoulder of a mountain still higher up and commanding a view in all directions. As he entered the living-room he found himself looking down the muzzle of a nine millimetre Luger in Bessonov's hand.

Bessonov looked at his young compatriot distrustingly and said,

"Don't imagine you can come and get me as easily as that."

Stefanov looked at the General uncomprehendingly.

"I haven't come to get you, General. I've brought you papers for South America. There's no point in wasting your time here. It's too late for the British game."

He invited the suspicious Bessonov to put his hand inside his pocket where he found the papers.

Bessonov handed them back, saying,

"I'm not going to South America. I'm waiting for the British to contact me."

Six years have passed since that day and I doubt very much if he is still there.

Stefanov informed me that through his own private channels he had learned that our friends Privalov and Brodnikow had both been executed and that Fiodr was in the clear.

Up till three years ago I received occasional letters from Stefanov, the last one of which told me that he was happily married and that he was going to reside in a place where nobody knew him and he could live peacefully away from the torrents of political intrigue. I sometimes wonder if this was not a cover behind which he intended to get himself more deeply involved in anti-Communist activities. At all events I have burned the address book with his eternal changes of name and address for, whilst I am far too busy minding my own business—which includes avoiding politics—I should not like to think that anyone who thought it worth while to raid my home for this now non-existent clue, might thereby have been led to his front door. I have no doubt that Stefanov will give me occasional signs of life in his own time. Wherever he is, my admiration goes out to him.

*   *   *

Soon after my return from Naples I handed in a document to the competent Authority concerning the traitor of Sonderlager 'A'—nor was I the only officer to do so. Although my hands were full at the time, I did this principally for the reasons explained on page 168, and also, to a great extent, as a debt of honour to those human beings he had betrayed. It can easily be argued that this was mere sentimental folly. It can also be argued that one need never raise a finger on any issue whatsoever.

My deposition against the traitor was as strong as the truth I have related. But for some unaccountable reason there was an amnesty towards a certain class of individual like him and my affidavit was never used.

The reason why I have withheld the traitor's identity and given those of Roger Bardet and Louis le Belge is the following. It is public knowledge that Bardet and Louis were released. Their trial was splashed across the pages of French pictorial weeklies at a time when the country was in a ferment of vengeance and now, in their freedom, all their associates are aware of their past. The case of the Sonderlager traitor is quite different for, apart from the inmates of our camp, nobody knows about his heinous past. It therefore seems to me unfair to rake up his case and spoil his efforts at building up a new life amongst people from whom he must certainly have kept this chapter secret. Though this man deserved to be executed, I still hope that he has been wise enough to benefit from his miraculous good fortune to turn over a new leaf, but my pity goes out to anyone who has to live with such black memories as his.

Keindl, the Sachsenhausen Commandant, was condemned to death by an International Court, but I am informed that thanks to his great experience as a German Camp Commandant, this was commuted to a life sentence by the Russians and he is now a Commandant of Concentration Camps in the Soviet Union.

Ravensbrück Concentration Camp has now been added to their number.

* * *

Of the 132 Prominenten, apart from those already mentioned, I have kept in touch with Baron von Flügge who, at one time, was in the running for the post of German Consul-General in London. I was sorry that this did not materialise as it would have brought him somewhat closer than Ankara where he lives; nor would this posting have brought anything but kudos to German representation over here.

Dr. Kurt von Schusschnigg died two or three years after the war, in the United States. Léon Blum has likewise passed on. General Garibaldi died within a few months of the armistice in Paris.

Count Leshek Zamoyski, who used to own a Palace and about 600 square kilometres of land in the Pripet Marshes, has emigrated with his entire family to Canada where he has begun life again on a small farm. He and his family are very happy.

I have met Pastor Niemöller once since the war and Lieutenant Fabian von Schlabrendorff has sent me a copy of his book.

Three years ago Josef Müller spent a day with us. Arriving at noon I left him at his hotel at 2 a.m. At this time he told me the story he had preferred not to spread around when our fate was still uncertain. Briefly it was as follows:

Long before the war he had disliked Hitler.

A regular frequenter of the Kaiserhof in Münich, he saw no reason to change his habits because Hitler had adopted the same beer parlour. He simply turned his back on him.

On more than one occasion Hitler's henchmen came over to his table in an attempt to recruit him for the Nazi stables, offering him the tempting post of Chief Justice of the whole of Germany. Müller turned down these offers.

A practising Catholic, he was also *persona grata* inside the Vatican. The Pope invited him to bring his fiancée to Rome and officiated at the wedding ceremony himself.

As a result of this strong tie Josef Müller journeyed frequently to the Vatican between 1938 and the beginning of the war in an attempt to warn certain countries of forthcoming plans to attack them. In this way he was instrumental in bringing about the Swiss mobilisation which nipped Hitler's aims at that country in the bud. When he then planned to attack Belgium a German aircraft was sent to "force-land" on a Belgian aerodrome and papers were left around by mistake on purpose to warn Belgium of what to expect.

When hostilities had broken out Josef Müller continued his journeyings to the Vatican, now bringing peace-feelers to the Allies. This activity was discovered by the German Abwehr, run by Admiral Canaris. Canaris sent for Müller and suggested that the latter should give up his lone-hand peace attempts and join forces with his department when he could avail himself of their aircraft and their passes to do the very same thing that they, the Sicherheitsdienst, were doing.

Müller complied and it was during one of his absences that the Gestapo raided his home and found documents clearly indicating that his activities were not helping the German war effort.

It was for this reason that after months of imprisonment he found himself in Flossenburg.

On the day before we arrived in the cell-block and knocked on his door with the good news that the Allies were not far off, Müller had been peremptorily taken off to the hanging shed. When he realized what was about to take place he shouted at the guards in the style they were accustomed to hearing from superior officers and told them he insisted on a proper court martial. He was led to the Kommandantur where, in his turn, he was shouted down by the "Butcher" of Flossenburg.

Back he was led to be hanged and again he persuaded the hangman that he could not proceed with such a crime. Once more he was led back to the Kommandantur.

Although this visit met with no more success than the last, Müller saved his own life by the very delay he had caused. On his return to the hanging shed, the assistant hangman was no longer there and the principal hangman said,

"You're in luck. It's off for today. A new intake has just arrived and all the guards are needed for them."

Josef Müller told me the very words he had prepared to tell the hangman in the event of this being his last journey. But these are words that one man may tell another when both have lived in the valley of the shadow.

*   *   *

Lieutenants Stonehouse and Sheppard (page 207) had recognised me from the London office. I knew neither of them, but they reminded me of the incident a month later in London. If I did not give their names, a dozen relatives whose sons were reported missing after capture in the French Resistance would write to ask if it might not have been their son. Such encounters were important. They put a date on the last time a man had been seen. After the war it was the job of certain people to trace those who did not return. To some this job was a labour of love. An outstanding example of this attitude was displayed by Squadron-Officer Vera Atkins, Croix de Guerre. After modest beginnings at the French Section Headquarters, she became so indispensable that she ended up the war as number two to Colonel Buckmaster. She knew us all, and our individual captures left their mark on her so that she made it her duty to trace those who had sailed off gaily into the field never to return. Nor was her long and arduous pilgrimage in vain. Going from prison to prison and camp to camp, she questioned, cross-questioned and interrogated dozens of people including

Camp Commandants. Thanks to her efforts all relatives of our companions in the Resistance can rest assured that no stone was left unturned to discover the fate of those who were lost but not forgotten in the hour of victory.

*   *   *

The man I have kept purposely until the very last is one of the most outstanding men I have ever met—Paul Steinert.

The German Catholic Padre of Fresnes continued his kind offices to the prisoners long after my departure. His constant infractions of Gestapo regulations in bringing comfort and messages to relatives of those inside, resulted in his being relieved of his post and being sent back to the Eastern Front. This great punishment, kept hanging as an eternal threat over the heads of those lucky enough to find themselves elsewhere, held no fears for the priest. The honest battlefield with all its dangers, bloodshed and icy cold was almost a relief to his compassionate mind, tormented for so long by the sight of wilful starvation and torture.

But before leaving the prison he saw Odette off when she was sent to Germany. He knew she had been condemned to death and as he gave her his last blessing, he promised her that, if he survived the war, he would get into touch with her children.

When the war ended and Odette and I were flown to Paris in June, our first thoughts and enquiries were for him. To our dismay we learnt from three sources that he was dead.

In the light of this information, confirmed by my three unanswered letters, I arranged for a mass to be held in his honour in London and we mourned the passing of this good man.

Some three years after the war on our return to London after a holiday in France, Odette's mother told us that she had had a mysterious visitor.

A tall young German had been led into the drawing-room clutching a large parcel. He introduced himself as a cousin of Father Paul Steinert. My mother-in-law explained who she was.

Undoing his parcel he produced two dolls, saying,

"Madame, I have no right to enter this home. My visit is a pilgrimage, for I bring these two dolls made in captivity by your daughter to Captain Churchill. She gave these dolls to Paul Steinert as a Christmas gift for his nephew and his niece, but when he saw her depart on her last journey, he decided to keep the dolls for an occasion like this. In bringing Paul Steinert's sad greetings to Captain Churchill I beg to salute the mother of such a daughter."

My mother-in-law smiled through her tears, for she was not only touched by this sincere gesture that brought back the memory of her own years of anguish and uncertainty, but realised that the man we had mourned so deeply was also alive.

When she told her guest of her daughter's miraculous survival he was overcome with emotion.

So it was that a German priest and a Frenchwoman that were lost were found again. Each a hater of violence, they both epitomized the supreme power of the human spirit.

Father Paul Steinert has no time for holidays, nor would it be a kindness to interrupt his long days of continual self-abnegation in his large parish of Karlstadt where he is priest and teacher alike. But he knows that, if in his endless sacrifice to humanity his health should fail, there is a home waiting for him in England where two human beings would consider it an honour to have him under their roof.

14